# QUICK BRIGHT THINGS COME TO CONFUSION

## *The Sequel to Fortune's Fool*

*Mary Pagones*

Copyright © 2016 Mary Pagones
All rights reserved.

ISBN: 1535052368
ISBN 13: 9781535052368

And ere a man hath power to say "Behold!"
The jaws of darkness do devour it up.
So quick bright things come to confusion. (*A Midsummer Night's Dream*, I.1: 141-149)

Here we may reign secure, and in my choice
to reign is worth ambition though in Hell:
Better to reign in Hell, than serve in Heaven. (*Paradise Lost*, I. 258-63)

*For Benjamin Winter, Olivia Inglis and Philippa Humphreys*

# NOTE TO THE READER

One of the challenges of writing equestrian fiction is the question of how much the fictional world should or should not resemble reality. I've always thought of Simon's world as a kind of parallel universe to my own, set in the twenty-first century (as is evidenced by the presence of iPhones and other technology) but a little bit different. While some people in my own world might be present in his (or in slightly altered form), and the names of some competitions remain the same, Simon's world is still its own unique place. This is important because I don't want to take away the victory of someone who won, for example, Rolex or Red Hills in 2012 or 2015 by making Simon the winner.

The question of fiction versus reality is also important because the sport of eventing is changing so much, literally as I write this introduction. I don't think by the time this book is published that it will be called 'Equestrian Triathlon' but who knows? Regardless, as always, I can only relate to the reader what Simon chooses to tell me from his world and in that world eventing is still called eventing with three distinct phases of dressage, cross-country, and show-jumping. Some of the events Simon competes in may have different names and when the rules come up as plot points they are hopefully explained to the reader's satisfaction. Those rules may have changed by the time you read this book but again, I can only tell you what Simon is kind enough to convey to me, no more and no less.

# CHAPTER 1
# I BUILD MY HOUSE OF STRAW ...

I've always said if you can't pick a stall with one hand while eating a slice of pizza, you're not a real horse person, but straw is something different. Every barn I've ever worked at, and there have been a lot of them, always used shavings for bedding. Shavings are easy, light and moderately absorbent, and there is a limit for even the most determined pig of a horse in terms of the mess he can make of shavings. Horses have to resort to pooping in their water buckets to really make your life miserable. I'd never mucked a straw-bedded stall until I came to Hans Fuhrmann's eventing barn.

The barn's located smack-dab in the middle of Germany, a country I'd never much thought about except for sleeping through a unit on World War II in high school and watching Quentin Tarantino's *Inglorious Bastards* over and over again. And there are some punk bands I like that use German in their logos and designs, which I thought would mean ... something ... some common ground.

Weeks before my working studentship began, I drilled myself in Rosetta Stone German. I smiled and tried not to be a total inglorious bastard myself when the Germans gave me a hard time for wanting to carry my new monoflap saddle, the nicest one I'd ever owned, onto my Lufthansa flight. (I didn't trust the airline not to lose it or break its tree in the baggage area, although I did concede my dressage and older jumping saddle to ride with my clothes and stuff.) I read everything I could get my hands on about the German riding philosophy, watched tons of German riders on YouTube to see what I was getting myself into. The Germans are the best, I was told by my mentor, Daniel McAlister. McAlister took me from a stupid, ignorant, arrogant, eighteen-year-old working student who was wet behind the ears at Preliminary and made me into a competent Intermediate-level rider. So I believed whatever he said.

Hans Fuhrmann is legendary in the eventing world—he's younger than Daniel (in his sixties rather than his seventies) but looks much older; he's heavier and almost bald. But all of the top riders from Germany, and quite a few Americans and Brits too, have trained with him and swear by his system. I kind of suck at dressage (it's always bored the hell out of me), and his riders always place at the top in dressage at events, so I told myself this might not be exactly what I want, but it's what I need if I'm going to succeed as a professional.

I want to stress that I came here with the right mindset. I've worked hard all my life, and I only recently came into some money when my father passed away (I didn't know him that well, so I don't mean to get heavy or anything so soon). This enabled me to take the time to educate myself and enslave myself to a German who could make me more competitive.

But straw? Every day I find myself arguing with the straw. It seems like such a waste. First, you have to use a lot more straw to bed a stall. It's heavy as hell, and you can't really pick it properly. And I was always told that lots of horses are tempted to eat straw bedding when they're bored, which could make them colic very easily. When I told my boyfriend Max, who is a vet, that Fuhrmann used straw, he agreed with me. "Simon, the nastiest colic I ever saw was from a horse that ate his straw bedding," he said, and I repeat those words in my mind every day as I pick up my pitchfork at 5:30 a.m. The straw isn't just annoying, its presence is ... illogical.

But from the mucker's perspective, the worst thing about straw is that it is super absorbent. And since I'm handling it all day long, my boots, jeans, and t-shirts all stink of horse piss.

All. Day. Long.

I'm almost glad that Max is not here, because I can hardly bear anyone touching me I stink so much, and again, I'm used to standing in horse shit for hours a day from my last position. The dinky shower in the little cottage I rented doesn't even make a dent in the smell.

I'm not sure why the Germans use straw. According to Ingrid, the other working student here, it's better for composting; farmers use it for fertilizer, and vegetables—especially mushrooms—love it. I hate vegetables. Especially mushrooms.

I throw my last heap of manure in my wheelbarrow and clank-clank down the path to the muck heap. Ingrid and I aren't done, not by half, but it's almost time for breakfast. Actually, we're never really *done* done. Having to pick out the stables is a constant battle, a battle Ingrid and I can never win. That I'm used to. What I'm not used to is that my boss thinks my work is half-assed even though I'm hypervigilant that things remain white-glove clean. At this point I wouldn't be surprised if Mr. F ran a white glove over the tack room to check for dust. Even my worst enemies at previous barns never complained about my horsemanship. It was my people skills that bothered them.

I nod at Ingrid as I pass, but she doesn't acknowledge me, as if I'm no one and nothing and transparent as a ghost. When I came to Germany, at first I loved the fact that people rarely smile here. I've never been much of a smiler myself, and it was a relief not to have to walk around grinning like an idiot, like you're supposed to in the United States. But Ingrid and I have been working together for a month, and she looks straight through me. Of course, the fact that we can't engage in small talk doesn't help. Ingrid has almost as little English as I have German. But I know that she has some sort of certificate to teach riding that is required in Germany, and the German system is very rigid and particular about the qualifications required to be a horse person. The contempt she feels for me as an American wafts off of her. It's a stench just as potent as the ammonia on our clothing. The fact that I've been on a horse since I was two years old means nothing to her.

In all honesty, I wouldn't mind the straw or the work at all if it weren't for my sneaking suspicion that she and everyone else here feels that mucking stalls is all I'm good for and that my work isn't an exchange for something, but rather a way of keeping me busy and out of the way until my time is up. I came here to speed up time, but things seem to have actually slowed down.

The stable provides us with breakfast. I've sort of picked up that Ingrid and I are expected to eat together. Coffee and bread. I don't like coffee so every day I pour myself a glass of milk and everyday like I'm doing it for the first time Ingrid gives me a look with her empty blue eyes. I kind of sense that she thinks it is weird but in the absence of my usual Mountain Dew in the morning, I feel I have no choice. I just don't get her. She looks younger than me but I think she's in her twenties. She's really pale and as flat-chested as a teenage guy but acts like one of my most annoying high school teachers. I always knew I'd get a D in a class if the teacher made a big deal about what color folder you'd need. Ingrid's the type of girl who would always have the right colored folders and pens.

Because the work is constant despite the fact it's not physically hard, I'm always hungry when they feed us, so I eat. There's butter and sometimes cheese for the bread. They call it Brotchen and it cuts the roof of my mouth, kind of like Captain Crunch cereal, only less tasty. Then it's back to cleaning.

It's the riding when my real life begins, however. There's a list as regimented as clockwork that I follow and it's sort of comforting to know that at 9:30 am every Tuesday I'll be on Audi, a stocky five-year-old mare, followed by a baby called Gunnar who's just done a couple of show jumping competitions. Every now and then Mr. Fuhrmann will watch me and dispense a couple of notes, like to drop my weight behind the vertical when I'm working at dressage or to collect Gunnar more when the gelding gets too excited and isn't careful with his feet. On the small practice cross-country course occasionally he'll ride by and bark advice as well. Although he's pretty fluent in English, you'd never know it. He gives orders to me in short bursts of sound as if he only has a handful of English words he's allocated to use on the working students. And me, well, I just have my Rosetta Stone German so when he rattles off long paragraphs and paragraphs of advice to Ingrid, I have no idea what he's saying or why she deserves more coaching than me.

It wouldn't be so friggin' annoying, galling, if Ingrid was a much better rider. She's okay but her leg is kind of floppy, even when riding cross-country and you need some security in the tack, and when she's riding dressage she almost looks like a parody of a dressage rider, her leg barely grazing the stirrup. She has won stuff, apparently. But despite my awards I sort of have a feeling my Americanness cancels out any advantages I might have in Mr. Fuhrmann's estimation. The last time I was sailing around cross-country on another horse named Dusseldorf he just looked at me, shook his head, and said, "You ride like a cowboy." Like that's a creative insult to give to an American rider. I don't think I've ever heard him call me Simon but once or twice. It's not a complicated name.

Despite the thirty stalls we clean every day (which again, take longer because of … straw) there is no music, no sound system for the barn. I tried wearing my earbuds to listen to music on my phone the first day because it's not like Ingrid is going to make small talk. Then Herta, the stable manager yelled at me, saying that I needed to be alert in case a horse got into trouble and they wanted me quickly. Which is just bullshit. The real reason is that she doesn't want me listening to music, period. I guess it looks bad for me to have the earbuds hanging out of my ear, music blasting. So, whatever. I know enough music so I'm always playing it in my mind. Right now, it's "Psycho Killer" by Talking Heads because that's how I feel.

After riding three horses, I turn the animals out, take in the next three I'll be riding after lunch, and feed them so they'll have digested it all and be ready to work. I put the first ten horses on the hot walker, which I'll supervise while eating my food. That's fine with me—at least I don't have to stare at Ingrid while eating. Lunch is provided for us as well, some weird kind of sausage meat in a different kind of scratchy black bread. I have a chocolate bar in my pocket and, staring at the endless merry-go-round of horses, I call my brother Sean back in America, since the time difference works. Even the chocolate doesn't taste good, like American chocolate.

I've tried to explain to Sean why it feels weird here. Back at home, when I was a working student before, even though I was working hard as hell, I could at least talk with Daniel. Daniel had a resume longer than Mr. Fuhrmann but after a couple of days he just became a person to me and I could crack jokes or whatever around him, he'd insult me, and I could relax. And I could make a sarcastic remark around the other students and they'd at least sort of get it, or at least sort of tolerate me being me.

"It's like being in church here," I complain to Sean, shoving a hunk of candy in my mouth. "Riding church."

"When was the last time you were in church?" he laughs. Sean runs on his college cross-country team which means when I talk to him he's usually eating, waking up from a nap, or in the middle of a practice. "You got yourself into this."

"I feel like I'm learning, at least when I'm riding, but I'm bored. Even the horses seem bored." I miss having my own horse too, something to ride during the downtime. Although there really isn't any downtime, since any moment we have when we don't have a specific chore, we're supposed to be sweeping or cleaning tack. "I came here to move forwards but I feel like I've moved backwards."

"Are you eating something?"

"Some kind of chocolate. Chocolate is weird here."

"You do realize that most normal people go to Europe for the food."

"It's weird."

Sean dated a couple of girls from Russia and France and Ireland he met in college in rapid succession so he's convinced that their culture has like, rubbed off on him or something. It's one of his things, girls that don't speak English that well, maybe because they can't understand at first what an asshole he is to them. One of my jokes that isn't really a joke. I mean, my brother is my brother and I'll always have his back but I'd never date him.

There's another thing that bugs me that's even harder to explain, something I can't even put into words for Sean. Back in the U.S., in high school and at Daniel's, I was always the one who would turn my nose up at the other kids because they'd rather be at the mall than cleaning tack or because they'd rather listen to Taylor Swift than some industrial band. I always thought I'd fit into Europe so easily because I could ride (which I considered a kind of international language) and because I didn't like normal American stuff. It's not like I pictured it at all.

Ugly American, I think, catching a distorted image of my reflection shining on the side of a steel water bucket lying nearby. Sandy nothing hair, pale, washed-out freckles. I'm nothing much to look at but even less so in the face of the bucket.

I take a picture of the horses on the hot walker and send it to Max. Max is a vet and is—was—my boyfriend back home in Vermont. I say 'was' only because we weren't sure how realistic it would be to try to stay together, what with me being over here and not knowing what I'd be doing and where I'd be going afterward. But we still communicate just about every day.

The plan is to use this experience to become a better professional rider myself. But at this point, who knows. Yeah, I've got two more horses to ride before lunch. But I haven't even laid a finger even on Fuhrmann's halfway decent horses, unlike Ingrid. I rode everything at Daniel's, he trusted me. I mean, I guess technically Daniel's best horses aren't competing on nearly as high a level as Fuhrmann's right now. But still.

*how I feel* is the caption for my Instagram picture of the horses going in circles on the walker.

*Rome wasn't built in a day.* Max writes underneath my caption, as always, with grammatically correct punctuation and capitalization. I wonder where he is and what he is doing. He's not as good about sending photos to me as I am to him.

I don't want to build Rome, I think, I just want to ride.

Mr. F merely stares at me when I'm schooling one of the just-broke horses in dressage today. He says nothing good and nothing bad.

The truth is, I'm used to being the biggest fish in a small pond. I kind of knew that I'd have my ego knocked around here. But I feel as though I'm not even swimming, just treading water. To hell with being a small fish, I'm like, phytoplankton at this point.

During the day I can keep up enough sarcastic working commentary in my head, in English, to amuse me but at night the loneliness is somehow unbearable. For all that they say about straw being better for the horse's breathing it seems to be choking me. This is what I longed for when the kids used to make fun of me for being me and now I'm here and it isn't like what I pictured at all.

I watch the bright sunlight gradually thread through the crack between the curtain and the wall, waiting for it to be time for me to go to work again. I'm looking forward to the barn because no matter what, it's better to be around horses than not be around them. But I always said that one reason I didn't want a job job, what my brother calls a real job, is that I didn't want to be stuck in some box of an office 24/7. Sometimes I think I've just found myself another box. But unlike me, the horses have no choice. I do have a choice. I can always get out of this if I need to. There has to be a better way to get ahead quickly.

## CHAPTER 2

# DESPERATE TIMES, DESPERATE MEASURES

Maybe it's the language thing. It's like I'm always speaking twice, first in my mind to say what I want to say, then translating it into what passes for my crappy German and then saying it aloud. Ditto when I hear other people speak German. It's like … pause … think of what they are saying … wait … and then make the German into English so I can understand it. I have enough problems dealing with humanity in American, I tell myself.

I mean, if I weren't here, what would I be doing? Working for another eventer back in the U.S. But given my resume, probably not a top one. I have no additional qualifications to make me extra special, competition-wise. There were a couple of barns that expressed interest in me when I was at Daniel's but for various reasons by the time I was done, either they didn't have an open position for me or I knew it wouldn't be the right situation. Of course, I could always buy my own new horse and try to train it now with the money I inherited. But money, even inherited money is finite and it's not enough just to train *a* horse and to be *a* rider; I want the kinds of experiences that will make me the best. According to the lists of the sport, which is all that matters ultimately, I'm way behind kids that have been on a consistent mount for ages.

I'm glad Max isn't here, because that would make me too comfortable with what and where I am right now and I don't want that. The fact is, without advancing in my riding, I'm not myself, or at least not a self that I like, a self that I feel is justified being in the world.

The next day, when I look at the board of my rides I see that all I have is walking the baby horses around and doing some up-and-down stuff with them. Fuhrmann's getting ready to go somewhere—to look at some new horses he's considering buying—and he sneaks up behind me as I glare at the board.

"Make sure you properly cool down those horses," he barks, even though I always do. He doesn't even call me by my name. At least yell at me for a mistake I actually make, I think. I feel this is just something generic he says to all foreign working students.

One of the barn cats walks up to him and rubs against his legs. The cats here are skinny but they do their job keeping the mice away, unlike the fat, fed barn cats at most American barns. Mr. F, to my surprise, coos and picks up the cat and strokes it. With the heavy ring he wears on his finger when he's not riding, I think he looks like some kind of a James Bond villain and I suppress a giggle.

"Mr. Bigglesworth, I presume," I say, looking at the cat in his arms.

"Excuse me?"

"Nothing." I'm still sniggering to myself. Of course, the cat has no name because it doesn't matter, it's a cat and won't come when you call it—Fuhrmann's sensible that way. Just like he never bothers to name me, because who am I, here, really? Who am I to him?

I attack the straw stalls. Yes, the song "Psycho Killer" seems like a good choice. Stable manager Herta hasn't seen that I'm listening with my earbuds yet and if she dresses me down and tells Mr. F, I really don't care.

As I throw the straw in the pile I think what great composting for mushrooms it's supposed to be ... kind of like anything dead. Of course, if someone hadn't died, I wouldn't be here. Being in this isolation tank's really making me morbid this morning and it makes me think of my father, working day in and day out, stacking up money and resentment on a pile and then making it all bearable with booze and spending the whole night out with his friends from work. And taking it out on mom, mostly, and Sean, and me too (I was always better at hiding than both of them, though). And that's all he had to look back on when he got sick.

The point of doing something I love was not to be trapped and angry and resentful in a cubicle and having to pretend to be someone I'm not, yet here I am. I was hoping to speed up the time I needed to become my true self ... *to win* ... to go Advanced ... but I seem to just be wasting time instead. Just closer to rotting. I turn my wheelbarrow around for more dirty straw.

## CHAPTER 3

# MILTON

My first excursion for Herr Fuhrmann to a horse trial is as a groom, not a rider. I was riding at Intermediate level before I came here but when I do ride, I know I'll be taking one of the more inexperienced horses around at a lower level. This is one of the biggest events of the year, with lots of international competition. Riders are shipping in from all over Europe.

Fuhrmann still competes internationally but not today. His doctor still hasn't cleared him to ride because of some minor operation he had before I arrived so Ingrid's taking over. I mean, Michael Jung rides with a broken leg but I guess Fuhrmann's old, so whatever.

Ingrid's at the top of the leaderboard after dressage. The bay mare named Isolde is green as grass but a pretty mover. Fuhrmann has an earful for Ingrid after she goes and she takes his criticism silently, nodding like a bobble-head doll. Cross-country gets her only one time fault, which still leaves her competitive. Watching her, though, I can't help but think that only Ingrid could make riding across such an amazing cross-country course look boring. Her expression doesn't change, it seems, through any of it, even though the mare's ears are pricked forward and happy. I guess Izzy (my nickname for her, no one else's) is finally happy to be out of the stall and free, even though Ingrid is on her back.

One interesting thing does happen between the different phases. There's a big field where they set up a bunch of small jumps (the biggest isn't more than 2'3), only they lean boards against them, kind of like ramps.

"It is for the skijoring demonstration," says Ingrid brusquely, handing Isolde to me to walk cool. She looks at the jumps and kind of shakes her head.

At first I don't quite register what she's said. I hear 'smorgasbord' or something like that, and I'm thinking like a smorgasbord of jumping or whatever, probably with little kids because of the size of the jumps. But then this guy comes out on his horse—only the horse is wearing a thin harness attached to two bungee cords that are pulling another guy on rollerblades, a guy with a helmet and knee pads. For a second, I'm like, *he isn't going to*—but the horse and rider make a big courtesy circle, just like they were warming up before a standard low hunter course back home ... and begin to jump.

The horse is super-quiet and rhythmical. You'd never guess he was jumping over jumps pulling the rollerblader behind him if the skater dude was cut out of the picture. The guy riding is just calm and steady, never getting left behind or falling forward and the rollerblader hanging on back there is pretty chill, too. He gets a little bit airborne over the jumps, like he really is skiing. This is just about the most awesome thing I've seen in the entire time I've been in Germany. They're playing some weird Eurotrashy crap in the background for musical accompaniment but other than that and the rail the horse takes down at the end (totally the blader's fault, since he was not balancing correctly), it's damn near perfect.

Ingrid walks by me and glares. "You are supposed to be walking Isolde cool for me. Not watching."

"I was just watching for a minute or two," I say.

"This is not really skijoring. This is just a silly thing," says Ingrid. Of course she thinks that. "It is supposed to be on the snow. This is silly. There's no point to it."

"No point to it other than the fact it's totally badass." I sigh. "I don't know how you put up with her," I say to Isolde. The mare snorts and shakes her head. Goals. If I stay here any longer, that rollerblading thing is *goals AF*. I mean, yeah, there really isn't a point to it but still ... I just want to try it, just because.

I finish my duties as a groom, leave Isolde with the professional staff at our stall area and then go back to watch the competition. Right now I'm debating if I'd rather be the guy rollerblading or riding. I guess riding because I really haven't done that much rollerblading in my life. As a kid, I had a skateboard and I taught myself some basic tricks like how to do an ollie. I'm kind of preoccupied with this question when the big black gelding comes out of nowhere at a gallop.

Everything is so calm, so regimented here, he takes me by surprise the way horses seldom can anymore. He's in a saddle with the stirrups down and swinging, and a bridle with the reins flapping on his neck, but I don't recognize him from any of the competitors I've watched. Sweat is pouring off of him and his veins are bulging. "Easy boy," I say, and raise my hands. And just as suddenly, he stops.

We kind of regard one another for a second or two and I grab at his bridle and he ducks and lunges away but not far. I follow him, stand still, make another motion toward his bridle when I feel like he won't move again but he eludes me a second time. We play this game of chicken for a bit and I hope he'll start to get tired but he's fit and seems to draw energy from our game, rather than getting exhausted.

Suddenly, even though I know it's dumb and I'm not wearing a helmet or even riding boots, I grab at the saddle instead of the reins and vault myself up. He's a big guy but I have long legs and enough athleticism that I can do it without dragging over the saddle too much, despite the fact he's bunny-hopping around. I settle and wait for him to buck or run. He gives a good one but I have a Velcro ass from all of the horses I've ridden in the past and I know how to sit it. I don't bother with the stirrups because I know they'll be too short. The horse tries to spin but I turn him into the nearby fence. For a second, I think he's going to foil this little trick of mine because he keeps going, doesn't slow down and I'm like hell, Simon, you're going to crash yourself and a strange horse but he stops at the last minute. He stands there gathering his thoughts.

I'm trying to calm myself. For the first time since I came to Herr Fuhrmann's, I don't know what's going to happen while I'm on a horse and it's been a long time since I felt that way. I missed it.

Slowly, we start to walk back to the show grounds. After a certain point, reluctantly, I slide down and walk rather than ride him. I don't want to, but I know whoever he does belong to won't take kindly to finding me on his back. I'm also not wearing a helmet. Although that never used to stop me in the past from doing stupid shit, I had a concussion less than a year ago and if I'm going to get another one, you better bet damn well sure it's going to be in pursuit of a prize.

It's not hard to find who the horse belongs to. There's a tall, very pissed-off-looking guy in breeches, a helmet, a bright red showjumping jacket, and boots, with a nervous, chunky, middle-aged woman with red curly hair with a sloppy bun trying to keep up with him. He bounds ahead of her as soon as he spies the black horse. I know they're not German before they even speak because their expressions are way too obviously emotional.

"Is this who you're looking for?" I say, cheerfully. The man grabs the horse away from me as if I were a thief.

"Jeez, I was only trying to help," I say.

The woman is a bit more apologetic. "We just bought him a few days ago through an online broker ... we're taking him home with us after the competition to our barn. We brought him here to get used to the atmosphere."

"I guess he's not that fond of it," I say, cheerfully. "He's a pretty mover from what I could see of him running around." The man glares at me more deeply. They both leave as suddenly as the black horse came to me.

Something clicks in my mind. Matthew Stevenson. Easily one of the top twenty-five eventers in the U.S. I think he's based in Maryland somewhere. I feel like an idiot. He normally rides a big bay horse named Geronimo. Although Geronimo must be old now because I remember seeing pictures of the two of them together when I was a kid. Geronimo has had such a career, he's kind of legendary for his staying power and endurance and so far as I know, Geronimo is both his show and barn name, kind of in testimony to the fact he was such an awesomely predictable jumper in his glory days.

Mr. Stevenson was also—many, many years ago—one of Daniel's working students. Just like me for a year. But I never heard Daniel talk about him, unlike lots of other riders that went through the program. Matt's never been one of the top riders I most admire. Not for any reason, although I certainly respect him.

Stevenson has a nickname. They call him the Iceman because of his pale eyes, hair, skin, and his constant cool expression, no matter what is going on around him. Even the few times I've seen him fall off his face never changes.

As is usual for any event involving horses, I haven't eaten all day, but I manage to find a vendor that sells French fries slathered in mayo (*pommes frites mit mayo*) and I stuff my face with that as I watch. Ingrid passes by, her face immobile, as if she doesn't care that she didn't win. I guess I shouldn't complain about her not caring. I have to admit that I don't really mind that much if Herr Fuhrmann's horses get first or last. Right now I'm thinking more about *Pulp Fiction*. So it was true what they said about fries and mayo, they do drown them in it over here.

It occurs to me that it's not that Ingrid is Fuhrmann's favorite that really bugs me—I kind of know that he has enough national pride to want her to beat me. It's that even she hasn't improved, not one bit, since she's been here. Fuhrmann's good for tips but he's not what I would call a great teacher. He might have this fabulous reputation, but it hasn't transferred to people just by virtue of being in his presence. And since I'm honestly not that crazy about how Ingrid rides, never mind her attitude, will I really get better here? Is this what I'm supposed to aspire to, I mean?

"Why aren't you riding?" I turn around and see the woman that took the black horse. At first, I wonder if she saw me on the horse but then she adds, "Matt and I saw you ride—was it a grey horse at Intermediate a couple of months ago? Everyone was talking about that story."

"Yeah, I guess Eventing Nation and a couple of other sites were impressed by the fact that I did so well on a horse that was supposed to be good for nothing that I bought for a couple grand. I'm not the first, though. Slow news day. But he's back home."

"What was his name?"

"Fortune. Fortune's Fool."

"What was his story before you got him?"

"He was sold to me as an eventing prospect that had to be taken up the levels again because they didn't think he was good for much, he'd been such a nightmare for his previous rider. No brakes. Pretty stiff and messed up with bad training. He couldn't even carry himself like he should in a Training level dressage test—they'd just shoved him in draw reins to make him do it. Plus, he pulled like a train when you'd jump him and had a nasty habit of taking off with his rider cross-country. We did okay together. I'm a working student here." I smile a little bit and stuff some more fries down my throat. "I haven't earned the privilege yet of riding the string in competition with Mr. Fuhrmann." Then I admit, "I'm not sure I ever will get a chance to compete for Fuhrmann. There's part of me that just makes me think I'm being taken and he'll use me for free stall cleaning until my time is up." I realize I shouldn't bad-mouth my employer. The words just kind of come out because I haven't had a chance to talk in English with someone who understands for so long.

She doesn't seem to care. "I'm not riding here either. This will be Geronimo's last international competition. He's getting too old to ship at this point. We're taking Milton home with him as a potential Advanced mount. I'm Lisa, Lisa Knight by the way."

"Milton is your horse, the black horse?"

"Matt's horse. When he saw you on Fortune's Fool, Matt was impressed by your riding. Well, impressed by the fact that you turned Fortune around and made him over so quickly, in less than a year." She laughs a little bit. "If you know Matt, very little impresses him." She hesitates. "He doesn't want to impose upon your time. He doesn't know what kind of a relationship you have with Mr. Fuhrmann or what the rules are for you … but he was wondering if you'd be interested in trying Milton out. If your schedule allows it. Early tomorrow morning before we leave."

I know this is Lisa's casual way of offering me a job interview, without actively seeming to poach me from my employer. Even though Matt obviously is.

I jerk my head up out of my food. "I'll be there. I would shake your hand but I'm covered in grease," I say. I don't ask what happened when they rode Milton around the show grounds. She looks older than I would expect for a working student so maybe Stevenson doesn't want to break her into too many pieces if the horse acts up again. I also kind of wonder if my reputation for getting on horses most people won't go near at Daniel's has permeated the eventing community. Best not to ask too many questions. "Please thank Mr. Stevenson."

"Matt, just call him Matt like I do."

By the time the event's all over, there's one guy named Ben Hillard that comes out on top at the Advanced level. He's twenty, barely a year older than me and he's as skinny as I was in high school so he looks even younger. But he can ride.

I learn a couple of things about Ben from the gossip wafting around. He's from some cute little nothing town in Connecticut. His mother also rode when she was younger as a pretty successful ammie but now works as some kind of a therapist. His father's a lawyer. So they aren't ultra-rich but well-off enough.

The Hillard family has a small farm, kind of a suburban hobby farm where they keep a few horses and chickens and stuff like that. They have horses at home, but Ben's new Advanced horse Quicksilver Springs (barn name Jasper) is stabled at a big eventing operation where they have multiple trainers for every phase. Ben is technically a student at the University of Connecticut majoring in engineering although at this point it seems to be more of a fallback thing; he's been on a leave of absence forever. He's just finishing up a couple of months' stint as a working student at some eventing stable near where I am in Germany. This will be his last ride here for his old trainers before he goes back to Jasper again. He's doing everything right, I guess. Got all his bases covered.

Unlike me. I must be doing something wrong because I've gone from riding at Intermediate to being head stall mucker. God, why didn't I stay in Vermont?

There's an after party where they hand out the awards and there seems to be more members of the equestrian media—Eventing Nation, Eventing Connect, the Chronicle of the Horse, Horse & Hound, Heels Down Magazine—than riders. I see Mr. F in a corner holding forth about something to a crowd of people but mostly I watch Ben. They give him a big check and douse him with champagne, like he's won the World Series or something.

When I was going over the candy cane-colored fences at schooling shows at fourteen, Ben was trailering over to a nearby cross-country schooling facility from his eventing barn. There are eventing barns where I grew up in New Jersey, of course, just not nearby where I lived, and my mom, of course, was all about the hunters and jumpers.

Ben's an awesome rider so I can't exactly hate him at first sight. In fact, he's kind of, well, more than kind of hot. All sculpted cheekbones and clavicles but with a nice ass and hard skinny thighs. He needs a haircut. His bangs hang in his face and that just makes him cuter as he grins and politely navigates the media. He talks about how all his hard work is paying off. He might be my age, but you can kind of tell that he is prepared for this, that his trainer or maybe his parents have taught him the right way to behave. He's modest but graciously appreciative of his success and hits all of the expected notes even though he looks really young and his jacket and tie are slightly too large for him. He even speaks German to the German press, although even I can tell it's kind of bad German, with a really strong American accent.

It's like I'm challenging him, asking him questions in my mind, questions the media isn't asking him, or really more questions of myself. Why are you there and I am not? And the real cross examination is of myself, as I keep looking at him and wondering, *Who am I? What am I, without this?* I always said that what I liked best about eventing was that for the most part it was an objective measure of a rider's skill. But that means that when you don't succeed there isn't anyone to blame other than yourself. Sure, I could say that I lacked money and backing, up to this point. But there are no asterisks, ultimately, besides the winners of the horse world. Either you've won or lost and I haven't won enough.

I'm tired—usually at events, I don't ever feel fatigued because I'm so pumped up from competing, but doing this groom thing is all the exhaustion with none of the payoff. In fact, watching Ingrid make mistakes that I know, deep down in my heart, I never would, and seeing her ride with such little passion was ten times worse than competing. I've never had bad show nerves, either, only good ones. There's no nerves here, just a kind of dead and longing desperation.

The party goes on and on so I leave to sit in the stabling area. I don't feel like going back to the hotel rooms Fuhrmann has rented for us. I know that we'll be pulling up and leaving tomorrow and it will all be back to the usual. I don't even feel the peace like I normally do with our horses, so I wander around the grounds, hands stuffed in my pockets, half-hoping to be stopped by a security guard or something just so I can spar with someone.

I go to where the horse Ben rode for the competition is stabled and expect to see someone there, like a groom to guard stuff, but it's just his barn's horses. And there is his German barn's big warmblood, a large bay gelding named Escapade with a kind eye. I look around, can't believe I'm alone with the horse. I put out my hand, touch the gelding's nose. He's got huge dark eyes, seems like a pretty mellow guy. Gently he takes the cuff of my shirt in his teeth.

I smile.

Then I hear the laughter. Shit, I think, and look around for a back way to slip out but there isn't any. There's a big tack trunk nearby though, more like a chest than a trunk. It's almost as tall as I am. Without thinking, I grab the sides as far up as I can reach, hoist myself on top of it and pull one of the blankets lying on it over me. Well, they always said that basketball would be my sport, if I ever wanted to do one besides horses. I could always jump high, even without a horse beneath me.

It's Ben and some girl. She's really short and ghostly pale and has black hair hanging down to her ass. So long I kind of disapprove because when girls have that much hair it looks weird stuffed in their helmets. They stop by Escapade's stall. I hear Ben unwrap some candy and the girl giggles.

"He lives to eat," I hear Ben say.

"What do you live for?" She giggles again. I guess she's an American. I didn't think she won anything today but then again she's won Ben for the night, and since Ben is like, the eventing equivalent of Harry Styles or whatever pop star teenage girls think is popular now, that's something.

They start to kiss. Shit. Shit, shit, shit. I'm going to be stuck here for a while. From the crack of light I allow myself under the blanket, I can see her put his hand on her breast and she's got her hand on that perfect ass of his. She's really going for it. Although to be honest, Ben just kind of stands there, almost awkwardly.

She pulls him into a nearby stall and after what seems like hours I hear her moan. I pull the blanket even tighter over myself. Coming here was a bad, bad idea. I hear one of the horses start to stamp. Whatever Ben and pale chick are doing, they're doing it standing up because no equestrian with half a brain would ever go for a true roll in the hay—far too scratchy.

Just hurry up, Ben, and get out of here.

They finish and I see them start to walk out together, hand in hand. She's muttering to him, bites him on the ear, and giggles again. Jesus, this girl does not stop.

I know it's not wise, but I keep looking from where I am, hidden away and above, from the crack of light I've made between blanket and trunk. Even in the darkness, I can still see enough. I can see the bones of Ben's back ribcage through his shirt. And I tell myself, despite the gulf between us, that I get it, Ben. We're not so different. Too much time riding to eat or spend hours at the gym getting buff. I've probably lost a good ten pounds I couldn't afford to lose since coming to Germany despite living on candy, bread, and French fries. We have kind of the same build, only you're a little shorter. We're not so different. You're not some magical fucking unicorn.

Looking at the arms wrapped around Ben's skinny waist, I feel, I don't know ... there was something about him that made me wonder, I can't explain why, if he might be gay. Okay, I hope every guy I'm attracted to is gay. I admit it. But I guess Ben is just as hetero as all the guys that used to call me a faggot and throw the basketball in my face in gym class. Of course, they learned pretty quickly that I could out run and outshoot them, making up for what I lacked in technique with the strength I got from hauling water buckets all day in the barn and sticking a buck on a greenie. But that didn't stop them from calling me "faggot" in the halls all the same.

Ben and the girl looked so fucking wholesome, I think, the most fucking wholesome thing I've seen since the glass of milk I chugged for breakfast a million years or really two days ago.

When I'm sure they've left for good I come out of hiding. I know I should hurry away, in case they return, but I stop by the gelding's stall instead, as if the horse could tell me Ben's secrets, the secret of being effortlessly awesome.

I walk back, pull out my phone and start to check out Ben's Instagram account. Like a total creeper. It's all pictures of him on his various horses, smiling in every one of them so much my jaw hurts. *good luck can't want until you are back in the USA* one of the comments says. I don't think he needed your luck.

I need to stop pissing around. I worked hard in my last position but on my downtime I'd always head off to the woods to hack around like ... like Mr. Fuhrmann would say, like a goddamned cowboy. Too much time on the back of my horse Fortune's Fool at a gallop rather than in serious and purposeful work. Fool is right. Too much time having fun with Max afterhours as well.

From this moment forth, every moment has to be devoted to getting better at *competing*. I don't even have Ben's luxury of a fall-back degree at some fancy school. This is all that I am and without it, I'm less than a groom. I'm no one, hidden in the darkness. From now on every thought and every action ... well, every other thought and every other action I take will have to be devoted to making a name for myself.

But there's Milton, I think. There's that. I don't care if Mr. F approves. If my reputation for riding bucking broncos gives me a chance to get out of this, I'm taking it no matter what.

## CHAPTER 4
# MILTON KEYNES

"He's highly reactive to sound. Something that you and I barely register—a rustle in the bushes—he'll stop and swing around, no matter what gait you have him in or how forward he is to your leg. That's the problem, well, one of the problems with Milton. But he's talented when he is doing what he's supposed to be doing and has good breeding. This might have been the best—or the worst decision to buy him, I don't know. Only time will tell," says Matt Stevenson.

From what I gather Milton Keynes actually placed decently at a couple of two- and three-star events here when he was younger. Then for whatever reason, he started to lose it and his rider had two falls in a row—the first one was just schooling before the event even started, too, so it wasn't a fault of the course design. Stevenson's going to take him down a level or maybe two when he competes him again back in the U.S. Milton's obviously got something, somewhere, but how and why he's been hiding it, no one knows.

"Well, Mr. Stevenson …"

"Matt, please," he says. I relax slightly. Despite what Lisa said, I still feel odd calling Matt by his first name.

Since I had relatively little trouble riding him myself for that brief period during the show (which I don't mention to Matt), initially I just assume that Milton is one of those horses with a bad reputation, one of those horses that people like to exaggerate how bad he is to make them seem like better riders. It usually goes one of both ways—either people claim that a big, fire-breathing horse is really "nothing but a great big bag of mush" and stress how much he loves to eat peppermints out of the hands of kids or they say he's Satan himself.

We start him over some warm-up stuff. Milton has a big powerful jump and for the first time since I came to Germany I feel like I'm using my skills again, rather than just riding the lower-level horses by rote like I've been doing at Herr Fuhrmann's. A part of my brain suddenly gets distracted and thinks, "I have hope." Beneath me I can feel the excitement and suppleness of a really forward horse who wants to move but has the conformation to do it in the right way, unlike just about everything I've ridden and owned in the past.

Then Milton suddenly stops on me in front of a jump, taking me by surprise, which hasn't happened in ages. I'm not the prettiest of riders, still, but horses usually want to keep going when I'm on their backs. I try to whirl him around to pop over the relatively low 1.10m combination but he's planted, still skittering away from whatever he spooked at.

"You see what I mean," says Matt. I'm pissed at myself for getting complacent although I feel happy, no matter what, to be in an environment where I can get feedback about my riding. We take the fence again easily, Milton is tense and hollow-backed, but at least we get over. Then he stops again.

Honestly, by my standards, the whole thing is kind of a disaster so I'm kind of surprised when Matt says again, "All things considered, that wasn't too terrible."

I'm sweaty and red-faced but I burst out laughing. "Why did you buy him?"

"Geronimo's getting too old for Advanced. I'll have to sell him to a lower-level rider soon. That will leave me only with Nebraska Sky and I can't have just one upper level mount because you never know with horses. Milton does have a good record and I think I could easily syndicate him once I get him back on track quickly."

Matt offers me a job. With money. A little bit of money. And while I'm not desperate about money like I have been in the past, I know that the fact he is offering a young kid like me a salary at all is testimony to the fact he wants me. Or rather, I know he needs someone to get Milton show ring ready for him ASAP. I have a feeling, based upon what Lisa said, that the speed with which I progressed with Fortune is my main asset in his eyes.

I pause for a minute. Do I want to leave Europe already? I was supposed to have this great opportunity, to learn new things, learn a different style of riding. I can't even let go of Milton's bridle though. I'm already planning in my mind what I'm going to do with this supposedly difficult horse once I get on him again.

"Think about it," Matt says. "I know you have another commitment."

"I'll take him—I mean, I accept," I say. I'm a little surprised he's so eager to get me, I'm sure he could find someone else with a longer resume. But at this point, I don't care enough to ask questions. Maybe he's surprised how eager I am, like a dying man flailing for a life preserver.

"Why is his show name Milton Keynes?" I ask Lisa as I prepare to leave, walking with her out of the temporary stabling. "That's weird."

"He's named after a town in England. A really mundane town. I suppose it's like naming a horse after Greenwich, Connecticut or Topeka, Kansas, in the U.S. Matt's other up-and-coming Advanced horse is Nebraska Sky, so it fits—names of places—and we aren't renaming him." I can tell that Lisa has traveled around by the way she tries to explain the analogy to me; she's been to all these locations. "I agree it is a weird name. Someone had a sense of humor, I guess. He's certainly not a mundane horse."

"Sense of humor? Obviously not a German." That much I've figured out.

## CHAPTER 5
# CONFUSION

The setup at Matt's is a bit more like what I'm used to; I'll pick a stall or clean a bridle if the staff gets overwhelmed because his operation is so small, but there are other people around with those specific duties and my main job is to ride, train, and teach. I can eat what I like, I can do what I like so long as it isn't obviously unprofessional (i.e., I can listen to music on my iPhone so long as I don't crank up the volume and if I'm training a client's horse or a client happens to be watching I take off the earbuds.). If someone does something stupid Matt's more likely to make a (nasty) joke than act as though someone's profaned the temple of horses.

I was a little bit surprised how tiny the barn was, given the size of Matt's international reputation. But nothing is perfect and I'm not here to ride perfect horses, so whatever.

And ... Milton? Some days he's great; other days he acts as though someone screwed his head on wrong. He'll be fine over a series of jumps and then he'll stop, spin, and whirl with a spook at the slightest thing, no matter how forward-going I have him. He's actually somewhat better at cross-country than at show-jumping since the faster we go, the more he has to occupy his distractible brain. But even then, no matter how many times we try to desensitize him, he gets completely thrown by certain obstacles that look kind of weird like skinnies and water jumps. Dressage he's not as bad as the horses I've owned in the past (but again, that's not saying much) so long as there isn't any scary-looking sunlight anywhere near the letters. If he were three, four, even five years old, it would be somewhat understandable. But he's nine and should be in his prime, not scatterbrained as a baby.

When I tell Daniel I'm back, I'm kind of worried he'll be mad, since he wrote a recommendation for me to go to Fuhrmann's, but he is philosophical about my not liking Europe. "I can see how it might be kind of a culture clash. And a clash of personalities."

"You mean that Fuhrmann's personality is like, the prince of darkness," I say.

Daniel laughs. "I told you before you went he was very old-fashioned. I warned you."

But when I tell him I am working for Matt, Daniel goes uncharacteristically quiet.

"He was your working student, too," I say, expecting him to tell me stories and be happy about that at least.

Instead there is nothing but silence. "Kind of a personality clash there as well," he finally says.

Really? Matt curses all the time, Daniel curses all the time. Both of them can be kind of sarcastic ... granted, Daniel is more into teaching his students and more passionate about horsemanship stuff and the state of eventing, but he's much older and no longer really competing so that makes sense. He has that luxury, the luxury of time. I thought they were kind of similar in many respects, Matt and Daniel.

"How so a clash?" I ask.

"He was very flexible. Ethically. And he has gotten a reputation."

Now that doesn't seem fair to me. "I've been working my ass off with Milton and Matt hasn't said anything about using lots of gadgets. Or drugs."

"Sure, drugging Milton too much to make him dopey would take off his edge and Matt wants to preserve that, and so far the horse hasn't gotten hurt enough to have to work through pain," grunts Daniel. "Just be careful that nothing sticks to you."

"What do you mean by that?"

"You're young and still developing in this business."

I think of all the empty hypodermics in the stalls at my old show barn way back when—there would always be one or two when I was mucking out. The ground after a show would be littered with empty bottles of Perfect Prep around the horses. Matt's operation isn't like that and I tell that to Daniel flat-out.

"What did Matt do to you?" I ask him. But Daniel won't say.

I feel kind of bad, as if I am defying Daniel after all the work he put into me but I can't go back to where I was, with Ingrid and her vacant China doll eyes and the endless slow cantering of Mr. F's baby horses while he rides everything worth riding.

"You know, Simon … ." And that really gets my attention, because Daniel doesn't call me Simon, not ever. "You still haven't started to think like an eventer. This is an endurance sport, from the point of view of the rider as well as the horse. There are many skills involved. You can't expect instantaneous results with an animal or with yourself. This is a sport, in spite of all its speed, for athletes that are willing to take their time. Time to bring an animal around. You don't take horses to a show and get ribbon after ribbon."

That really hurt. Ribbon after ribbon? What does he think I am, some hunter princess? But I am where I am and there's no turning back.

Pause.

"Your precious Milton damn near killed his previous rider running into a jump in Europe."

"I didn't know that. He's balky but he's never been like that around me. And that was before Matt had him. That's not Matt's fault."

Daniel doesn't tell me to be careful with my own neck, because if I were careful, I wouldn't be doing what I'm doing. But I know he's concerned, which worries me for a second because, honestly, Daniel rarely is concerned about stuff like safety. And then I put that out of my mind, not because he isn't wise and I don't respect him—I do—but because worry is the real death when you're riding.

When I tell Max I expect him to be happy but it's him, not Daniel who really gives me push-back. "You lasted in Germany, what five minutes?"

"Wow, I'll really glad to see YOU again, Max. You do realize I can visit you more now."

"Simon, it's not that I don't want to see you, of course I do—"

"Coulda fooled me—"

"But you gave me this whole speech about how going over to Europe was going to be like your college, your education, and how determined you were. I'm just surprised, that's all."

"I am determined to succeed. That's why I'm leaving. It would be nothing but watching horses on hot walkers for months while that German girl rode whatever was halfway decent. Why should I stay? Just so I can say I was a working student in Germany? Well, I was and it sucked."

"So, tell me about this Milton." Max listens quietly, asks me questions about the horse's tack and if the horse's problems might be physical. "Maybe he's a slow developer, warmbloods sometimes are."

I know Max deep down isn't that crazy about eventing. Unlike Daniel, he actually wishes I'd do show-jumping which he regards as marginally safer, statistically and all. (He knows me well enough that I would never be happy doing anything slow-moving and deliberate like pure dressage or hunters.) And Max knows the statistics because he's a vet, and of course just like he studies whatever is the most effective wormer, according to recent research, he also knows that the risks are higher going cross-country versus even the biggest and weirdest fences in an arena because at least stadium fences fall apart. I know the math too but I also know that eventing is the ultimate test of horse and rider and it's the only thing for me, the only thing. Matt knows he has to tolerate my obsession and accepts that because he has no choice. Just like I have no choice but to accept the fact that he's thirty-four years old and wears glasses.

Max's reaction continues to annoy me because I feel his disapproval whenever I talk to him, either over the phone or through his curt text messages. I mean, I thought Max and I had a relationship. I thought he would support me no matter what. I'm also kind of mad at him for not running down to see me (even though I know how dedicated he is to his job as a vet) plus all of the quitting stuff he says.

My mother just says, "You never did have a very long attention span," and sighs.
"What's that supposed to mean?"
"I'm sure you'll make your own way," she says. "I can't talk long. I'm at the clinic and have to tack up and warm up soon." My mother teaches riding and now she finally has some time to brush up on her skills. I know she's riding in the 2'9 division at some elite hunter clinic in the area. She's staying at the low levels because she says she hasn't been judged in a while on her equitation. She's been the one doing the judging instead as a trainer.
I know Mom is kind of disappointed, deep down, not that I'm back but that I'm not doing the hunter-jumper thing. But just like she warned me it was a mistake not to go to college, she just makes her wishes known and then lets me do what she knows I'm going

to do. She's a lot less directive of her kids than she is of her horses, but I guess she figures that Sean and I have a responsibility for taking care of ourselves, unlike her animals.

I seem to have let everyone down, I guess. Except Matt. Even though I don't exactly like him, at least he seems grateful to have me. I'm the only one crazy enough to get on Milton day after day, and I've never been unseated by Milton Keynes, which I gather is an improvement on the record of his previous riders.

I call Max again late one Monday night, which is technically my day off, even though I spend it at the barn anyway, riding a few horses that still need to be worked. "I was thinking about Fortune," I say. "I'd like to go up and see my horse soon. Would that be okay?" I know Max is doing paperwork in his sterile apartment and I hear him take off his glasses with a click and I think he's rubbing his eyes. I've been with him long enough to know that the work of a vet never ends, especially since Max is the youngest guy at the practice and gets all of the cases none of the other vets want. "And see you as well if you're not too upset about dating a quitter."

"Simon, you're taking my words out of context and twisting them around."

Max tells me about riding Fortune, how he's getting better at balancing him at turns in show-jumping and is more confident galloping on the flat. "I'm sure having me ride him is quite a comedown, but I'm actually thinking of showing him, just at a small schooling show. Just in the jumpers, at one of Daniel's little informal, unrated events. Fortune always won everything when you rode him in the jumpers so perhaps I can fool him into thinking I really know how to ride long enough to do respectably well."

I miss having my own horse, I miss having Fortune. Of course, if I really wanted to, I could move back to Vermont, continue working for Daniel and live with Max. It wouldn't be a bad life. But there are too many 'buts.' Not enough exposure to the elite levels of eventing. Not enough time to work outdoors because of the snow. Not a fast enough track to move me to the top. It's kinda sad that Fortune didn't quite have what it took. It would be a great story, but it's not the story that happened.

I stop by to see Milton when I'm doing my Monday night errands—in other words, going to the supermarket for junk food and soda for the week. I honestly feel marginally more like a grownup doing this, versus purchasing groceries at a convenience store and ordering pizza every night. Milton's standing there, staring into the corner. If I were back at Daniel's, I'd take him out again for a short, unapproved hack but I know I'm not allowed to do that here. There's some stale doughnuts left over from breakfast this morning. I go in, grab one of the plain cinnamon ones, break it up and offer it to him. Milton takes it gingerly, bite by bite.

I can see one of the grooms, a small block of a man, staring at me. I vaguely wonder if he will mention this to Matt, since I know that Matt's very careful about what the horses eat down to the last bit of grain and SmartPak supplement. But I think he just thinks it's weird that I'm here when I don't have to be, after I've spent all hours of the day at the barn as it is. Horses are just a job to him, probably the only kind he can get. Just creatures that dirty up stalls as far as he's concerned. It occurs to me that he's probably never ridden one, and I feel sorry for him all of a sudden.

I have an apartment, a nice apartment, but I'm hardly ever there. A normal person would have bought a house with their inheritance. Equity or whatever. I don't want the hassle of taking care of one and I don't know where I'll be in the next couple of years. Matt's barn is located in Maryland, which is a good place—not too hot in the summer and not too cold in the winter—but I want nothing to root me down.

The supermarket's pretty dead late at night. It's just me and a mix of weirdos, people coming back from working night shifts, college kids getting food to cushion the booze they'll be drinking later in the week. The guy ringing up my food is about my age and has a textbook beside him with some awful title like *Principles of Management,* so I guess he's in college too. The man in front of me looks like a day laborer in a stained flannel shirt and baseball cap that covers his eyes. He's counting his change to pay for his rice and generic bag of potato chips and cans of beans which I guess is his dinner for the night. As he digs in his pockets for more quarters and dimes, I say, "You know, don't worry about it," and tell the cashier to put his order on my tab as well. I feel almost guilty how grateful the guy looks as he scuttles out of the place. Of course, we're not dressed so differently. I just smell of horse and he smells of some weird chemical fertilizer and grass. Even though I've showered and done laundry, I know I will never get rid of the odor of the barn.

    The college guy ringing up my purchases is really tall and thin, even taller and thinner than I am. "That was nice of you," he says. He has a big nose and pasty skin and I don't know if I'm just tired but he looks weird and disproportionate to me, almost like a cartoon. I hurry the hell out of there with my cart. No matter how big of a mess I make of things, at least I have the horses to take me out of myself every day, to connect me to something outside of the numbness of the rest of daily life. I think of that cashier sitting in class, hoping that some stupid degree will get him a stupid boring job that will buy him some kind of respect. Whenever I dip into the world of civilians, no matter how briefly, I always realize how lucky I am.

## CHAPTER 6
# THE WHITE RIBBON

Matt's working student Lisa (his actual work-for-nothing-student as opposed to his paid-almost-nothing rider-me) is different from all the other working students I've known before. For one, she's old. And I mean old old, like forty, with streaks of grey in her frizzy red hair. You can even see them through the hairnet she wears when she's riding. She looks more like a client or someone's mom. Not my mom, who looks really young, but the moms of people I knew at school who used to come home and, I don't know, cook and do laundry and vacuum and all the stuff my mom never did because she was teaching riding after work. People used to mistake Mom for my older sister when she was a bit younger and they weren't joking.

I don't know what Lisa's doing here, why Matt pulled her out of nowhere. At first I was worried about her throwing out her back (all the older riders used to complain about either their back or knees or both) when she was lugging a bucket of water or whatever. But when I offered to help a couple times she glared at me and brushed me off. And Lisa never complains, not about her back or her knees or even when Matt tells her she looks like a sack of potatoes wedged in a dressage saddle.

Mostly Lisa's always okay with me, even though we have nothing in common. It vaguely occurs to me that she's actually not that far from my boyfriend's age, but because she has the body and the attitude of someone who seems like they've been working in an office for eight hours a day rather than moving around a great deal, she seems ancient.

I still can't entirely figure Matt out, either, even though I work for him. I'm still looking for signs of the reputation, why he and Daniel came to hate each other all those years ago. It's unsettling because I liked Daniel so much and felt I understood him so well. I immediately pegged him as a kind of crusty old New Englander, and although I wasn't a perfect employee by a long shot, I did see quickly that the way to his heart was to ride anything and everything he gave me, to make sure that my leg didn't slip back over jumps, and to leave the stalls clean without throwing away any useful bedding.

Matt's not as cheap as Daniel and his demands are more inconsistent. He doesn't say I look like a sack of potatoes on Milton, though. I have a feeling that he's desperate not to make a fool of himself after this new purchase was talked about so much in the media although sometimes he'll chew me out about the other horses, like when he saw me bringing back Electric Slide (Lexi for short) after a schooling session. Lexi's a young OTTB, a delicate-boned chestnut mare who is very much true to the stereotype about TB chestnut mares, which is a good thing, in my estimation. She has hooves like teacups, is all leg, and you couldn't put fat on her if you tried. With her prominent blaze and nearly orange coat color, she's quite striking and it's lucky for her sake she's too fast with too high a head carriage, otherwise someone might have tried to make her into a junior hunter.

"You've hardly been on her, Simon," Matt barked at me. "I'm not paying you for just a pony ride."

"I always try to end on a high note when I'm working on a young horse, even if I only ride them for twenty minutes, and she did everything I asked her," I protested, surprised because he'd never said anything during the other times I'd worked her. But he kept bawling me out and then gave her to Lisa the next day. I admit that I was dying inside for a little bit, but he didn't take Milton away from me and that's all that matters. Was this how he and Daniel had a falling out? I wish I knew.

Lisa and Lexi had a really good session and that's how she ended up Lisa's project. Which annoys me to no end. If I was the sort of person who cared about how people look on horses—which I'm not—I'd say Lisa looks too heavy for Lexi, even though the mare carries her fine. But then again, even when I was on her, I'm sure Lexi was thinking, *this is like the fattest jockey ever.*

Matt does have a habit of exploding at the grooms because the tack isn't clean enough or because his mounts aren't ready and waiting for him to ride immediately, even though they've had a legit excuse like attending to a sick horse. Still, it feels like he's letting off steam more than has an agenda. Lots of people who work with horses have a short fuse and it doesn't mean anything. Of course, sometimes it does but it takes a while to find out what group they fall into.

"I think Matt's PMS-ing today," I mutter to Lisa on one of his off days. She hesitates, then she laughs. Lisa's competent and does what he tells her but seems slightly scared of him. I bet that's a hang-over from her days in middle management or whatever they call it, since he's her boss.

Matt and I haven't had much of a real conversation yet. Daniel would go out hacking with his working students every now and then. Matt goes to the gym every day to lift weights, inspects the barn, goes and rides, has lunch, then teaches, then rides some more, ticking off his to-do list by the hour.

But when he watches me ride, even though he's rude and brusque, he's a way better teacher than Fuhrmann was for me. The first lesson Matt saw me ride a dressage test he said, "I can see you're faking the connection."

Matt is paying me more than I got as a stipend at Daniel's but what would be barely a living wage if I didn't have the other income from what I inherited. I know that he knows I must have some sort of money because I'm not totally scrimping by. I'm here because I want to learn and ride, not because I desperately need the job. And unlike Lisa, I'm young enough that if I had to, I could find other places to take me on. Hell, I could even just pay someone to train me, although that's not really my style. But while I have the money I inherited, I'm not rich enough to coast by on it for my whole life if I want to stay with horses. Still, the money gives me a kind of power over Matt, I have realized: the power to say "no" just like I did to Germany and Mr. F. I get a feeling that Matt doesn't like this, but without it, I wouldn't be here.

Of course, the power isn't that much. If I want to become who I want to become, if I want the ride on Milton, I still need to please Matt. Anytime you want anything, it gives someone some kind of control over you.

One day, Matt tells me that I should go to the gym with him the next morning. If I have any downtime, I usually spend it reading science fiction novels, looking up sports scores on my phone, and reading the Chronicle of the Horse and Eventing Nation online. I resent that time being eaten into, so I protest. "My brother runs, I hate stuff like that."

"You can't rely on being young forever, you know. All of the top riders do more than just ride. I hear that Michael Pollard does CrossFit and runs a half marathon every month. You have to put in some effort into yourself, not just the horses. I'm trying to help you."

Honestly. I doubt that. Trying to show off, more like it. Show that he's fitter than his younger, up-and-coming rider. At least that's the vibe I'm getting.

When I show up at the gym, Matt's not impressed. "Don't you even have real sneakers?"

I'm wearing a pair of puke green Converse from high school. They still have rude stuff about some of my teachers written in pen on them. I shrug.

Honestly, I'm not that impressed either by Matt's workout attire. He's wearing these ridiculous orange shoes, a grey top, and a pair of shorts that are tight enough to leave nothing to the imagination, and trust me, I have very little imagination in that regard.

I watch Matt stack up some plates on a bar. My boyfriend Max is into this stuff, so although I rarely do it myself, I know what I'm doing. I could always lift more than Max, anyway, without trying too hard. I never really worked out exactly, I'd just step in every now and then just to piss him off. My brother and I were always really active as kids and good at things that involved moving around.

Matt works on his front squat. After he struggles with his last set of five and stops to take a rest, I walk over. I know it's more than I've done in the past, but I tip my elbows up and sink to the ground easily then up again; I've always been pretty rubbery and flexible that way.

One of the other guys in the gym, a lean buff guy with a shaved head and tattoos, mutters *nice* and I kind of smile inside although I just shrug and make my face numb as I re-rack it. Again, I think of all the guys in high school gym that used to call me *faggot*. At least it's not like that in here, I was kind of afraid it would be. I put more weight on the bar because I know I can handle it. I didn't want to come here, but now I'm kind of into this. I want to see how much I can take, if I can make myself break a sweat.

"So you've been hiding your talent from me," Matt grunts, as we walk out to the parking lot. I watch the sun rising ahead of us and I try to think how to politely navigate this with my boss. "I thought you said you didn't work out but you were bullshitting me all the time."

"I've always been strong from all the barn work I do," I say. My brother always used to say that I was freakishly strong because I could lift more than him, even when we were both in high school and I was so skinny my arms were practically convex. "They call it 'farmer strong.'"

"I have trouble picturing you roping cows."

"I actually have gone team penning." A long time ago, with my brother. Of course, I insisted on riding in my English saddle, even though I do know how to ride Western, thanks to having spent so much time riding with my brother. I try not to let anyone know that. Penning was pretty disastrous, anyway, given the temperaments of the horses I like to ride. Most OTTBs think cows smell weird, and I can't say I blame them.

Matt doesn't tell me to go to the gym the next day or the day after that, and I guess with my performance I've successfully avoided him getting on my case. I'm okay with that. I don't need to be Matt's friend, his buddy. I've never really needed friends like other people, I tell myself. And he's helped me get better at riding. I can now look like I am doing dressage versus just performing a series of motions strung together. I feel more confident navigating technical jumps cross-country. I've changed even in the short, few weeks I've been here.

I've never held it against people who don't have … warm … personalities. I know that I don't. My brother used to point out that there were other obviously gay guys in high school (unfortunately, none of them were particularly attractive), guys that weren't out like me, but who everyone knew about … and they didn't get bashed as much as I did. He said I had a habit of rubbing people's faces in things and he didn't mean the fact I was gay so much as the way I'd sleep in class, get up, answer a math problem correctly, go back to sleep. The way I'd wear my barn clothes to school without even bothering to wash them. "You come across as an arrogant fuck who's just putting in his time," he said. Which I was, in high school, just doing time, as far as I was concerned.

Also, for Milton, for all of his stopping and weirdness and spooking at the sun ... when he is going forward I am aware of something, some talent, that I have never experienced with any of my other horses before. I am beginning to sense what makes an upper-level Advanced ride, I think. I am finally moving into my future; I am finally where I should be. I'm not trapped anymore in a box of straw.

On my first weekend off, I go to see Max ride in one of Daniel's schooling jumper shows. I actually drive up to the show right before Max's getting ready for the class. It's not formal; he's just in a polo shirt and breeches but it's one of the few times I've seen him in tall boots, ever, versus half chaps and paddock boots.

"Your boots are muddy," I tell him.

"Like you're anyone to criticize someone for how they dress," he says, looking up and smiling at me.

"What's that supposed to mean?" I'm in ripped jeans, my shirt that says The Hungry Puppy (which I got free from a feed store), a flannel shirt, and work boots. I dress nicer at Matt's than I used to since I'm not doing as much hard labor but that also means all my nicer stuff is in the wash. At least I'm wearing clean things. "Horse show is different, that's the only time how you look really matters," I say, looking around for a rag in his tack box. "You'd never go to a vet appointment with dirty hands, would you?"

"I think that's kind of a different thing. i.e., a matter of life and death."

"Not to me, it's not. Missed me, buddy?" I ask, putting my hand on Fortune's nose. "I've been cheating on you. I have a new boy."

## Quick Bright Things Come to Confusion

"So how is Milton?"

"Kinda flattered that they think I can handle him, in all honesty," I say.

"I doubt there is anything you can't handle in terms of horseflesh, Simon," says Max. He looks nervous about the schooling show, which I find endearing.

"You better win this. You have the best horse," I say. "He can jump a course like this in his sleep if you just pilot him around correctly. I'll be watching you." No one is around except us so I slap Max on his ass as a reminder.

I haven't been away that long but I feel like a million years separate me from my past as I watch the competent amateur riders and pros with greenies hop around. Max has improved a lot as a rider and Fortune is still the same. For all Max's joking, it's not like my horse has regressed, I think, as they sail over a green-and-blue oxer. I know Fortune's hard to keep together and prevent from getting strung out and Max does a good job.

I flinch as Max goes for a long one and Fortune bangs a rail. Max gets flustered and slows down in the turn, but they still have a clear round. Two thirds and a fourth. Not horrible for their first outing, I guess, but I'm a little disappointed. If only Max had really gone for it in the end and not gone so wide in some of the turns, they could have won.

"What were you doing out there? Did you suddenly think you were doing a hunter course in the end? Was it really necessary to travel into another time zone to take that last oxer?"

"I wanted to play it safe after we almost pulled a rail. White ribbon, white horse," says Max.

In a way, it is hardest to be around Daniel at the show. I want to corner him at some point, to ask him about why he doesn't like where I am now, but he's too busy with his students and managing everything for much of a real conversation.

Although I was looking forward to returning to Daniel's, I'm glad to leave, I hate to say. I know there's no way I could go back to this, much as I miss having my own horse nearby. "You know, I bet Daniel would have you back," says Max. But it's too remote, too off in the middle of nowhere. It would be like going back to school, and this time I'm really done with that.

Even lying in bed with Max, I wake up in the middle of the night feeling smothered, the sheets twisted around my legs like I'm hobbled. I'm usually a pretty deep sleeper when I do have time to sleep, but I get up, throw on a pair of pajama bottoms and sit on Max's functional couch, which always looked to me like something you'd find in a hotel room. Like a place you'd just pass through on the way to somewhere else. Max always likes things really clean with everything at right angles. Everything just as it should be, contained. I am the one exception to that policy.

I hardly have time to read or watch TV anymore but I'm slowly making my way through *The Scorpio Races*. It's a fantasy book. I only like reading fantasy and sci-fi unless it's a horse book. What's the point of reading if you're still stuck where you are in real life? *The Scorpio Races* is really good because it's kind of both fantasy and horse stuff. I turn on the light and take it out of my bag. I love books where characters can overcome everything against them just by brute force or a magical spell. No matter how uncertain their circumstances, I know it will end well. Maybe the authors have figured out something I haven't in life.

I go ride Fortune the next day. Fortune is still stiff and unbending but a machine cross-country. After riding a horse that I can't trust for so long, it's nice to have one that I can for a change.

I remind myself that Milton, for all of his faults, can do what he is expected to do at an Advanced level. Fortune might be almost the same color as Jasper but he can't compare in any other way to Ben Hillard's horse.

I linger at the door of my car when I'm saying good-bye to Max. He tells me he loves me, he wishes I was here with him. I hear my voice say the same sort of things back like an echo.

I'm not sure how I would feel in the environment I am in right now, where I have to be so guarded, with Max around. I know Max wouldn't like Matt Stevenson any more than Daniel did. Maybe less, and he'd let me know it constantly, in his own, quiet Max-like way.

I plan on driving home without stopping but I'm too hungry and restless and end up pulling into a McDonald's to stretch my legs, use the bathroom, and eat. I'm impatient and starving. Matt and Max share that one thing in common—they think you're supposed to be so careful with what you put in your body because you're an athlete and all, but even though it's not what I'm supposed to feel I know eating this is what I need right now and it feels good and sometimes that's all that matters, no matter what anyone else says. I can't deal with hunger any more than I can deal with stillness. I shove one hand in the bag, ease the car up to ninety, and lick the salt and grease from my fingers periodically, keeping one hand steady on the wheel.

## CHAPTER 7
# DIRTY STOPPER

Matt will be away for the next two weeks, doing a series of clinics. Clinics make money and get him lots of publicity and hopefully draw the interest of the media. Media attention is a good thing; media attention means possible syndication of the horses, wealthier clients, and so forth. Not as much as winning a major, major event but something.

I don't know why, but I feel as if I can breathe easier, not being watched, when Matt's away. I get up earlier than I'm supposed to and tell the grooms I'm going to school Milton over some of our practice cross-country jumps. I don't start Milton over anything major, just keep him forward and in front of my leg. The jumps we school are really for the babies. They're way beneath his level but I keep him fast enough over the little coops, tables, and a splash of a water complex so he can't even think too much to refuse. He's athletic enough that he isn't even sweaty by the end of it and it's still early morning and quite cool.

I think things are going well and I'm almost about to quit until he screeches to a halt in front of a perfectly innocuous rolltop. Like a Beginner Novice level thing. I dig in my spurs.

You little shit, you're fitter (and saner) than that. You have no excuse. We get over but he gives a few colossal bucks to express his displeasure. I head for the jump yet again, without giving him time to think and he pops over. Victory.

"I didn't recognize Milton," says Lisa. "He was going in a straight line. You've done a nice job with him these past few weeks."

This is supposed to be a nice job, I think? He's going well today but overall … I've never had a good horse make so many stupid refusals.

I watch a bit of Lisa's work with Lexi. She's a good rider, her leg is as stable as if it were planted in concrete, and she has sensitive hands. I think she means what she says when she praises me and I think she knows what she's doing.

At Daniel's, there were two other working students, Megan and Cynthia. Megan is now working for Daniel as the barn manager, although she was off on her honeymoon so I didn't get to see her when I was there last. I liked her alright, she was funny and a good worker. Cynthia (we called her Cindy), the other student, left eventing and went back to doing hunters. Even though she didn't have the guts and strength to excel in my sport, she's winning much more than she did before. Her leg is stronger, her position is less exaggerated.

Cindy used to say I helped her, I taught her too. And I feel a little bit good when I see her latest ribbon and championship cooler in a photo on Instagram even though we inhabit different worlds and I know that her easy going horse would be lost galloping where I'm off to … Her father was some sort of talk show host who they say might run for president someday or something like that. All his money couldn't buy Cynthia enough real guts to even get up to Intermediate. Again, I stand by my belief that people are easier to fool than horses. Cindy went through horses faster than I went through breeches and still couldn't find the "right match" for eventing, which means she didn't know how to ride.

A good rider can ride anything, I tell myself. That's the dividing line between pro and ammie.

The day is even longer than usual because, as well as training and the usual lessons, we've got to take over Matt's work as well. I don't mind, I kind of like teaching and this means I have some upper level riders I wouldn't be training normally.

The only bad thing is that a few of the girl riders are disappointed that it's me, not Matt. I can see it in their faces. It's funny but while I can appreciate that Matt is objectively good-looking—tall, sandy hair with only a few streaks of premature grey, blue-eyed, suntanned, and muscular from all that gym crap as well as riding—I don't feel that attracted to him at all, not even in a detached way. He is, in his own way, just as unpredictable as Milton. He'll be fine and then turn on you but I guess for some people that's what makes him hot. I like games with rules and certainty, though, not ones with subjective scoring. Like I said, I have never liked hunters or dressage versus jumpers and that carries over into just about everything else in life.

Lisa asks me if I'd like to have dinner with her that night. I'm actually so surprised I say "Yes," although I'm not even sure I want to. She offers to drive.

"You can tell how horse crazy I am by my car," she says. I slam the door of the blue Ford Explorer shut.

I'm kind of confused. It's sensible and truthfully kind of boring, even more boring than my own car is here. I was so tempted to get a sports car but I thought about all the little matchbox cars I'd seen crash in Vermont in the snow when I was living there and got an SUV instead, a Subaru, which the guy said you could practically drive across a sheet of ice.

Lisa can see the confused expression on my face and she says, "What I mean is that if I didn't spend so much on the horses I could have afforded a really nice car, just like everyone else where I used to work." She talks to me a little bit about her former position, something at a company I've heard of, vaguely, a place that manufactures what she calls 'personal care' products. Anyway, she apparently was making a six figure salary, "But between all the coaching, the horses, the shipping out for schooling, full training board since I couldn't get to the barn as much as I'd like, it all added up. I didn't even have enough time or money left over to dye my hair or fix my chipped fingernails at a decent salon, so I got out of the habit of that," she says, gesturing to the white streaks in her hair and her short nails, which of course I hadn't noticed until now, because I never notice those things on women of Lisa's age. "Got out of the habit of dating as well, for lack of time."

"So what made you give up corporate life?"

"I got downsized and—"

"That's like, a fancy word for fired, right?"

"Yes, Simon, that is a fancy word for fired. And my horse was getting old and no longer competitive. So I sold him to a lower-level rider, sold my house, and decided to take a year to do what I'd always wanted to do, which is be a working student. We'll see what happens after that. Hopefully work as a trainer at least part-time, find another horse to compete on. Try to find a way to better balance life and work."

"I've never had much of a life, only work, so I wouldn't know," I say, laughing.

"Well, you're Bridget O'Shaughnessy's son so you're to the manor born."

That kind of pisses me off. I did inherit money when my dad died but most of the time we were really poor by the standards of the horse world, and poor poor by any standard for a couple of years after the divorce. Lisa doesn't know that but I guess she figures because I'm a formerly famous rider's kid, we were loaded. "I wouldn't say that."

"I mean, in terms of reputation, not money." I relax a little bit. She says, hesitating, "You know, I competed against your mother when I was a junior. She was something else. They thought she was going to be like Beezie is today. She could make even a rank horse handle like a dream."

"She still works as a trainer," I say. Ever since she got a bit more money from the inheritance ... Mom was divorced from Dad but I gave her some of what I got ... which I don't want to talk about because that subject always makes me feel weird ... she's been able to work less and train more. But I know it's been so many years since she was seriously competitive as a rider she'll never be where she was or what she could have been if she hadn't taken such a long break. The barn she ended up teaching at was cheap, the kind of place that has both Western as well as English riders. It never sent people to any kind of finals but the barn owner let her board our horses in exchange for almost nothing and let me ride almost anything so it sort of worked out even though I left it to work for a fancier place as soon as I could drive.

"I could see you were her son the moment I laid eyes on you. I was like, 'I know this kid from somewhere.' You ride like her. Not like a typical eventer. You have textbook equitation."

"Thanks, but they didn't think so at my last hunter-jumper job. Or when I was in Germany."

"Well, you have a release, which is more than some eventers have."

"I'm not as defensive as some, I guess, but that's more out of a careless attitude towards my own neck than any kind of grace."

We pull up to the restaurant. I'm starving. Like usual on a busy day I haven't had any time to eat a real meal since the two candy bars and chips I ate for breakfast.

Lisa orders a bottle of red wine. "To unwind," she says. I refuse and just order a coke. "You're making me feel bad," she says. Sometimes I wish I liked drinking wine more but most of the time I think I make enough bad decisions without it. After a glass or two, Lisa begins to tell me more about herself. "I kind of got away from horses because of college, and then when I bought my first OTTB, he was definitely not the hunter type—"

I laugh. "I know what you mean."

"And eventing was relatively cheaper. Relatively, of course, when it comes to horses. I never had the right look for riding hunters and the equitation anyway. Always kind of short-legged and fat. Even though the hunters are supposed to be about the horse, I always felt it counted against me. So I slowly moved up the levels, and now I'm here. There have been a lot of conference calls on my phone in the tack room while wearing my breeches since then. I feel lucky to have been picked by Matt."

"I feel lucky to have found Milton," I say, looking around, waiting for my food to come. Because it seems to go with the earlier comments about my mom, I ask, "Do you have kids?"

"God no, no. I couldn't be doing this if I were responsible for anyone but myself."

"I have a horse but he's back home with my old trainer."

"Daniel McAllister?"

"Yep."

"You trained with him? No wonder you're good. Is he as crotchety as they say Matt says he is? I know Matt was Daniel's working student."

"Crotchety in a good way. But then again, I'm kinda crotchety myself."

Lisa laughs. "That's not a bad description of you, Simon. For a young guy, you have a very old soul. You're always either serious or sarcastic."

"I just have a low tolerance for bullshit." Well, except with horses. I'll tolerate some b.s. with Milton, at least for now. Because he occasionally shows these flashes of brilliance and brightness and then it's all back to resist, resist, resist, and push, push, push.

"Matt says that Daniel was difficult to work for, always holding him back," says Lisa, frowning. She's put down her fork and knife but I can tell she's still hungry. She starts to pick at the half of the plate of pasta she left. I still keep shoveling down my fries.

"Daniel was really supportive of me," I say. I pour lots of extra ketchup on my plate since I still have fries that need it.

"Simon, that's gross," Lisa says.

I shrug and keep eating. "Maybe it was Matt who was difficult."

"I grant you that Matt does have a temper but that's always true of the best trainers. He's just a perfectionist."

There are people who are perfectionists and people who are assholes. It's critical to be able to tell the difference, I think. "I really don't care as long as a guy puts the horse first, not himself." Diplomatic but not dishonest.

"No one has ever invested in me like Matt. I was always the also-ran at every barn where I rode. Here at least I get some personal attention. For my riding, you know?" She pauses.

"Yeah, that's what sucked about Germany. I always felt because I was an American Mr. F just didn't care. He knew I was going back to where I'd come from. I need to feel as if someone respects me."

"That's it, Matt respects me," says Lisa. "So different from other guys I've known." She can't help herself, she begins to eat the rest of her food. I'm slightly disappointed given that if she didn't want to finish it, I'd be happy to oblige. She eats with a guilty conscience, though, I can tell, she's looking side to side as if someone were watching her, as if she was doing something she shouldn't. "I know I'll have to go back to the grind and get a real job when I leave here but at least I can have my teenage horsey fantasy doing this working student thing for a bit, you know? Unless I can find another way out, which I doubt."

Her words sound familiar for some reason and then I remember it's kind of what I said to myself in Germany, I could always get out of things. Only I'm pretty sure that I can escape when things go sour. I'm young, I think, and Lisa's not. I'm lucky that way. I'm lucky in so many ways, unlucky in some.

CHAPTER 8

# NO SLIDING BACK

Going to my first event with Milton at Intermediate shouldn't intimidate me, but to be honest, this is the first time I've actually been somewhat nervous about my performance at an event since I can remember. All of the other horses I've ridden were at least assured to want to go over most of the obstacles without much prompting. Milton is still unpredictable, and although I don't really think that I will break anything on him or fall off I am kind of worried about making a fool of myself.

"Jesus take the wheel dressage," I mutter as I head for the judge. Don't fake the connection. Rhythm, relaxation, connection, impulsion, straightness, collection. I can feel his back stiffen and resist in every transition, and I know he's thinking about putting his head in the air as we canter, but I manage to send him forward enough that the movement at least looks correct and his unwillingness isn't telegraphed for all the world to see. Matt watches me and chews me out afterward but our scores aren't terrible and we're fourth going into the cross country phase. The field is very tight, though, and the scores of about ten of us are relatively similar.

I've done worse, that's for sure. Fortune once jumped out of the sandbox but I don't mention that to Matt.

Ben friggin' Hillard is there. And of course, I get to finally see the great Jasper in action when he rides him at Advanced. Like Fortune's good, not-evil twin, I think as I watch him on the slate grey horse. Darker, younger, and of course more athletic and better put together than the grey horse I own. Ben's also riding a big chestnut mare going Intermediate called Paparazzi. Paparazzi is a deep red and from what I see of her record and how Ben rides her when he's warming her up, talented. But not as talented as Milton.

In the starting box, Milton's ears are back and when the bell sounds he surges backward, not forward. I hear the crowd give a slight gasp as he tries to buck me off, a real buck; he's not just antsy and feeling good. But I'm not going anywhere but forward, I dig in with my spurs and we're off, over the initial tables and then up a path surrounded by trees on both sides, which would be beautiful if I cared about anything else but getting to the next serious question. A series of skinnies, then a splash … then lots of galloping ground and I can feel him relax even though I can't. "Good boy," I tell him, "Good boy," and finally the ears go up.

He nearly swerves and runs me into a tree at one point (so much for the benefits of scenery). But he has no problem with the series of coops and even the big water complex after another long flat field of galloping. He looks at the water but doesn't stop. "Christ on a cracker," I mutter. I lift my crop but it isn't necessary, he seems to decide that it's better to get that over with than make a fuss.

I pat him and praise him unreasonably after it's over. As if to answer me, he gives another good buck. We had a good pace despite all the attitude.

I get off and one of Matt's grooms takes the horse. Someone shoves a bottle of water in my face and I take it even though I don't feel thirsty or tired or anything, I'm still coming down from the high.

"For a second, I thought he was going to get you off before it even started." I turn around to answer, not really thinking and registering who is speaking and then I see it's Ben.

I'm not usually past words, at least not by choice, but I just stand there, wondering if I've hallucinated. He's smiling with his hands shoved in his pockets, his shirt hanging open, breeches bagging at the knees and looking for all the world like some high school kid dressed up in an eventing costume for Halloween (not that that would happen given no one cares about eventing outside of our bubble).

"I'm used to it by now," I say, when I've finally recovered. "Wasn't my first trip to that rodeo." He laughs and I take a swig of water to stall for time even though I can barely open my throat.

"I saw you ride in Germany," I say. God, say something Simon, before he walks away. "You were amazing." Well, that was dumb, but at least my lips are moving. "I was a working student there, too." I don't mention that I never competed and that I left before my time was up.

"Thanks."

I don't want to let him go so I say, "What about your new chestnut mare, Paparazzi?"

"Patty is her barn name."

"Back at my old barn we used to joke that when riding a chestnut mare it was always a question of whether you were going to get the good bitch or the bad bitch in her when you rode. We have a chestnut as well, Lexi." As soon as the words 'bitch' leave my mouth, I feel kind of awkward, as if I shouldn't curse in front of someone who is semi-famous, even though he's just about my age, but Ben just grins and runs his fingers through his hair.

"Patty's not all that bad. Not like the stereotype at all. I don't know why chestnut mares have that reputation."

"Is she named for the Lady Gaga song?"

"Of course," he says. "She originally started out as a jumper but then she came over to the dark side so I got to rename her."

Pause. I can't wish him good luck on Patty because I'm competing against her, of course. And Matt's competing against Ben and Jasper on Nebraska at Advanced.

"Simon, I need you." I hear Lisa yelling for me. Suddenly I realize I haven't introduced myself. "I'm Simon O'Shaughnessy," I say. "I ride for Matt Stevenson. I was part of Daniel McAllister's working student program last year." (Since that is still my main claim to fame.)

"Simon? Like Beezie Madden's horse?"

"Exactly like Beezie Madden's horse." So you can remember me.

Jasper is at the top of the leaderboard after all of the Advanced horses go. Patty's second at Intermediate, followed by Milton (we were slow due to his erratic path and lost critical seconds). Lexi is way down in the rankings.

Matt is particularly hard on Lisa and Lexi when he critiques both of us and I feel bad. I try to say something nice to her but she just shrugs and says, "Sure beats a performance review in an office any day," and smiles in a way I know is totally fake.

I look at Lexi in her stall and the bridle hanging on a hook beside it, ready to be cleaned. "Was Lexi not tacked up by her usual groom? That's not the bit you normally use for cross-country."

"Matt wanted something stronger because she was running out last time we were schooling," says Lisa.

Well, obviously it worked too well, since you had so many time faults, I think. "She actually has a pretty soft mouth from what I can remember when I was riding her."

"How many horses have you ridden Advanced, Simon?" I start and turn around to see Matt.

"Forget it, Matt, I was just running my own mouth," I say.

"How many?"

"None."

"That's what I thought."

For fuck's sake, I had a genuine fucking question. You don't have to be an asshole about it. There's no way to cover for myself, though. I just nod and shrug like I'm a good soldier that never thinks for himself.

The next day, Matt pulls a rail in show-jumping so he ends up fifth on Nebraska; Milton kind of sucks back, but by giving him leg at every jump and taking barrel-racer turns, we still manage to go clear, doing even better than Patty and Ben. And so we win. Lexi pulls two rails during stadium and doesn't even place at Prelim.

But of course, Ben the golden wonder boy wins on Jasper at Advanced.

I tell myself it's amazing that Milton has made it this far in such a short period of time. When I started riding him he was pretty much not competitive at all.

I still feel a weird stab of jealousy, combined with a kind of heart-stopping desire to grab Ben at the same time, when I see Ben's grinning face as he rides his winning horse for his victory gallop. There's a blue ribbon around Jasper's neck.

After everything is put away and the horses are settled, I go back to my hotel room, lie down on my bed. I pick up my phone, look at the background, which is an image of Brandon Flowers from the Killers. He's my favorite singer and they're my favorite band. I stick my phone's earbuds in my ear to listen to music.

I put on some music. "For Reasons Unknown." The Killers. Always, always the Killers when times get really tough.

I can't stop thinking about Ben. Because Advanced is better than Intermediate, and Intermediate is better than Preliminary … that's just the way it is. Maybe at the lower levels you can pussyfoot around and pretend you're only competing with yourself if you're just a recreational rider like Sean or our friend Heather back in high school. But it would be b.s. if I said that about myself.

I vaguely realize I haven't talked to my brother Sean or my mom in a while and even though I'm tired I should tell Mom that I won today. I turn on my phone to text her and then my heart stops. It's a text from Ben.

*its ben hillard nice job today*

"Holy crap," I mutter.

I sit up at attention on my bed. How the hell did he get my cellphone number?

More to the point, how am I going to navigate this? And I forget about my family and even my future for a second.

The phone rings and I literally jump, more scared of this than anything I've seen on a cross-country course all day. But when I say "Hello," I hear the voice of my brother instead.

"Look, I don't know where I am," he says.

I expected him to know I was competing (I think I told him), and the fact he doesn't congratulate me further disturbs my sense of equilibrium, like my phone has a social life of its own.

"What? Aren't you at school?"

"Dumbass, yes, I'm at school. What I mean is, I went running and I lost track of where I was and now I don't know how to get back."

"Jesus, you're in a city. It's a grid. Ask directions."

"Um, given the area I'm in right now, I don't think that's a good idea." I hear a beeping over the phone.

"What's that?"

"My Garmin."

"Well, if someone tries to rob you at least you can bargain with your overpriced stopwatch."

"I can tell you're really concerned."

"Just take the T back home."
"If I can find it."
"How long have you lived in the city of Boston, college boy?"
"Forget it. I hope you find it funny when I die." He hangs up.
I take a shower. As I'm dressing, he calls me back.
"So I'm on the T now."
"You managed to find your way back out of the great wilderness."
"Shut up."
"How many miles did you run?"
"Only sixteen. I was going to run twenty but I haven't eaten all day. I think I'm lightheaded."
"I guess it would take too much planning to stick a Snickers in your pocket? Or do the cute little shorts that you're wearing not accommodate that?"
"Whatever. Why did you sound so disappointed when you picked up the phone?" Well, I guess Sean wasn't totally out of it if he noticed that.
"I was expecting someone else."
"A guy."
"Yes, a guy. And you don't count."
"I've been meaning to ask, what happened to Max?"
Beat.
"I'm not sure what's happening with Max."
"Too sane for you?"
"Maybe."
"I liked him."
"Well, then date him. I liked Heather and you broke up with her."
"Look, I gotta go. It's getting too crowded to hold my phone." Heather was my best friend in high school that Sean dated for about five minutes before finding someone new. Typical. Of him that is. I had no social life in high school, and up where Daniel is

in Vermont, it was pretty much just me and Max so I couldn't have strayed, even if I had been so inclined.

"Make sure you scatter crumbs of protein bars so you can find your way home next time."

My phone goes dead. I didn't put it into too many words until now but the truth is, I just don't feel the same pull towards Max the way I did when we were living closer together. I'm finding it harder and harder to explain to him what I do all day. He feels farther and farther away from everything that is relevant in my life right now.

All joking aside, I'm glad Sean found his way home. I smile and picture him wandering around with his pasty white thighs in some 'hood in his short shorts, his huge Garmin on his wrist, and only his cellphone for company. Yes, that wouldn't have ended well. Although I'm sure any danger he was in was totally exaggerated by his running high.

I'm not like Sean. I always know where I'm going. I have a good sense of direction. I could be in the middle of a dark forest in the middle of Nowhere, Vermont and I'd still find True North.

## CHAPTER 9

# NOT STRAIGHT ENOUGH

Back to more important matters than my brother, I think. I text Ben back:

*thnx*

I know I need to say something else. Nice going ... on your path to becoming one of the best eventers in the world before you're like, twenty, or something? So I write:

*Jaspers amazing*

Yes he is, I think staring at my words on the screen. Yes he is.

I don't get any messages back but I'm too restless right now so I decide to go out for a slice of pizza close to the hotel room. I kind of jump when I see Ben and a couple of the riders from his barn walking down the street although it's not totally weird he is there. Lots of eventers are staying in the hotel and the streets are full of us. You can always pick out the riders—some of them haven't bothered to change and even the ones that have put on civilian clothes are all suntanned in a certain way, have baseball caps on, and are wearing polo shirts or some other part of the unofficial uniform.

The two of us make eye contact as we pass and to my surprise he says, "Remember Milton, the black horse? This is his rider."

"He's pretty," says one of the girls. "Why is his name Milton Keynes? What does that mean?"

"It's a place in England—a kind of ..." I try to think of Lisa's language. "... a boring town. Some kind of barn joke back where he first came from. I didn't name him," I say.

"Ya wanna come with us?" says the girl and grins. She's wearing a baseball cap with some kind of horse logo on it, has her flattened straight hair in a ponytail and could be any one of the nine million horse girls I've known in my life.

I shrug, take the path of least resistance, keep walking with the crowd and she starts chatting with me. She's nice enough. She comments on the Red Sox hat I have on. But I wear it to disappear and she wears her hat with the logo of her barn to blend in with others. Ben's now oblivious to me. He's talking to another girl, a girl with a blonde bob. She's more athletic looking than the ghost-like girl whose bones he jumped in the stable in Germany, but as far as I'm concerned, they're both the same animal.

I honestly don't feel like socializing that much, so I grab two slices of pizza to go and sit and eat at one of the empty picnic tables out behind the restaurant. It's cool outside and there's no view except for the back of the other buildings. I feel more alone than I did by myself in the hotel room.

But then Ben is beside me with his pizza. "Why'd you leave?"

I shrug and take another bite. I consider saying something like, "I thought I'd be in the way. That you might want to be alone with your girlfriends." But this isn't just a guy, a cute guy, it's one of the top eventers in the country in front of me, even though he's just like me right now in jeans and a shirt and one of his boot laces untied.

"Where's the rest of the bunker?" Ben asks.

"Bunker?"

"That's what my trainer calls Matt's barn."

"Whaddaya mean by that?"

"Just that Matt doesn't socialize with people that much and his riders usually don't either." Ben deftly takes a bite, managing to drip tomato sauce and oil on the paper plate he's holding, not on himself, which I also regard as fairly impressive.

"I didn't mean to be standoffish," I say. There is a beat of silence between us. "I own a grey too, but he's not with me now. I took him as far as he could go. We got to Intermediate together, but in all honesty, that was pushing the upper level of his skills. He's back where I used to be a working student at Daniel McAllister's and is happier just being a jumper up there."

"Gotcha."

"My ex-boyfriend rides him," I say. This is the first time I've called Max my ex before. The truth is more like we're not officially dating but when I go up to visit him, well, it can't be like we never had anything, right?

It's the first time I've been this close to Ben and can look at his face for a long time without seeming creepy. Even in the dimness, I can see Ben's tan and the street lamps reflect against his light brown hair. Now that I'm very close I notice he has weird piercing eyes. I act like I'm playing it cool, and the truth is I'm so hungry that whatever desire I'm feeling isn't affecting my appetite. I finish my food, crusts included, throw away the paper plate, and sit back down next to him. He eats more slowly than I do, tosses the crusts. Then we get up and begin to walk together, as if thinking the same thoughts, which I think we might be.

Suddenly, I'm not afraid, and Ben is just a guy to me, not someone I've been watching like a spectator. "Congratulations on today," I say.

"I'm lucky to have found such a good horse, so early in my career," says Ben. There's still a part of Ben that has a very practiced sound, as if he's been around adults and the press so much he's forgotten to talk like a real person.

"You're not lucky, you're good," I say. We're moving through some kind of little park, and I sit down on a nearby bench. I suck the last dregs of the soda from the wax cup I've been carrying and toss it out. "I've been lucky." There is a pause between the two of us. He sits down beside me, close, close enough that his jean leg brushes against mine.

I lean over, look around to make sure that no one can see us and kiss him. He doesn't pull away. Lucky me. My mouth is still cold from the ice and I can taste the garlic from the pizza in his mouth but since we've both eaten the same thing it doesn't matter.

I'm not exactly a fan of hooking up outside in a strange place, but one thing leads to another and we stop for a little bit to find a place in the park that's out of the way of most of the streetlights, near a playground that's totally empty since no little kids are out this late at night. Except for the squeaking of the swings in the slight breeze it's quiet and dark enough that I can forget everything around me except the thought, *Holy shit, I can't believe this is happening.* It's almost as sweet a feeling as winning earlier today and much, much more unexpected. The plastic, pointless castle in the background that kids are supposed to climb up and down makes the whole thing even more surreal.

I can hear drunk people laughing and shouting as they walk through the park so I zip up my pants quickly. "Fuck," says one of them, a guy's voice. I'm not afraid, God knows I've gotten into my share of fights with idiots but I feel, I don't know, weirdly protective of Ben right now so I just stand there until they pass. I mean, they might not care what we're doing but I can't help reacting defensively.

"I should head back," Ben says.

There isn't much more to say; both of us will be leaving tomorrow. I'm not sure about a lot of things, if Ben is even fully out or if he considers himself bisexual or whatever (not that I believe in bisexuality, exactly, even though I know that's not what you're supposed to say … although Max always said when it came to other people's sexuality I just believe what I want to believe and I guess at least about that one thing he was right).

I don't want Ben to go. I grab him by the hand, the hand that feels almost fragile with its long, bony fingers, the hand that has such a sensitive touch on the reins. I can tell he's more inexperienced than me, which sort of surprised me—Max was older, so I'm used to being the less aware one. I kiss Ben again and consider going back at it since we're by ourselves again but I can sort of tell he's spooked. Ben stays by my side and we walk out of the park together, not wanting to be alone. He stays with me until I'm at the foyer of the hotel. "See ya," he says.

I still don't know what the hell happened other than the fact it felt good as I stumble into the hotel lobby. "We're leaving at 5 a.m.," I hear Matt bark at me.

Oh, God, Matt. During the time I was with Ben I had seriously forgotten Matt was alive and in my world.

I'm guessing Matt's been in the hotel bar for a couple of hours but he's only slightly drunk. He's a pro and knows how to pace himself. Probably doesn't want to be hung over when we're transporting the horses back tomorrow. I know his style by now. I'm back in the bunker now. "Yes, commandant," I mutter when he's out of earshot. "*Jawohl.*" Pretty much all the German I can remember.

## CHAPTER 10
# THE EMPTY TRAILER

I'm supposed to visit Max the following weekend and I'm not looking forward to the conversation I'm going to—have to—have with him. The truth is, Max is a great guy, I'm just ... bored ... restless ... I'd rather be seeing Ben even though I know it's not exactly like we're dating. I'm not even sure what Ben is to me at this point, although he sends me pictures of his horses from time to time and funny little messages and all. I just know that although most of my brain is occupied with my job, when my brain does stray, it's preoccupied with Ben, not Max. Well, with food and sleep and stuff like that too, of course.

Matt's little trailer, which he let me borrow, bangs behind me like an empty tin can. What's really bugging me, of course, is my horse. It's not the thirty-day boarding rule of having to sacrifice the month because I didn't give notice. I just kind of wonder how he will fit in at Matt's. I have already talked to Matt—there is an opening in the lower barn.

It will be so awesome to have a horse to hack on my own, I tell myself. It doesn't make sense to leave my horse with my now ex-boyfriend. Even though he doesn't know he's my ex yet.

There's part of me that feels sorry for Fortune. I won't have time to ride him like I did when I was at Daniel's. I feel sad for horses in general, all of a sudden. It's amazing how something like the sex lives of their owners can have such an impact upon their futures, how they're trained, how they live, even if they live or die although I'm determined that as long as he lives, my horse will have a home with me, somehow and somewhere.

I don't even know how to have this conversation. *We have to talk?* That sounds like such romantic bullshit from a movie.

Max isn't home so I go to Daniel's to see Fortune. I think of how last year I used to go careening through the woods, without a care in the world, and it seems like a lifetime ago. How I used to worry about money all the time and where I was going to be working next. Now that I have savings and a job, I should feel less worried, but I don't. I feel like there is this extra, aching responsibility at all times to justify what I'm not sure I've earned. It's pressing down on my chest constantly, just like the fear of being stuck in a box of a job having nothing to do with horses used to dog me. Oddly enough, even though statistically eventing is a dangerous sport, nowadays the only time I don't feel on edge, ill at ease, is when I'm riding. At least then and there I know the worst that can happen; at least then I have a prayer of answering all the questions that might be posed to me.

I see Daniel, standing with a slight stoop due to his old, injured hip in the middle of the freshly-dragged ring (the work of his latest working students, I can appreciate). Max is on Fortune, who looks (almost) clean and two other ladies, one on a bay and one on a chestnut, are halted next to Daniel. I don't recognize their horses, so they might have trailered in. The fences are set to about .90m.

I watch Max go first. His first jump is kind of a bad distance, but he stays with my horse. Then Fortune starts to settle and they're ... moving as one pretty nicely. Max manages to hold the big horse together, he stops Fortune from rushing or getting too heavy. Fortune's almost compliant and Max isn't just a passenger hanging on, like the girl working students used to be when they tried to ride Fortune. Standing and watching from afar, I wait for the other riders to jump the course, and then I come closer to the fence. Max spots me, starts, and then smiles. I feel like hell. He looks so happy to see me.

I want to ride my horse so badly. Even if he's not perfect. I mean, together we tried and he taught me so much.

"God, I love this horse," I say to Max as he walks him cool. Watching Fortune from the ground with Max riding feels like such a weird role reversal.

"Don't you love your current one?"

"I do but our relationship's a little bit more complicated."

"I thought you hated that word, complicated, and any complicated relationships." At first I think Max is criticizing me but then I remember he's referencing a conversation the two of us had a long time ago, when he was talking about a relationship he had with a 'straight' guy who was married for five years. I said I would never submit myself to such bullshit and I feel guilty because my relationship situation is pretty complicated right now.

"Milton isn't my horse," I explain. "Matt's operation is dependent on a very few horses; it's pretty small, and every ride counts. There's no riding for fun."

After we untack my horse, Max rubs my shoulders and kisses me on the neck since we're alone in the barn. The women are gone, Daniel's back in his house. Max touching me still feels good. I'm aroused, but I know I can't exactly sleep with Max and break up with him immediately afterward. I mean, technically I can, but ...

We walk back to the grassy field that doubles as the barn's parking lot, where Max's battered old SUV is parked along with my newer car with the small but shiny trailer hitched up to it. I remember how I only had a rickety bicycle when we first met. It was useless for most of the year in Vermont, given how much snow we got that year.

"You want him back. Fortune," says Max. "I thought I heard a trailer when you came in."

"You have hearing like a dog, Max."

"One of my few professional assets."

"One of many."

"When are you going to find time to ride him?" he asks, kind of casually. "Then again, I know you, you'll be galloping around the fields and the woods at midnight. I always said you were half-highwayman."

I'm not sure what a highwayman is exactly, I think it's some kind of a thief. I think of the setup at Matt's. I know it won't work the same way at Matt's as it did at Daniel's. It will be at least a half a day, getting Fortune on the trailer and off again, parking, observing the restrictions of the trails, dealing with stupid Maryland drivers on the road who crawl up the ass of a trailer even though there is a horse's butt hanging out of it.

It's not going to be the same, having Fortune with me now.

"There's someone else," says Max. And I know he doesn't mean Milton.

"No. Yes. Sort of." It's … complicated. Again, I hate that word. But the plainest truth is that I want Max when I'm around him but not enough when I'm not. Not enough. And I know he doesn't fully understand the cold hard drive within me, pushing me ahead, the sense that my days are numbered. Sure, there are plenty of old guys riding horses, but that's only because they're cashing in on all of the success and time they put into competing and winning when they were my age. My time at Daniel's, my inheritance … the way I grew up at Mom's, I feel like everything has been pointing me in a specific direction, even the things I didn't really earn myself and I have to follow that path. I have to be one of those old guys still riding at the top level someday, and that means I have to work my ass off now with blinders on.

I can see the parallel universe I shut out when I left here—I could have stayed, worked for Daniel McAllister, competed on Fortune as best as I could at Intermediate, and bought a better horse to take me to Advanced—but I can't say I regret leaving it. Max is safe and kind but I've outgrown all this already. This isn't me anymore. It's too far away from where things are happening in the industry and where I want to be.

I don't say all of this, of course. I just kind of shrug and walk back to the barn. Fortune's in there, eating his dinner. "I'll wait to let him out when he's done." He hates to be confined inside. He's like me that way. No malice, just needs space.

"I'll miss him," says Max. I can hardly look at him, I'm so uncomfortable. Max sounds cool and I know instinctively that there isn't going to be some kind of farewell fuck to end this all.

"You're right. It wouldn't work. I can't bring him home," I say. "Not where home is now. Take him."

"I can't afford a horse," says Max. "Time-wise or money-wise."

"Daniel isn't charging me that much," I say. "And you're not the only one riding Fortune." This is all true. Daniel's begun to use Fortune in the occasional, upper-level lessons, thanks to Max's consistent riding of him. Fortune doesn't pull like a train as much as he used to. He's come a long way for an animal my own mother called a POS (piece of shit) horse when she told me I'd be better off getting a used Ford Fiesta for $4,000 bucks (or something like that). They thought he was broken, they called him an eventing prospect when they sold him to me, even though he was old and had evented before so I knew that in horse sale language eventing prospect meant no brakes and hopeless. Hopeless like me, like I was back then, a junior that had ridden all sale horses and jumpers.

"You keep him. I'm certainly not selling him. I owe him that much. I wouldn't be where I am now as a rider if it weren't for Fortune."

"He'll always be there for you, if you need him again." I'm not sure if Max is saying, "*He'll* always be there for you, if you need him again," as in," *I* won't" or if he's saying something that's true about them both. He's sort of using something between the voice he uses only with me and the voice he reserves for his clients. Clinical.

It doesn't matter, really. I'm already gone inside. I know I've driven all this way for nothing. I feel as empty as my borrowed trailer. I lean over to kiss Max good-bye. Yes, I'm already gone. I've gotten good at leaving things lately.

## CHAPTER 11

# BAD WORK ETHIC

The next week, I do get Matt's permission to take Milton out to school cross-country at a nearby horse park, where they have a series of courses of varying levels of difficulty. This absolutely blows Milton's mind and he stops at the first jump. I whirl him around, show him the jump, tap him smartly with my crop and then approach again. He clears it easily, without incident and is great for the rest of the school.

"I hate a horse with a bad work ethic," I say to Lisa after trailering him back. Interestingly enough, Milton is actually pretty easy to cram into one of those shiny rattling boxes and will load without much of a problem. Lexi's much more inclined to have a meltdown and require a lunge whip and the assistance of another person. With Milton, it's once we get there that the problems arise.

"Did you always have a good work ethic in school?" Lisa asks.

"Hell, no," I say.

"Well, we get what we deserve. What goes around comes around."

I laugh. "I'm sure my old high school teachers would think Milton doesn't treat me nearly as badly as I've treated them. He didn't fall asleep halfway through, for example."

"Karma's a bitch."

"Nah, I think Karma's a chestnut mare, based on Lexi's last school that I saw."

I reflect upon Lisa for a minute. At first, I dismissed her as an amateur playing professional, and an old and out-of-shape one at that. But she's surprised me. She's actually a pretty good rider even though she doesn't look like much in the saddle, and Lexi's been so difficult recently. Sometimes I wonder if Lisa regrets her life before this; I vaguely wonder if she had been like me, didn't care what people thought about her at all, and just hit the ground running with her riding, become a working student immediately after high school or even college, then maybe things would be different for her. Maybe she'd still be lean and fit and brave enough to ride horses like Milton. Don't get me wrong, she's not like the middle-aged ammies that have to plod around on packers. But very, very few people get to the elite levels of my sport. I know there is no room for detours. I'm still not entirely sure why Matt thought enough of her to take her on, and I wonder if that thought torments Lisa as well.

I walk pass Matt working Nebraska Sky in the dressage ring. He's cursing a bit under his breath—I can tell even though his face is expressionless, his lips are moving slightly. The horse is way above the bit, resisting him, not in a frame. It's ugly. I know Nebraska is much more compliant than Milton, and Matt'll get him where he should be after a few turns around the ring, but every now and then, it's nice to see that Matt is human, that even the Iceman has to sweat.

Lisa seems to hear what I'm thinking. "We all have our bad days," she says. "But even on my worst day, I know I'm lucky to be here."

## CHAPTER 12

# CHASED AND CAPTURED

I've never wanted to *be that guy*. You know, the guy that hops in his car and surprises someone even though we're very clearly not dating, just messing around. But on my next day off I kind of have a dilemma. Because I don't have a horse, it's not like I can just hack around and although I could watch some lessons or watch Matt school, I know it would feel weird and he would ask me why I was doing it.

But there's no way I can just stay in my apartment, doing nothing. Sitting and watching sports on TV, reading a sci-fi paperback, eating junk food. I'd have no idea what to do with myself. I don't do downtime, I just don't. A normal gay guy would find a more convenient hookup using Grindr, Simon, I remind myself, as I get in my car early in the morning.

My heart kind of feels funny but that might be from the amount of Mountain Dew I chug driving up to Connecticut. The sign on the farm where Ben rides out of says *No Trespassing* on the front. Long View Farm. There isn't a gate with a punch-code at Long View like at Matt's so I drive in.

When I walk in the barn I feel all eyes turn on me. Ben's there, in breeches, boots, and a polo shirt, holding Jasper and talking to a woman who looks like some assistant trainer or something. Suddenly I feel even more different from Ben than I did before because he looks so confident, in his element and I'm clearly an interloper. We make eye contact and to my surprise he doesn't look surprised.

"Oh, Monica, this is my friend Simon. He said he might drop by," Ben lies, smoothly.

Then Ben introduces me to his trainer, a guy called Patrick Everett, mentions I worked for Daniel McAllister. And about my record. Everett hesitates. His eyes narrow when he hears Matt's name. I can feel him looking me up and down, placing me in a peg as competition but not in serious competition with Ben.

I know Patrick much better than he knows me, of course. He's no longer competing, one of those people who has more of a reputation as a trainer than a rider. But he's supposed to be a great teacher.

I watch him watch Ben as Ben works with Jasper on adjustability over fences. Everett's not a screamer. Actually he's kind of quiet and it sort of surprises me after a certain point how little he can say and yet affect Ben. I'd do anything to be in the lesson myself, I think, I feel more longing for that than for Ben himself for a moment.

After Ben cools Jasper out, one of the girls asks me and Ben (she calls me "your friend") to come to lunch but Ben just shakes his head. I follow him home in my car. He says the house should be empty because his parents aren't home and his older sister is at college. I know that Ben's not super rich, not like some kids who ride, but when we pull up the gravel driveway, I see that there are two horses in a stable in the backyard, a miniature goat eating grass in a round pen on the front lawn, and a big orange cat jumps up on the front of my car before I've even taken the key out of the ignition. Everything is very clean and nice, too, the house, the fencing, and the quaint little red shelter for the horses, and I know that to keep even a tiny place like this up in the Connecticut suburbs takes some money.

"Who are the horses?"

"Those are just mine and my sister's retired horses from when we were kids. We'll go trail riding on them for fun, but we don't seriously compete on them. My dad rides them mostly. Mom can't ride anymore." Ben picks up the cat and kisses him on the head.

"That cat is so fat it has its own zip code," I say.

Ben laughs. "He's very spoiled."

I'm still interested in the horses. "Your sister events as well?"

"She actually did the hunter-jumper thing. Now she's a senior at Wesleyan University. She doesn't live that far. She comes home on the weekends and sometimes she comes home just because she hates people, or having to live too close to people in a dorm. She's not really doing anything much anymore, horse-wise other than hacking. She's a vegan. Shoo, Sigmund," he says to the cat, putting him down and latching the farm gate behind us. "We have a bell on him as you can see for the chickens."

"A vegan, what, is that like a major or something at Wesleyan?"

"It could be. If you ever meet her she'll go on about the merits of synthetic saddles and, I don't know, hummus. I think she majors in English. I try to stay out of her life."

"Morrissey," I say.

"What?"

"Morrissey is a vegan. The Smiths? Their album *Meat is Murder*? One of my favorites."

"Are you a vegan?"

"I live on pizza and hamburgers. But you really haven't heard of the Smiths? You must have listened to some of their stuff. I'll have to educate you."

"If you're not a vegan, we have more than enough free-range eggs that the chickens laid last night."

"What would I do with those?"

"Eat them? We're lucky my mom isn't seeing any of her clients today and she's not at home. There's a door out back that leads to her office in the basement. She's a psychiatrist."

"If I see her I'll make sure I don't say anything crazy." Pause. "You said your mom doesn't ride or that she used to ride? Did she get hurt?" I think of my old trainer Daniel McAllister, who had a bad hip, the result of getting busted on a greenie when he was in his late sixties. He still rides, just not at the level he used to and he's in his seventies.

"Nah. She has lupus." The name sounds vaguely familiar to me.

"What's that?"

"Hard to explain. It's like when the body attacks itself, mostly the joints. It's really painful. It was hard for Mom to stop because she loved riding so much. Dad rides but it was Mom who was really into it. She used to event, even when she was doing her residency, which most people don't. She'd ride at really crazy hours, just to get the training in. Lupus, it's a weird disease. They weren't sure what was happening at first. Mom actually kind of figured it out before everyone else."

"I'm sorry. But she can still work and walk and everything?"

"Yeah, I know, I'm sorry as well. It's not like she's crippled. She looks normal on the outside; she's just in a lot of pain most days. If you see her, for Christ's sake don't say that she doesn't look sick, like some people do."

"What kind of an asshole would say that?"

"I don't know, people say stuff if they see her parking in a handicapped parking lot because she doesn't have a wheelchair."

He looks down at the street.

"What?"

"My dad's law office is close by, too. I love my parents but it feels like they're always around. Just making sure dad isn't stopping by for lunch."

"Do you miss being in college?"

"I'll go back to UConn next year ... maybe ... unless things continue to go well."

"That would be a pretty powerful incentive for me to continue to win. I barely survived high school. I'm sorry I just turned up out of nowhere."

"I thought you might one day. You seemed like the type."

"What type?"

Ben just smiles.

Ben goes to the stables, checks to make sure his horses have enough water and hay and throws some food out for the cat, "the worst mouser ever, we really shouldn't feed Siggy but we do," and makes sure that all of the chickens are still in the coup. The stable is really more of a lean-to—the horses have shelter but they can walk out and in freely. There are no doors.

"You can't blame your cat for being fat and a crappy mouser if you put a bell around his neck for your birds."

Apparently, these are super-fancy chickens, because Ben gives me a whole rundown of their breeding and history, just like you would a horse. "Most of them are Rhode Island Reds, what they call a heritage breed." He tells me his mother is a real hobbyist about them and put a lot of her horse energy into them when she couldn't ride anymore. I also kind of wonder if she put a lot of her horse energy into Ben, too. I know Jasper was a find but he couldn't be cheap and the retired horses aren't old nags, either, even if they aren't competing anymore.

Ben's house horses are both big bays around 16.3 hands, one a mare, one a gelding, one with a star, the other with a blaze. The more powerfully-built one, the mare, was Ben's. She packed him all the way up to Training, he tells me. The horse's show name was Paradox but her barn name is Doxie. Ben's sister's horse is a more elegant-looking animal but the same color (almost like the horses are sister and brother although they aren't). Show name Lost in a Maze, barn name Larry.

Long ago, when I was a kid and Mom was still married, we also used to keep horses at home but our barn was a rehabilitated version of a very, very old stable with big box stalls and stuff. Even though everything isn't brand new, this all looks like it has been bought from some sort of a catalogue because it has the same kinds of cutesy little designs on it and stuff. The chicken coop looks like some kind of a Victorian house, I've never seen anything so elaborate even though plenty of people kept backyard chickens in Vermont.

I take off my boots at the door because Ben has kicked off his driving moccasins and I kind of get the idea you're not supposed to wear shoes in the house. I'm in a threadbare pair of jeans and a torn t-shirt, and suddenly I'm lurched back into high school, an alien amongst perfect, preppy kids. Ben's polo shirt has come unbuttoned, exposing the muscles of his chest as well as the bones of his clavicles and what I like best about his breeches isn't the label but the fact they leave nothing to the imagination at this point when he's out of the saddle. I realize I should have worn something nicer, but I didn't want to come looking like I was dressed to ride on one hand or that I was dressed like a civilian who knew nothing about horses on the other. There was really no way to look good doing this.

The kitchen is kind of old but not, and it seems like the place has been carefully designed to look like a colonial farmhouse. There's brick and wood everywhere, and in the living room there's lots of little figurines and glass bowls and other things I'm afraid to knock over.

Ben sits down on a couch, puts his stockinged feet on the table. I grab him by his legs, pulling him to the ground where there's nothing to break.

"So, what was the deal with that girl you hooked up with in Germany?" I ask him when we're (sort of finished). I'm not entirely comfortable just laying here, but Ben seems cool with it so I kind of have to trust him on this one that we're not going to be walked in on and things aren't going to get awkward.

There is a long pause and I know I've kind of shocked him but I don't care. "How did you know about her?" he asks. And then I tell him about going to see the horses and hiding under the blanket on top of the tack trunk. It's kind of embarrassing for me, but I've felt weird concealing it from him, too. I'm a pretty bad liar. I've been sort of worried he'd hate me and I try to emphasize I didn't know what the hell to do. He looks at me, arches his eyebrow, and says "What are you, like a ninja or a spy in your spare time? You're something else."

"Yeah, that's what a lot of people have said and not in a good way."

"She was just—oh, I don't know. I had had a few too many drinks at the party. It was whatever. She'd been after me for a long time. She's still in Germany working for my trainer there. Sometimes I miss Germany."

"I don't."

"I learned so much there."

I'm not going to let him change the subject, especially to my own sore spot. "What, you were too polite to say 'no'? What goes on in Germany stays in Germany?"

He shrugs. "The people at my barn know I'm gay, if that's what you're asking."

"I just wanted to make sure that I didn't have some big secret to keep or something. I don't have much patience for closet cases, I've dealt with enough of that."

"Oh, I seem like a closet case to you," he says.

"Nah, just really gay and preppy."

"So I must have surprised you after you saw me with Elise?"

"Nothing surprises me. I'm a ninja, remember?"

Ben moves away from me, goes to pull on his shirt and breeches. I stop him from doing this for a minute, put my arms around his. I know he's surprised by how strong I am, most people are. I hold him to me for a good minute, kiss him again, and then let him go.

Ben's phone has been making sounds the entire time we've been at it, and as I get dressed, he starts answering messages.

"Who are your texting, your next hookup?"

"What do you take me for? I'm texting my trainer. And I'm answering some of my friends."

"Your new girlfriend, you mean?"

"Shut up."

"What about that girl who wanted to go to lunch with you?"

"We're friends. We went to the Chase School together. We've known each other for a long time and because she events as well. She goes to UConn too, although she's still in school there, not taking a leave of absence like me."

"What is the Chase School?"

"My high school."

"Oh, a prep school. Figures."

"And I suppose you're going to tell me you went to some school in the projects or something."

"What's that supposed to mean?"

"You and your bad boy attitude."

My old puke green t-shirt has the name of one of my favorite bands, The Clash, emblazoned in red across it with the words THE FUTURE IS UNWRITTEN on the page of an open book on one side, with a picture of gun on the opposite page, and the words KNOW YOUR RIGHTS underneath the trigger.

"This isn't an attitude."

Ben goes to the kitchen and starts making himself lunch. "Do you want anything? I'm sorry, but if I don't eat, I'll pass out soon." He grabs a jar of peanut butter, a fancy little jar of what looks like homemade jelly from the refrigerator and a loaf of bread that's weird, misshapen and I guess also homemade. I watch him carefully cut his own sandwich into quarters. I want to do something to mess up how perfect he looks. Even his hair has fallen back into place from when we were on the floor.

"You cut your sandwiches into quarters? How adorable."

"Is that wrong?"

His phone lights up again and I grab it. "Lady Gaga is your background. See, you're such a cliché." I read the text which I assume is from a girl because it says:

*your friend is cute who is he*

I'm tempted to answer it but I don't. "Aw. I'm apparently cute."

Ben takes the phone. "You're just as much a cliché in your own way, Simon."

"What does that mean?" I start eating his sandwich as I watch him text back. "No one's ever called me a cliché before."

Ben makes another sandwich for himself and doesn't answer. I finish mine (or what was once his), pick up the spoon lying on the counter, take another spoonful of peanut butter, put it my mouth, roll my eyes, look at him meaningfully as I lick it with my tongue.

I leave soon afterward. It's a long drive and I need to be fresh for work tomorrow. Ben needs to ride horses all afternoon. I want to know when I can see him next but of course I don't know when that will be. It's just not practical to pin down a date and time.

Still, I feel high on it all—high on the speed of my driving as my car climbs steadily, eighty, ninety, ninety-two, just hovering there, that's a good pace. High on an impulse paying off. Like choosing a slightly dangerous choice of a distance or sharp inside turn to make time. High on the fact that somehow I've convinced Ben that hooking up with me is something he wants to do, even though I'm sure if he really appreciated who he was, he'd realize he could have any other guy on the planet. And obviously any girl. He's never known anything but success. He doesn't know how rare that it is. He's never been anything else but perfect. And loved.

It's just because he's hot as hell, I tell myself, but even I can't convince myself that's the only thing drawing me in. Wanting to be someone, wanting someone. The line is as fine as a tripwire.

## CHAPTER 13

# ELECTRIC COMPANY

Lexi is stone cold lame the next day.

Unlike at Daniel's, Lisa and I don't have the responsibility to take care of her or even call the vet. I just have to get the next horse ridden, so I'm up on Roxana next, trotting her in spiraling circles, cantering and counter-cantering, trying to get this deadish horse to move out. I can't stand a lazy mount but that's the reason I'm riding her today, because she's been dragging. I can't stop thinking about Lexi and after I've ridden all of my morning horses (Milton is scheduled for the afternoon), I find Lisa and ask if anything has been done about the mare. Even though Lisa's been riding Lexi for ages now, I still like the horse.

Lisa looks blank. "She's fine now."

I notice when Lisa rides her that Lexi is indeed not lame anymore but she's careless with her legs and raps a couple of fences. That's not like Lexi—if she doesn't want to do something, she's usually more inclined to run out. The mare is slow with her changes and stumbles a few times.

There's nothing dramatic but the whole experience leaves a bad taste in my mouth. I have a package of Pop Tarts shoved in my jacket that I forgot to eat for breakfast and I give Lexi one, first making sure that Matt can't see that I'm giving the horse junk food. I like Pop Tarts cold. I smile as she licks the brown sugar from her lips.

As she eats, I give her a quick scan. I realize I'm looking for … something … I don't trust Matt.

I feel under Lexi's stable sheet. There's a small bump in the area between her shoulder and neck. Her skin is so fine it shows everything. Her veins are like a map under my fingers. Of course, it could be nothing. I feel the bad leg. It still feels hot even though she doesn't react. In fact, she doesn't move at all when I ask her to lift it and I have to lean hard, like she was a pony that was resisting having its feet picked by a kid.

"Sorry girl," I say to Lexi. "I'm sorry about it all."

At the hunter-jumper barn where I worked in high school there were horses I knew were Aced up to the gills, or who I knew had more than their fair share of Perfect Prep stuffed down their gullets before a show day. While that type of thing isn't common in eventing, you never know about painkillers. It would be stupid, to work a lame horse just for a schooling session even though Lexi's record has been pretty crappy and she needs all the work she can get. That might be Matt's rationalization? I don't know. This might be nothing but I do know that with Matt and horses, they're just a means to an end for him. He can always get another one, just like he can always get another me. Disposable. Lexi's not working out, I know she needs to go, and she needs a couple of wins under her belt to recoup his investment. There's nothing I can prove, I just know I'm in a place where things can't be trusted and I hate that.

## CHAPTER 14

# FIRST ADVANCED

Eight months later, almost nine, Lexi's still there. So is Milton. So am I.

Some things change, some things don't change. The biggest change is that we've finally moved up a level, where we should be. Advanced. Playing with the big boys. That is, playing with Ben.

Or rather, Milton's back where he should have been for months and I've finally moved up with him. Or I've brought him back from falling down the levels. Depends on your perspective, I guess.

"Whoa, Whoa." Milton is rushing. He's getting excited but I prefer that to sucking back. He doesn't fuss about any weird looking brush or go crooked over any skinnies. I ride him hard at a gallop over the flat and open land because I know the next complex is tricky and will require some serious half-halting. Of course, I can't be too aggressive and override him because then there is the off chance he'll stop, stick his head up, and relapse into the Milton I used to know, when we first were negotiating our "complicated" relationship.

We're heading for the water complex when suddenly I hear, "Hold on course, hold on course." Damn it, things were going so well. They write my time down, one of the faceless people on the sidelines who are more characterless in my eyes than the trees and grass—I notice the colored flagpoles more than the volunteers when I'm in motion. I pace Milton back and forth like a panther. He's sweating, foaming, and so am I.

But we finish clear. I stay with the groom while they cool him down.

"What was the hold for? Someone fell?" I ask Blondie, the groom.

Blondie giggles, which annoys me sometimes, but she's competent and workmanlike. Her real name is Vicki. She doesn't know it but Blondie was also my favorite nickname a long time ago for a pretty spacey dun mare I used to ride and Vicki reminds me of that horse. And Blondie's also one of my favorite bands. So it's kind of a compliment, an endearment if that's what you want to call it and kind of not.

"Yes, a fall. Ben Hill something or other."

"Ben Hillard?"

"That was it."

I had calmed down before hearing the news but suddenly I'm sweating again. "Is Ben—I mean, is Hillard, is the rider okay?"

"Yeah, I think so."

"Can you find out?"

Ben and I haven't been texting much in the week or so leading up to this. Hell, I've hardly had time to eat or sleep much less think about—but suddenly I'm breathing hard, my hands are shaking, as though I'm nervous. Which I'm not. But I'm surprised I care so much.

"Blondie, what did they say?"

"About what? I hate it when you call me Blondie."

"Victoria, how is Ben Hillard?" I try to smile and drawl out her name but I don't feel like joking now, not one bit.

"He's fine. Horse is being looked at by a vet."

"Okay."

"Pretty horse. They don't think he's broken anything but maybe strained a suspen-suspen—"

"Suspensory ligament?"

She giggles. "Yeah, I was gonna say a suppository but I'm like, that wouldn't make any sense. Something S."

"Gotcha." Ben is okay, Ben is okay. And I hope his horse is okay. Now focus, damn it, I tell myself, and I'm in the chute again in my mind, the tunnel of competitive drive, where no desire can reach me.

Cross-country Milton's time was rock star solid.

Matt and Nebraska have already gone and Matt comes over to me as I'm still decompressing. I'm grinning and squinting in the sun. "Time was good," Matt says. He's with Freddie Whitechapel, a British guy who is based in America because his wife's from around here. Freddie's one of those people who is genuinely, flat-out hot as hell and has no idea that he is, with his pale skin and blue eyes and mop of curly dark hair to set it all off. His wife isn't even as hot as he is (not that I am an expert in such matters), and when you see a hot guy with a less-than-hot wife, you know he fully doesn't understand the power of his attractiveness.

Freddie says, "I recognize you from last year. You were working for Daniel McAllister then."

"I was Daniel's working student. I work for Matt—Mr. Stevenson, now. He's my boss." I'm not sure how Matt wants me to refer to him in front of other people.

I had wanted to work for Freddie at one point, then decided to go to Germany, and then ended up with Milton. I still admire Freddie, his riding, his ethics around horses, his accent, and the way he looks right now in a pair of breeches. My face is beet red but fortunately my secret idol will just think it's from sun, and the brim of my helmet's skullcap conceals some of it, I'm sure.

"My, that horse Milton has changed. He had quite an edge when I saw him last with his previous rider in Germany," says Freddie, admiringly. "Your program has done him a world of good." Matt grunts and I watch Milton walk past us in Blondie's capable hands. He sticks his head in the air and neighs. He spooks and nearly pushes little Blondie over but she pushes back. Even though whatever comes out of her mouth is kind of dumb, she's a great groom and takes no bullshit.

"Milton still has a bad attitude, but he's fast," says Matt.

"He certainly goes well for Simon," says Freddie. "They always say black animals are unlucky in the States although black cats are actually good luck where I come from."

"We did well today but that's not luck. We've been working hard as hell on that horse to recoup my investment and it's finally paid off."

"Jazz looked nice today," I say, referring to Freddie's current Advanced mount.

"I was hoping we'd do better this season. But … bloody Ben Hillard on Jasper. Until today. This is the first time we'll get a crack at winning something for a change. Not that I wish ill luck on anyone."

"Ben Hillard. I could snap that kid in two. Even Simon could," Matt says, gesturing to me. "He is arrogant as hell. He could benefit from eating dirt now and then and I don't mind saying so."

"Don't get any ideas, Matt," says Freddie. "Ben's obviously tougher than he looks."

Ben strides by. He smiles and nods to all of us.

Now that I know Ben is safe, I admit I feel a bit more relaxed in the entirely imaginary competition that exists between the two of us in my head. The fact that he can fall reminds me that he is, in fact, human. He can be touched by some things. Me and the ground for one.

Matt seems to be in a good mood even though for the first time technically we are competing against one another. I think it is because he still regards Ben as his major competition.

Ben and I have met off and on. When we have time. We have different days off and the fact he lives with his parents doesn't help much. He's come down to Maryland a couple of times. At least then we can be assured of time to ourselves, without interruption. But for two people who have known each other for as long as we have ... I feel I know him well and not at all; I know him because we want the same things and I don't know him because he's very sparing with the little bits and pieces he reveals about his inner life. Maybe he doesn't have one, maybe I should envy him that as well.

I want to see him right now, go over to him like a normal person whose boyfriend's just fallen off at a major competition, even if he isn't injured. But I can't.

In the morning, Milton sweats and frets in the warmup ring. A relatively low oxer and a vertical makes him excited and he doesn't like a lot of horses in what he considers his personal space. Which is sometimes the entire ring. He doesn't seem exhausted; quite the opposite, with every canter circle and transition he gets more and more amped up which could be good, or not. I can't get too confident or overly excited myself. As if to remind me of this, he knocks a rail down and I flinch. Fortune, as clumsy as he was on the flat, was a rock star jumping but when Milton's tired he doesn't respect the rails in the cups the way he does a solid fence.

There's still a part of me that is surprised when Milton does poorly at stadium. It's by far our weakest phase together. After all, I grew up doing hunter-jumpers, so in many ways it's the easiest thing for me mentally. I understood Fortune's hatred of dressage but Milton's different and kind of craps out in stadium. He's tired and he knows the jumps will fall apart so he doesn't care.

*C'mon Milton, be a competitor,* I think. I know you can do it. *It was just the warmup,* I tell myself. *Forget it when it counts.*

When the bell sounds Milton starts surging forward. The course passes by as I ride in a daze but we leave everything up, just barely (Milton raps the last rail pretty hard but it doesn't budge).

"Nice," I hear someone say as I pat Milton. More riders to go, I can't relax.

Then I hear someone say: "It's a shame about Hillard falling, it would have been nice to see the best rider here over that course, though."

"Happens to everyone at some point, though. At least the guy's not hurt."

"Figures it would happen when I come, though. It will be ages before I get to see another horse trial of this level in person, the way my work schedule is this year."

I get off and hand off Milton to Blondie. I can hear my breath rattling against my chest, I wipe the sweat off of my face, get sand in my eyes and it stings.

I'm first overall, Nebraska is third. Not only do these victories get Matt's barn some needed publicity—now we have a waiting list to fill up empty stalls, some up-and-coming new riders want to train with us, newer, better horses—I feel as if I've proved my worth to him finally. I have a victory I can hold onto, something tangible that can't slip through my fingers.

## CHAPTER 15

# THE BAD COLIC

Even though we win, I'm not expecting a victory parade or anything. I know Matt too well for that. Still, I'm not prepared for what happens during our next day of real work: Matt tells Lisa to ride Milton and I get to ride Lexi. What the hell did I do, is my immediate reaction. I mean, I can understand criticism if I lost, but I won. Like a kid, I think, it's not fair.

Again, Lisa's a good rider but she gets intimidated with the crap Milton pulls on her when she first gets on. Eventually I have to take him. Matt seems really pissed and I can't do anything right in his eyes although secretly I don't think we do that badly. I know that he's angry on some level that Milton's going well only for me, that he can't trust someone else on him. And I know that Matt's reminding me that he owns Milton, I don't.

The day after, I'm supposed to flat Milton and I think all will be right in the world. But even before I tack up I notice something's off. When I tell Matt he says, "You can be a real old woman." But when he checks him out, as if on cue, Milton starts kicking his belly and he realizes I wasn't whining. He sends me out to work one of the client horses.

I watch Milton arguing with the groom, trying to lie down as Blondie works to keep him walking. After I'm done with the horse I'm on, I take the lead rope from her, yank it, and remind him that I'm the boss including the boss of his health.

"I need you to work the other horses," says Matt. "Not lead a pony around." I ignore him, pat Milton, and begin to walk.

Walking isn't always the best way to deal with colic. There are so many things that can cause it—gas, a twisted intestine, and impaction—I know that my old boyfriend Max said that lots of times it isn't even recommended because it's just exhausting. Sometimes it just tires the horse out. But the way that Milton's been rolling and thrashing, walking is actually probably less tiring for him, so walking—very slowly—is what we're going to do, old skool.

We're all hoping it's just gas and goes quickly away at this point. It's been less than an hour and a half, and I've already died a thousand deaths inside.

I go to lead Milton outside. It's too close in the indoor. I'm choking in here myself and can't breathe even though I've made my face impassive, even annoyed to the outside world.

Milton stops dead in the aisle for a second but doesn't seem to be about to throw himself down. I try to coax rather than pull him forward. I remember how intimidating he looked to us all when I first saw him when he was running away, all those months ago in Germany. He looked more like a photograph or a statue than a real animal. Well, he's definitely real now.

"C'mon buddy."

I hear Matt in the distance, and Lisa's voice—she's finally come back from riding Lexi.

"I hope he's okay," I hear her say.

"He'll be fine. Simon's just being a …" And I can't hear what he says, just the tone so I can guess.

There is a pause and nervous laughter from Lisa. At first stab, I think it is because she's worried about Milton but then I realize it is more discomfort than fear. "Well, I wouldn't say ... that."

"There's enough of them in the dressage and hunter-jumper world," he says. And now I know he's definitely not talking about the horse.

I stand there for a minute but Milton takes advantage of my momentary weakness and tries to lay down again. Someday, I'll have my own place, I think. Even if it isn't huge. Even if it is just the size of Daniel's farm. Someday, I won't have to deal with this shit.

Well, that's not really true. No matter how famous you are, horses can still colic. You still have to deal with ... shit ... I think ... which is what I'm praying Milton passes soon.

The vet says it *is* gas, it's not an impaction or twisted intestine. It's not anything that requires surgery and we all, even Matt, kind of relax together and can finally breathe again.

"Just being dramatic," I say to Milton, relieved, trying to make a joke in the dead quiet of the stall. "He's quite a drama queen." The vet laughs but Matt is silent.

"He may have ulcers, though," says the vet, an old, crusty guy, who is the exact opposite of Max. More folksy than cool and clinical but that's typical of vets who have been there and seen so much over the years. "I'd recommend doing some tests ... and in the interim, be sure he always has something to eat, to prevent too much stomach acid from building up. We're gonna have to baby the big guy a little while"

I touch my hand to Milton's muzzle. He's standing quietly for a change. I can tell he still feels like hell.

Although he's passed manure, Milton seems listless for the rest of the day—even Matt doesn't say to do anything with him. Milton hardly eats or drinks, which is a bad sign, since keeping something in his stomach is key.

At first, I was so worried about Milton, I didn't even think what it would mean for me, but now I've had a chance to mull it over in my own brain, my mind working like the juices of Milton's overactive gastrointestinal system. It's beginning to sink in. Matt has the other two horses at Milton's level at this barn—Nebraska Sky and Geronimo and Geronimo doesn't really count because he's been demoted because of his age and soundness. I don't know what's going to happen to Geronimo since he's soon not going to be useful to us. Perhaps Matt will sell him to a lower-level rider.

Lexi is Lisa's project and has no record to speak of. The other horses I regularly ride are mostly sale horses at the lower levels and client horses. Matt's really hit a dry patch, horse-wise, and he's never had a big string. If Milton goes, I'm back to where I started, almost worse than where I started. "I've really screwed myself over with you, Milton," I say as he stands there, his eyes vacant, staring into space.

I need to call someone to talk about this. Certainly not my brother. Not Ben. Of course, there's one person I know who knows more about colic than I do. I shudder a little bit but I have to do it.

Max identifies himself over the phone like he usually does but before I can utter the single syllable that's his name, he says, "Simon? Is that you? What's wrong? Are you in trouble?"

Jesus, he does have hearing like a dog, he can tell it's me by the way I breathe. "It's not me, it's my—it's Milton. He's colicked and he's still not quite right although the vet said it wasn't something that required surgery most likely. He's passed some manure but he's not eating. They think he has gastric ulcers."

"Does the vet seem competent?" I feel slightly honored that Max values my opinion although it's true I shadowed him on enough rounds the year we were dating.

"Yes, yes, he is," I say.

Max tells me the type of medication he'd use (omeprazole) which is what Milton is on right now. I feel comforted hearing his voice tell me that.

"Is Fortune okay?" I ask.

"Yes, I had a really good ride on him yesterday."

I hear music playing in the background. "Is that the Pixies?"

"Yes, it is." But then I hear something else, a man's voice. God, I'm such an idiot.

"Well, I better go." I'm just too tired even to feel anything. I hang up.

It's just like Max, that the Pixies would be his idea of hot date music, I think, one of the things I liked most about him, that we could communicate by talking about music.

I gently lean on the wood of Milton's stall door and smack the front of my skull against the surface. God, I'm such an idiot, I think again. I look at the big, sick listless black horse. With a great rush, I remember what it felt like to be free, galloping around on my own horse in the woods of Vermont with Max. I realize I'm standing in a box, trapped with this horse Milton and who knows what's going to happen to the both of us. I've been trying to avoid boxes all my life and somehow seem to have made one for myself just the same. "I think you'll get through this one," I say to Milton. "I think we'll get through this one okay." He looks away from me into something beyond as if he knows something I don't.

I'm exhausted. I don't recall the last time I felt such bone-tiredness. Lisa looks pretty tired as well, and I can feel Matt's eyes on us as we sit slumped on one of the carved benches in the center of the stable. They hardly get any use except when there are visitors.

"C'mon," Matt says, "Let's go out to dinner."

I know he means to be compassionate but truthfully, having to put on my game face for my boss for the next few hours just feels like another chore. Still, I can't say no.

Without asking either of us, Matt orders a large plain pizza, beer, and wings. Both he and Lisa dig in but my stomach feels too sick and knotted to eat.

"Simon, I can't have you keeling over on me. Eat something," says Lisa.

I mutter something about not feeling well.

"You're as skinny as a jockey. It's unfortunate you're not shorter," she says. "What are you, six foot?"

"A little over that, yeah."

I'm so jealous of tall guys," says Lisa. "I'm only 5'5." I actually thought she was smaller. Another unfortunate thing about Lisa as a rider is that she's all torso with stubby legs but I don't say anything. I close my eyes. A Taylor Swift song is on in the background. "Shake It Off." This is the worst day ever, I think. Almost. The only redeeming thing is that nothing and no one has died. "Shake it off?" Fuck you, Taylor.

As if he can read my thoughts, Matt says. "Milton's still alive, Simon."

"It's my nature to expect the worst."

"I agree it would royally suck if Mr. Milton Keynes decides to leave us soon. If he does, it's just for spite. It's not a serious colic. There's no twisting of the internal organs."

After a couple of beers, Matt begins to loosen up and talk about himself. His father used to breed racehorses and he grew up breezing them. He's never known anything else but horses. Sometimes I think that if Matt felt he had other options growing up, he'd have taken them, but he's one of those people who have never viewed horses as a choice, they've always just been there and a way of life.

Matt looks at his phone. "No messages from the barn, so I assume Milton is still alive, Simon." He picks at the screen a bit more, shows me a photo from Eventing Nation or Eventing Connect, one of those types of websites. "Well, it seems *his* horse is healthy enough."

I start a bit. It's a picture of Ben and Jasper. Ben's sandy hair is shining gold in the sun and the greenness of the huge brush fence makes Jasper stand out even more in the photograph. Jasper's a dark dappled grey, darker than I ever knew Fortune to be, but his white parts are nearly blinding. "B—Hillard's a nice, sensitive rider," I say, choosing my words carefully.

"Sensitive, yeah, he sure is *sensitive*. He's a pretty boy. That's why the eventing press likes him," says Matt. "You beat him last time and he's still their featured interview this month."

"Yes, yes, I did," I say. "I won."

Back at the barn, the three of us check on Milton. He's eating and drinking finally like he's hungry, and he's passed some manure and doesn't look like death warmed over anymore. I stand there for a long time and, uncharacteristically, he walks over to me of his own free will. I put out my hand and he rests his muzzle in it. I breathe and sigh and so does he. I feel like he's asking me a question to something I don't know the answer for— "I don't know Milton, I'm a bad one to ask about a lot of things," I think. "I don't know."

I return to my apartment and finally I can eat. I go to the kitchen, pour a bowl of corn flakes with a huge amount of milk and slurp it down, standing at the sink. The milk doesn't taste like the milk in Germany, even though it's whole, not the sickly skim stuff. I remember liking the milk back in Germany. Again, I don't miss much of what I lost, even if I could go back, I wouldn't.

I look around my faceless rented apartment. Nice as it is, I've barely had a chance to unpack much less decorate it, for all of the time I've been here. So not much has changed in my habits since

I was a working student. I've come up in the world technically and my apartment rent is higher but it's just as messy as it was before and just as plain. It doesn't belong to me, it's just a resting place between events. It's just a nothing hole, a cell, like everything else that doesn't have to do with my job.

## CHAPTER 16

# BREAKING THROUGH THE KEYHOLE

I feel like the buzzer takes about an hour to go off but in reality it's only about an extra thirty seconds.

"He looks like a skeleton," I hear one of the spectators say, ogling both of us. Don't know who, the crowd's just a sea of waterproof boots and whispery rain slickers to me. It's misting but not really storming. For a half, brief dumb second I'm offended by the comment and then I realize it's the grease on Milton's legs that makes him look like he's wearing a skeleton Halloween costume.

Milton's hooves beat softly on the grass. Over a table and onto the real meat of the course, which has mercifully fewer spectators. The mass of gawkers will get thicker again around the water complex and any jump that has more than one or two falls (rubber-necking ghouls) but I'm going early and right now the hot chocolate and the big plastic glasses of wine being sold at the tent right in front of the starting box are just too good to resist. In fact, one of the sponsors must be a winery or something like that because the next (easy) jump is made to look like a bottle of wine lying on its side.

"A totally realistic jump that you'd be likely to come across when out foxhunting," I said to Matt as we did the course walk together.

"Don't make me want to crawl inside that thing after you've finished riding," he responded.

So far, nothing to drive anyone to drink. The next few jumps are less weird and we're up through a ditch so easily it feels effortless, like floating. The wind is against us as we gallop and Milton starts to get fresh, but I manage to give him just enough whoa that he takes the next gate as clean and pretty as if it matters how the two of us looks, which it doesn't.

We gallop past a grove of trees. Mud slashes into my face as we slice through the water. Now a skinny, now uphill, right to the next major question.

Blondie is there, waiting for us as we finish. No faults, and the fastest time yet. "You're way at the top of the leaderboard now."

Somehow I knew that even without her saying but I smile and nod and thank her. "Good boy," I say again, and scratch Milton's withers. I'm almost afraid to make too big of a deal about it, but he was such, such a good boy.

I have to wait. It's usually bad to be one of the first to go cross-country. The order is kind of messed up, too, because a number of riders have multiple trips on different horses. But despite their more favorable position in the order of go, right in the middle of the pack, Matt and Nebraska have a refusal. Ben and Jasper go at the very end, without a fault of any kind.

Matt says, "Nice work, Simon." His voice is cool and expressionless. "He can really move out when he wants to." For a beat I'm not really sure what to respond. I know it's always weird for him, me being ahead of him like this. I know I have to hide how I feel because I can sense Matt seething against his Iceman exterior. Blondie's walking Milton cool, and I watch the gelding's leggy loose stride. He's happy now. He doesn't care. He doesn't have to deal with all of the bullshit of the sport outside of the competition.

I call Sean that night to tell him the good news. But he sounds all weird when I pick up the phone.

"Are you okay?"

"I just got back from the ER."

"Shit, what happened?"

"Stupid foot again. Another stress fracture."

"So this means no running?"

"Not for another couple weeks until it heals. Could be three or four, could be six."

"You're fucking Cinderella, Sean, with that foot. How many times have you broken it?"

"It's kind of hard to run without a foot."

"No foot, no horse."

"Yeah, I expected you'd say something like that."

"Jesus, I was trying to be sympathetic."

"I figured. Well, the coach isn't going to shoot me, in case you're concerned."

"No founder or thrush, I hope."

"Asshole," he says.

"What did your coach say?" I know Sean really likes the guy. From what I understand, he's this really spiritual Zen type, not what you'd expect of a college cross-country and track coach at all. He never yells, for one thing. But he gets the team to run like a hundred miles a week and Sean even trains in the off-season for half marathons and once trained for a marathon, just to keep in shape. I'd be bored out of my mind. But the team seems to like this coach. The team's not super-competitive nationally, Sean's not going to be a professional runner or anything like that nor is anyone on the team, but he's still obsessed with it.

"Coach just told me that I had to trust that my body would heal in time and I had to accept that."

"Honestly, if someone told me that, I'd want to punch them." More than I would from any of Matt's weird toxic bullshit, I think.

"Well, I have no choice."

I've always been lucky, even more so than Sean, with my health ... although not with the health of my horses. There are some things you do have to accept, like the limits of how much you can push the horse but with my body, forget it, I'm just going to keep pounding on it as long as I can, until I meet my goals. That's what's worked with me up until now and until it stops working, I'm not going to change. I know Sean's had stress fractures before, little cracks in the bone that aren't real breaks, and deep down inside I always think that if it were me, I just wouldn't say anything and keep running. I mean, it's not like he can pound the bones of his feet to dust. Can you? I don't know but they always say that human legs are less fragile.

The following morning is cool and cloudy for stadium and that's a good omen for me; I don't need the sun. In fact, I prefer it when it's not too bright. Milton's nervous and pawing as we wait to go. There's a light, low-lying mist that I know will burn off soon but it makes things look strange and shadowy. I haven't really slept all night but the thoughts that kept me awake—like how long I've been planning and waiting for this, how just a few minutes can determine the course of my entire career—now feel cold and dissociated from me and I can watch them, clearly and calmly from a distance. All the tension within me has burned off already, even before the fog. It feels good to be doing something and not thinking.

The rider before me, I'm not too worried about her because she had a refusal cross-country. She goes clear this time, which isn't a bad thing. There isn't a specific tricky fence or combination that I'm anticipating. The main thing all the riders will be battling are fatigue and nerves at this point and I know Milton can get squirrelly when he gets tired. I warmed him up mostly on the flat, trying to keep him settled yet forward and listening to me.

I'm acutely conscious of how alone in the world I am. In a way, I'm the only person in the world who really wants me to win this without reservation, and of course, that makes me all the more determined and sure that I will.

Milton's tossing his head with his nose in the air but I manage to get it down as the buzzer sounds and we head for the first fence, which is just a simple red-and-blue vertical. He gives an explosive kick out afterward, I'm not sure if he's annoyed or pleased with himself, but I'm able to settle him and send him straight into the oxer in front of us without him even thinking of running out. He takes it long but not ugly. The course isn't that bad at all, almost routine. The only remotely spooky fence is yet another jump flanked by wine bottles, but Milton doesn't even look at it, I guess he's seen something like this before so it doesn't even register. "Wait, wait, boy," I mutter as we head to the in-and-out, then finish at a hard gallop over the final vertical.

"You guys were amazing," chirps Blondie, positive as ever. Blondie's sunny optimism occasionally irritates me but suddenly I'm grateful for it. I know Ben and Jasper are on course right now, and as if she is reading my mind, Blondie adds, "It will be hard to beat you."

It's out of my hands, although I admit I'm hoping Ben'll pull a rail. It's probably just the same as he was thinking right before I rode, I tell myself, to make me feel better. I also realize that I don't care that much about how Matt does, just as long as he doesn't disgrace the barn (which I know he won't). He can't beat me today, no matter how hard he tries.

I watch Blondie walk away with Milton as his glossy tail swishes beneath the oversized pale blue cooler.

I don't watch the rest. "Ben and Jasper went clear, but Milton Keynes is still ahead thanks to their time cross-country," I hear one of the spectators say behind me. I whirl my head around and see two women in sturdy Dubarry boots and matching rain slickers they must have bought from one of the vendors. They don't even know my name, but they know Milton.

When I get a moment to calm down after it's confirmed I've won, the first person I call is Daniel. It feels sort of weird to say it, since it seems kind of inadequate, but I say, "thank you."

"I always knew you could do it," he says. "That's some horse you have. How has Matt been treating you?"

"It's a mutually advantageous relationship, I'd say."

"You've become pretty diplomatic in your old age, Shaughnessy."

"He's kind of an asshole, but Milton can be one as well. No malice with him, though, Milton, I mean."

"Now that's the kid I know."

Lexi doesn't do so well. I've hardly noticed Lisa all weekend. She's still stuck in Preliminary. Off my radar.

## CHAPTER 17
# NOTHING TO SEE HERE

There's an article on Milton and me on every eventing website and also some of the general horse ones as well. One of them says OVERNIGHT SUCCESS. Yeah, I think. Almost twenty years of overnight success (my birthday's coming up although I don't tell anyone about it). And however many years they've been saying Milton is talented but useless.

I can't help but read the articles. They say it should be no surprise that I dominated stadium, given that I just did the jumpers when I was growing up (well, it was a surprise to me) and that Milton's better at dressage than the horse I rode at Intermediate when I was a working student at Daniel's (Fortune). "No shit," I mutter and smile. You mean he didn't put his head up and try to jump out of the sandbox?

I have a day off a few days after the event. I'm afraid it's going to be all weird with Ben. But I want to see him. I want the feel of him beneath my hands and there's something in me that needs to be released, some nervous and bottled up energy.

We're riding together this time and I wear my breeches. Then at the last minute it occurs to me I'll need my saddle and boots, which I left at the barn.

The barn's closed today—I have off and it's 5 a.m. right now (I have to leave early to make the drive worth my while) so it's just the barn crew ... and Matt's car. I immediately wonder if something's wrong because this is early even for him, he's usually at the gym at this hour if he's up (sometimes he sends me texts between weight-lifting sets).

I notice Milton's stall is empty. Is he sick or something again? My stride quickens as I head out back, looking for Matt. They're not in the main barn—I even check the wash stalls to see if Milton's being hosed down for a cut. Then I hear the swearing.

Outside, in one of the smaller rings, I see Milton and Matt. Milton's pawing, shaking his head, and pulling his usual crap as Matt tries to ride him over a relatively reasonable-sized course in one of the smaller schooling rings.

I flinch as I see Milton's front hooves leave the ground for just a second, not a rear, exactly, but he's thinking about it. Then he spins, trying to unseat his rider. Matt's ass doesn't move from where it is. *Good for you, buddy.* I'm not thinking about Matt.

Kind of an asshole thought on my part, I guess. But I can't help it. *Jesus, why is he trying to undo what I've been working on so long and hard? Bastard. Bastard with a side order of bastard sauce. The poor horse has finally learned to trust humans a little bit and now you do this, you fucker?*

Then I realize: *He thinks, I've fixed Milton for him. He thinks he can take Milton for himself. There's nothing I can do. Milton's not my horse, so I can't tell Matt to get off. I can't give him advice (even if I wanted to, which I don't). I have to go. Stop feeling like someone's cheating on you with your horse. He's not your horse, none of this belongs to you, Simon. Matt's still one of the best eventers in the country, stop being such a fucking know-it-all all the time. What would happen if I got all dramatic, barged in, and demanded he work him right? I'd be told to get the fuck out of there immediately and he'd be right to say it. He didn't even like it when I questioned that contraption he's got Lexi going in cross-country. Matt doesn't take questions. He's the Iceman.*

Milton starts to run. He's got a good bolt and his head's flying up, evading Matt's hands. Matt makes the horse go in smaller and smaller circles until it's painful to watch. Milton's got to get tired soon, I think. The horse gives up eventually, planting his feet in the ground, but he's having none of this jumping thing, none of this moving thing, if he can't go where he wants.

I can stay and watch and speak and lose my job. Or I can go and pray that Milton teaches Matt a hard lesson.

I get what I came for and leave. I know that if magically Milton behaves for Matt, Milton's not mine, no matter how good I am as a rider. And even if Milton leaves Matt in the dust, he's still not mine. I still need this horse. All the thoughts I have pop around in my head like popcorn, disconnected yet intense and angry and ready to explode.

I feel like my brain looks like the diagram of an atom I drew in physics class so many years ago. "I just need a good fuck," I mutter, because it feels satisfying to say that, and it's the one thing I can be certain of in the next twenty-four hours. It's not really true, I know, I've always been the worst liar, even to myself. I need so much more but maybe, just maybe I can be normal once and pretend. All normal civilians need are a good fuck and money for beer, I tell myself. It's only in the horse world that normal becomes eking out a few extra seconds ahead of someone on another billion dollar horse in a billion dollar saddle. I am so, so not normal in so many ways.

I turn up "Should I Stay or Should I Go" by the Clash. I ask the great Joe Strummer from the great beyond that very question. But the song provides no answer. I listen to it on repeat but the music just amps me up, it gives me no guidance.

The drive is long and I hear my old self talking to my new self. *Get out. You didn't put up with crap at all the old hunter-jumper barns where you rode all those years.* An image floats in my mind of me wearing one of my favorite band t-shirts, riding after hours, with my iPod plugged in my ears, the jumps hiked up, and saying fuck all because I knew I was the best (bravest) rider there and they wouldn't challenge me because there were some horses only I would get on, that would only go well for me (that is, when they weren't tranquilized or Perfect Prepped out of their minds). But where did that get me? As soon as the young or crazy horse was calm enough, he'd be palmed off to another rider who was willing to wear a nice shirt with a collar to lessons, smile, and do what she was told so she'd get a consistent mount and be able to compete in and win all the right things.

The old dream: what I really need is my own place, where I can own everything, where no one owns me. But even if I had the whole fortune left to me by my father to blow, I know that I couldn't afford to maintain a stable all by myself and keep it going without credit, support, a name. It's not like setting up a Wawa on the corner of a street.

Speaking of which, I've been several hours on the highway already and I'm hungry. I stop at a rest area, not a Wawa unfortunately just a faceless bathroom, burger place, and vending machine area, and look at my phone. Not that I usually bother to wait to check texts when I'm driving but I've been so absorbed in thought and the music has been playing so loud that I haven't responded to the beeping and buzzing like I usually do.

*see ya in a few hours love you*

My hand starts to shake a little bit. This feels, I don't know, weird. I get corn chips, Snickers and Mountain Dew. That will satisfy me for now. Just focus on the taste, the motion of my jaw, the emptiness of the open road and my speed. I'm not even sure I know what love means anymore. I thought I loved Max. I think I still love my old horse, so why did I leave him? When I began this whole journey from high school to this, I saw Fortune being ridden cranked up in draw reins and just bought him for a couple grand. Because no one wanted him. Love at first sight. That doesn't cut it anymore at this level.

It's best not to say 'love' at all but Ben doesn't know that, not yet. He's always done what he's supposed to, his parents have been able to pay for nice mounts all his life. He's always been around good people.

I meet Ben at his barn, park my car, and slide next to him in the small truck he's using to pull the two-horse trailer we're taking to some trails nearby. I texted him on the road so he's ready to go, and we don't waste any of the precious seconds we have together today. He says we're taking Patty and another mare.

As we tack up, he says, kind of out of the blue, "You're not the type of person I'd have pegged as belonging to Matt."

*Belonging?* "What do you mean?"

"You're a nice guy. Usually like attracts like."

I feel like I should laugh but I don't really feel like laughing so I don't. "Are you so sure of that? Give me time."

"You know what I mean. Everyone knows the only reason the two of you are staying together is because of Milton."

"Staying together for the good of the children?"

"Kind of like that. They know he wouldn't have you around otherwise."

"Who is 'they?'?"

"People talk."

"They know he doesn't like me?"

"Don't take it personally, Matt doesn't really like anyone. He has a real stick up his ass."

"I'd love to see his face if he overheard you saying *that*," I snort. Ben laughs. Hearing Ben say that seriously made my day. "Do they talk about us?"

"Probably."

"I don't want to ruin your reputation."

"Shut up, Simon. You'd love to ruin my reputation," Ben says, grinning.

"Well, not everyone is as perfect as you are, Ben. Not everyone is Eventing Nation's cover model."

"Eventing Nation called you an 'overnight success,' Simon."

"Whatever."

"You don't look so bad in photos yourself. You do know that every eligible female that hasn't clued into the fact that you're gay has a crush on you."

"That's such bullshit. And even if it were true, they'll live."

"So heartless."

"I've never been the kind to sleep with a girl just to avoid hurting her feelings, unlike some guys I know."

"It was an experiment. A German experiment."

"What was the result of the experiment, professor?"

"Meh."

"It's not attractive to spit in the pot after you've eaten from it, Ben."

"You asked."

"Is that what you say about me behind my back? Meh."

"You already know what I say about you behind your back."

It's the middle of the day so the trail's parking lot is deserted. We're the only trailer pulling up onto the dirt. I lean over and kiss Ben. We're alone and so we sit there, making out for a long time until Patty whinnies. As soon as I can feel his tongue and lips, I forget everything, even the horses, I can't help it. I can hardly keep my hands off of him.

We take Patty off first, then the second mare.

"What's wrong? Don't you like Tess?"

Stupid face gives everything away. "She looks like a horse I used to ride." The truth is, she looks like the very first real horse I ever owned, an OTTB named Damsel in Distress. She was a really nice jumper before she injured herself in a paddock accident in the middle of the night at my mom's barn and had to be put down. The first in a long series of events that resulted in me not having much of a career as a junior rider.

"Is Tess a Thoroughbred?" I ask Ben. "An OTTB?"

"Nah, warmblood."

"Looks like a Thoroughbred. I mean that as a compliment."

"Yeah, her conformation is good, but she's just kind of a common-looking bay horse, not very flashy. She's my friend Elise's project, although my trainer technically owns her. Elise thought some work off the property might be good for her so she told me to take her. This is the first time she hasn't been ridden in a ring since she's come. You don't mind?"

"That's okay, I've always been the barn's resident crash-test dummy, willing to get on horses no one else will ride. You won't get rid of me that easily."

"Tess is really a sweet mare, just flighty."

We saddle up and head onto the path and the highway, and all of the other stuff I was thinking of, even the fact that Ben and I are going to be competitors again very shortly sort of ebbs away. The early parts of the bridle path are pretty well-manicured but it's rougher and more tangled the deeper we go into the woods. Ben has a pocket knife with him and stops to cut us past some low-hanging, new, green branches that refuse to be held to the side. I watch him as he holds the reins in one hand, makes the first cut, quickly grabs the base of the branch, and then finishes off his work easily and I know he's done this many times before.

Despite all of his successes, I'd kind of pegged Ben as, well, a wimpier rider compared to me, given all the riding I'd done up and down in Vermont in the open but I can see by the easy way he moves that isn't the case. He may be preppy as a Ralph Lauren ad, but he has a kind of catlike grace and assuredness on his horse that seems much more than something that can be won just practicing for competitions. It occurs to me that I don't carry a knife when I ride out and I should. I say as much to him and he asks, "What happens when you get caught or something gets in your way?"

"I'd always managed to find some way around it, or over it, or been able to tear myself out."

"I have a spare knife in my tack box. Remind me to give it to you. You need something to cut yourself free when you get caught," he says.

"You're quite the Boy Scout. Always prepared."

And then we grow silent as we head deeper into the wilderness.

After a bit, Ben asks, "Do you like Tess?"

"Yeah, she moves well. And so far, not even spooky despite her reputation." A really stupid thought popped in my head before that came out of my mouth, which was that the years have settled her a bit. My old horse used to be really sensitive—she was a great jumper but not the type of horse you'd want cross-country and certainly not in the hunter ring. She'd have her nose in the air, be bent the wrong way half the time but she had a great heart. She'd jump anything. But that was when she was still pretty green from the track and I've been thinking of Tess like it was her, like my old horse had the years since I was fourteen to get used to the world a bit more. If we'd had the time.

"Is something wrong?" asks Ben. And I'm kind of surprised because no one around me usually asks me if I seem upset. They just assume it's me being me. And so I tell him.

"My mom bought me an OTTB mare when I was twelve which everyone said was a really stupid thing to do. We didn't have the money to do much real showing then, but I won just about every jumper class I entered on her when I finally learned to ride her. Just dumb, low-rated, local stuff and schooling shows but I thought I was the shit because no one else was willing to get on Damsel.

Didn't matter to me what anyone else said about anything else. Then she ended up breaking her back in a paddock accident, a totally freak thing. This was after my mom had spent lots of money on a special saddle for her, surgery for a floating bone chip, helped me train her. It was like losing a member of the family and years of our life all at once."

"I'm sorry."

"This was when I was a freshman in high school, too long ago to be sorry about it. Tess just reminds me of her, the way she looks. But she's a nicer horse really, and more sane." I pat her. "I learned a lot from that mare, including the fact you can never count on horses."

"Really? You seemed like the kind of person who would only count on horses."

"Well, I guess I think you can count on them more than people. Can't really count on anything I guess."

Ben stops and I stop next to him. He reaches out to me, squeezes my fingers and I feel a kind of weird, electric sensation in my heart. His long, boney arm is ropy with muscle and he's almost perfectly melded to the saddle. This is the first time I've really talked about Damsel with someone, I try not to think about the past in general and even I think it's dumb to be that sentimental about a horse. Right now, I don't care that Ben and I are going to be at each other's throats the next time we compete. I just feel sort of peaceful with him, like he gets me and I get him.

We pick up a canter when there's a wider path for us and the trees give way to open space. Without even consulting with one another, we urge both of our horses to gallop. The sun is in my eyes and Patty's just a thin chestnut line in my peripheral vision.

We have to trot when we spy a bunch of kids on dirt bikes coming the other way. Ben seems to know where he's going, so I follow him without asking questions. We don't get funny looks, so I assume people riding the trails is pretty common, which is nice. I was worried the kids would yell or throw stuff. I guess I always do assume the worse of people.

When we get to kind of a grove with trees on all sides of us and two big rocks that kind of look like steps—almost like a picnic area—Ben gets off and says we can let our horses graze. Tess throws her head up, snorts, looks around and for a brief second I wonder if she's going to make a break for it. As if Ben can read my thoughts he digs in his pocket and offers me a thin nylon rope halter I can put on her, so she'll be easier to catch but won't get the bit slimy. Patty seems totally chill with all of the surroundings although Ben puts a rope halter on her as well. He puts his arms around me.

I kind of worry about one of the people we saw coming too near when he takes off my shirt, but then I don't care. Everything sort of slips away except the feeling of him near me. Tess jerks her head up when Ben moans, and then he says, "Easy girl." There is a little part of his mind still on them no matter what we're doing. The sun's so bright I can feel it through the trees, and while normally I don't like it very much right now it feels warm and good on my back, and even if I have no sleep tomorrow and I'm burnt red and peeling, I don't care. I don't care about anything now.

We lay in the grass a long time afterward, unobserved by everyone except the horses, not talking at all, which is nice and it occurs to me that I don't want to go back. The temperature starts to drop—it's spring and although by my standards not particularly cool, the ground isn't comfortable anymore even with Ben's body heat. Both of us put on enough clothes to keep out the chill but Ben pulls me back into him. He lays his head against my chest and once again, just like when I was watching him ride, I'm surprised how strong he is despite his apparent fragility. He may be preppy and whatever on the surface but his muscles and bones and sinews are almost as strong as mine, even though you'd think he weighs almost nothing.

I wonder why I can't just be happy with this. Because I really, really don't want to return, to Matt and to constantly having to watch myself. To having to justify everything I do and to having to be better every single day, to make sure I never make a mistake in order to ride Milton. Even to Lisa, who's fine, but who's always scared about everything she's doing because of what Matt will say. To Lexi who is evidently not flourishing in Matt's program and who looks more screwed up than when she came because Lisa won't stick up for her. I just want to be here with Ben forever in this kind of stopped time.

But I know I would never have wanted Ben if he weren't such a competitor. So this whole just wanting out of the game is a lie, just like the way the sun is playing tricks with my eyes, making the horses' coats look weird and sparkly gold and making Ben's eyes blue and green all at once as I open my own eyes and look at his face closely, as if for the first time.

"Are your eyes two different colors? I just noticed."

"One's blue and one's green. Did you just notice that? I'm so offended you haven't looked deeply into my eyes until now."

"I have. I just noticed the color for the first time. That's all."

"Okay, I'll forgive you."

Eventually, we decide to go. Wordlessly, without consulting one another, we know it's time. We put on the rest of our clothes, bridle up, tighten the girths, and head back, warming the horses up again with a slow trot, and then easing into a canter when the footing gets better and they've remembered what their job is after their rest.

Suddenly, we hear shrieking.

Tess snorts and for a brief second she wants to bolt but I close my legs and drive her forward. Patty tries to pull the same thing with Ben—she whirls round and acts like she's going to run before he shuts her down by sitting deep in the saddle.

At first I think the screaming is human, but then I realize that it's birds. Right in front of us on the path there's a dead dog and what must be ten, twenty turkey vultures ripping the thing apart. My first reaction is relief because I know there is nothing for us to do, no 911 to be called, but then I feel sorry for the dog. It's a nice-looking yellow lab, must have once been someone's pet or something, and it's still recognizably a dog even with its bloody guts being pecked out. I guess the birds' shrieks were shrieks of joy. It still has its collar on with tags, a bright red nylon collar like a gash that blends in with the blood and flesh the birds are picking at. Definitely someone's pet.

We have to really muscle our horses past the scene because the birds are so excited they aren't even afraid of stomping hooves. They're predators, not prey, even though they don't kill, just pick at the leavings.

"I hate those things," says Ben. But they're just doing what is in their nature. Just like I can't get mad at the horses for being scared or hate Milton for whatever screws occasionally pop loose in his brain. There is no malice in it. It's just part of everything out here, dog eat dog, vulture eat dog, like everything in the world.

"It's okay, I think we've passed them all by now," I say. "I wonder what the dog died from. Vultures are scavengers—they don't kill."

"Still nasty."

"I hope the dog didn't die of starvation or exposure out here. That's an awful slow way to go. Better to go quick," I say.

And so I'm reminded how things can end and that I can't stay here forever. I have to keep moving or else I'll be picked to death alive. That's the answer, I have to stay where I am at Matt's to keep in motion. Even out here, there is no permanent stopping place, no living peace, and tomorrow I'll be on Milton again, I'm sure of it.

I mean, I guess Matt might take Milton back as his ride but I have a good feeling that he won't, based on what I saw this morning.

I suppose I should check my phone to make sure he's okay and Milton didn't dump him or anything after I left but I don't bother. Lisa and Blondie and the rest of them will be around to scrape up whatever Milton leaves on the ground before the vultures swoop in, I think and laugh a little to myself.

The sun is lower now—we must have been out longer than I thought. I'm lucky to have Ben, I think. I'm lucky someone loves unlovable me. Lucky to be loved and alive. I don't take that for granted. Although someone must have loved that dog once, enough to carefully put on a collar around his neck, just like I loved my old Damsel in Distress.

I help Ben trailer the horses back, groom them, put them in their stalls, and wipe down the tack, which has gotten sweaty and muddy. Ben does remember to give me the spare knife, which I stick in my pants pocket. It's red with a white cross on it. I'm sure I'll need it someday.

## CHAPTER 18

# JOGGED SOUND

When I get back, Milton is in his stall as usual. Matt stops to give me a rundown about how I should work him tomorrow. Everything is normal except that Matt looks kind of pale and queasy. Immediately, I wonder if Milton threw him, although I can't say that of course.

"How was your day off?" he asks, not because he cares but because both of us know he's just saying something you're supposed to say to be polite.

"Good," I say. I try to make my voice flat and toneless so I don't sound like I got laid.

The next day, I feel kinda bad about hoping Matt fell off because Matt calls me from the hospital. At first I think he's joking but then I remember that Matt doesn't have a sense of humor about himself, only other people. "Apparently, they're going to have to take out my appendix."

"Wow. Is there anything I can do?" I know that having your appendix out is serious stuff.

"Just keep things from getting out of control. I hope I'm cleared to ride two weeks from now."

Two weeks from now Matt's going to be riding Nebraska Sky at Green Valley. It's a pretty big deal. I don't have anything fake or chipper to say because I'm sure when they take an organ out of your body they don't recommend that you jump on a horse the next day. To be honest, I've powered through a concussion before but I've never had surgery.

I won't bring Matt down, though, so I don't say anything and tell him not to worry and all the usual stuff you're supposed to say to someone in the hospital. I also don't say thank God it's not me because I know if it were he'd be giving all my riding to Lisa and I don't trust her with Milton. Hell, I don't even trust Matt hasn't loosened a couple of screws in Milton's head.

I ride Nebraska first. It's kind of nice how things are more relaxed when Matt isn't around.

"He looks great," chirps Blondie as I finish up. "I've tacked up Milton for you to ride." I nod and slide down, pat Nebraska and give him to her. He's a weird, gold color, almost a buckskin with a small patch of white on his withers, which I scratch for being a good boy. "You look good on him, like he's your usual ride. For a second I thought you were Matt in the distance."

Without meaning to, I feel my face tighten into a scowl. I don't say anything because I know she means no harm but I'm instinctively angry.

Blondie immediately senses she's said the wrong thing and starts to babble. "I mean, you're obviously not Matt. You're younger."

That's not what annoyed me. My face is already showing wear and tear from being out in the sun every day, all days, since I was a kid, I know that. It's the idea that my riding style might somehow be so marked by Matt's influence that people could pick it out, even after I leave here—I never thought of that but then again, how could it not? And Matt's a great rider, I remind myself. I'm learning from him. Why should that offend me? She meant it as a compliment.

I put that out of my mind and get on Milton.

By 4 p.m. I have lost count of the horses I've ridden. I think this will be number nine. Good old Geronimo and then I'm done.

"I'm glad Matt made it out of surgery okay," says Lisa. Lisa has obviously been checking her phone, unlike me, out of concern for our boss. "Do you want to go and see him later? I just finished riding Lexi."

The truth is, I have no desire to see Matt whatsoever. So I just shrug and put a blank look on my face. I try to show concern as she talks about him. I mean, I guess from her perspective despite all of his jerkiness, he gave her a chance when no one else would so she's grateful for that. Maybe I should be. I don't know. Maybe there's something wrong with me, I think.

"I still have to work Geronimo, I'll be too tired," I say, even though I only have a light school on the flat planned for him.

Blondie's got more on her hands than usual because Matt is gone, so I cool out Geronimo myself. When I've finally blanketed him, I look for Lisa, and I find both her and Blondie standing in Lexi's stall. Lisa's giving her some sort of injection.

Lisa makes eye contact with me but doesn't explain herself. "What's going on?" I ask, but it's just like Ingrid with me back in Germany. Both women look right through me.

"Just to help her from feeling so ouchy," says Lisa. The baby talk irritates the hell out of me.

"If she's hurt, you shouldn't have worked her. Maybe that's why she was acting up."

"Work is better for her. She's better working it out than just getting stiffer from standing around."

I've watched Lisa on Lexi a bunch of times. Lexi's still in a pretty harsh bit cross-country. She still is inconsistent in her pace, either pulling or lagging. Unlike the girls at my old stable Lisa's never asked for my advice or shown any interest in practicing with me. The horse's endurance isn't great, either. She's frequently sore and just a bit 'off.' I know that both Matt and Lisa are disappointed with Lexi (and honestly, even though I have no stake in her, I am as well), and they'd sell her in a minute if they could get a decent price for her. They're hoping she'll do better and they can get rid of her whatever it takes although I have no idea what "it" is.

Lisa acts like I saw nothing and offers me a ride to the hospital from the barn as I gather my things. Seriously? "I'm going home," I say. "Say hi to Matt's appendix for me." Tell him to work it out, just like he told you to give Lexi whatever, I think.

"I don't understand you, Simon. Have a little compassion," she says. "I know you don't like him."

Compassion? That's a fucking joke.

I drive home, pick up some tacos on the way, put on the Killers as background music to eat and slump in my sofa, trying not to think.

There was something in Lisa's tone ... I mean, I get she likes Matt more than I do but why does she care so much? Something clicks in my head ... the look in her eyes ... God, I've really had my head up my ass not to pick up on it. I've been so busy with Milton I hadn't noticed anything. I admit I never thought of Lisa having any kind of a sexuality at all, kind of like my mother. But honestly, Matt's probably about seven, ten years older than Lisa. It's not so weird, I guess, even though it gives me the creeps. But not as much as whatever she and Matt have been doing to Lexi. But what can I say? Or do? I don't know what's going on. I can't put my finger on it other than the fact I don't like it.

I have no power in this situation. Other than walking away. From Milton and the track I've placed myself on. It's too late, I'm already on course, moving forward. There is no slowing down, no place to stop.

# CHAPTER 19

# IN THE VALLEY OF THE SHADOW

The next competition, Green Valley, isn't that far away from the barn, about fifty miles or so, but it could be on Mars as far as Matt's concerned because he's still not cleared to ride from his appendectomy. The week before, Matt called me every night to brief me on how I should be riding and exercising the horses, and I can't totally blame how pissed off he is at the world because I would probably feel the same way even though I pretty much hate him now.

"Fucking useless organ," he says, about the appendix.

"Look on the bright side," I say. "You'll never have to have it out again."

"This is probably the first time Matt's been in bed for more than six hours straight since, well, since forever," says Lisa as we ride together in the rig at 4 a.m.

No rest for the wicked, isn't that what they say? Before, I would have said this aloud to Lisa, but I don't now.

I'm actually slightly pissed that I'm not riding Nebraska and Milton but Matt said he thinks I'll have my hands full with Milton alone and I don't argue.

I always used to say I wanted a job where I never had to wear a suit except for a show jacket but for the jog at Green Valley, since it's a CCI, I actually do have to wear nice civilian clothes, especially since the press is really here in force, taking photos of us, and commenting on what we wear if it is sufficiently interesting. I have a black pinstripe suit, which I select solely because I tell myself it looks slightly *Reservoir Dogs*-ish and a pale blue shirt because someone—Max—told me I look good in that color. I sort of feel I haven't totally lost my street cred in it, although my badass reputation is probably solely in my mind. Anyway, what's most important is Milton jogs sound. Whether it is because of or despite Matt, you be the judge.

"You clean up well, Simon," says Blondie as we walk Milton back to the stabling area.

"Yeah, I scrubbed behind my ears and everything," I laugh. After seeing Blondie with Lexi, I'm beginning to feel that everything I say and do at the barn is a performance. No one is on my side. I try to joke to keep things normal but I feel as if I'm only really honest with myself when I'm alone with the horses.

I look over and see Ben walking with Jasper. He's wearing a grey suit that almost matches the horse and a pink shirt with just one too many buttons undone. His expression doesn't change, but he winks at me. Stupid heart, I swear it skips even though I don't believe in those sorts of clichés. Useless organ, I tell myself, kind of like an appendix.

"That man is so hot he smokes," says Blondie, when she thinks he's out of earshot. "It's hardly decent he's such a good rider. He looks like a model."

"Horse is nice, too," I say.

I know Lisa is a bit intimidated doing her course walk without Matt so I go with her. She's not in the CCI, obviously, but they run divisions as low as Novice concurrently with the CCI at Green Valley. Honestly, it's kind of a zoo here, even more than usual at an event.

I hear Lisa saying things like she's worried she's not fit enough, not practiced enough but I silence her and my own fears. I tell her that since we're doing it, there's no looking back, no point in worrying. As angry as I have been with her lately, I still want her to do well, for Lexi's sake, if nothing else. I know Lexi's not long for our barn, and I want the mare to have a soft landing, find a new rider who can handle her but who won't push her too much. It would be nice if she could get a few good wins under her name.

I go over my own course in my mind ... There's a three or four stride from a keyhole to a water complex. Then a ditch and wall ... five strides to a skinny brush. The questions come up thick and fast early. I'll really need to regulate Milton's pace and make up for the time lost between. But as often as I ride it in my mind, I know that Milton can be an unpredictable horse. I have enough time to envision several scenarios—if it goes according to plan, if he's fresh, or if he's being inconsistent, balky, and jumping everything to the left and right to start out with.

Milton is particularly good and we have such a fantastic dressage test that I enjoy it, which I never thought was possible for me with dressage. We score a forty-three but that's about the same as our serious competition, the judges are being pretty stingy here. He's supple and thinking things through with me. There's no fighting or coaxing on my part. He's light and easy in my hands. I actually feel as if we have a real connection and there's no forcing on my part. Lisa gets through her test without embarrassing herself.

"I think you guys do better when Matt isn't here," says Blondie. She says what I think.

Lisa just shrugs. Her face is pink and serious. "I can't wait to get this sports bra off. I'm wearing one that's a size too small to fit into this stupid shadbelly. I feel like I'm all bound up and choking."

"Ah, female rider problems."

Cross-country is the next day for the upper levels, show-jumping and cross-country for the lower levels.

At the first question, Milton's quiet and the four rather than the three works out but then once we get going he gets hotter and hotter and when he takes an airy trakehner with a massive over-jump I have to give him a pretty hard half-halt to steady him.

This course is steep and I'm a little bit worried about Milton's conditioning given that we haven't worked much over hills. It was so much easier in Vermont to condition a horse when pretty much everything was a hill but he doesn't seem to be flagging.

The next few big tables are almost like a rest, they're not particularly complicated even though a few of them are huge and I know they've given horses problems on this course before.

He doesn't even look funny at some of the types of jumps that bothered the old Milton, like coffins (he'd stare at them while going over). A few times he spooks at the cheering spectators, but nothing terrible, and I'm able to pull him back into focus.

The worst thing he does is drift when we're jumping a combination with an A, B, and C element, nearly missing the B. Good jump in over the log, heavy right leg to left hand and we make it over the brush skinny in the middle of the shallow water, sharp turn up and over a table, and we're an ugly clear but clear nonetheless.

Blondie is there to greet me at the finish. And Lisa. A very small cheering section.

After Milton's cooled down, I'm still flying. I can feel my breathing straining my clavicles, and I'm pumped up, high on adrenaline.

I feel several inches taller than normal when I stride past Lisa. It takes me a second to register the expression on her face.

"Lisa, what's wrong?"

"It's just—oh, I don't want to bring you down. It's selfish of me."

"Is Matt okay?"

"No, no, it's not Matt. It's just—things haven't been going that great with Lexi lately."

"Don't think of that, Lisa. Put that all out of your mind. You're a good rider, I wouldn't say that to you if you weren't."

"Thank you, Simon. I know that. That means a lot. It's just, I've given up so much to come here ... sometimes I feel very unworthy. I know many people would like to be in my place. Sometimes I ask myself, why do I think I'm so special? Maybe I should just go back to an office and give up horses altogether."

"Like sending yourself to prison?"

"For my bad behavior."

"Lisa, you and Lexi are still developing as a team." *Of course, it doesn't help that Matt keeps screwing Lexi up and you're going along with it,* I think.

"You can't understand. You've never settled for less than number one, and you're less than half my age. Imagine how it feels to be me, you can't. I just want to place in the top five for once at a low-level event. God, is that so much to ask?"

"Ultimately, Lisa, all we can do is kick on and hope for the best. Talking doesn't cure anything." *Neither does overthinking.*

"No, no it doesn't."

"You're a good rider," I say again. "Of course you deserve to be here. If you didn't, you would be like everyone else this weekend, I don't know, shopping at the mall or sleeping in, or whatever normal people do for fun. I wouldn't know." *I wonder if Matt ever tells her that she's a good rider or if he just sleeps with her. I can't imagine Matt saying anything nice to anyone. The idea of Matt in anything but breeches and doing anything but yelling at people kind of makes me cringe.*

I watch Lisa head off to jump her brightly-colored sticks. I can't hold Lisa's hand with this one. She's on her own.

On my way back to Milton, I almost literally bump into Freddie Whitechapel, who congratulates me. *Don't jinx me yet,* I think.

"You and your partner in crime seem to be doing well without your fearless leader. Where is the Iceman?"

"Iceman's in the hospital."

"Hospital? I hope he's alright."

"Oh yes, it's not a riding accident or anything. Just having his appendix out." Freddie seems to like Matt, so I try to keep my tone as neutral as possible. But then again, Freddie seems to like just about everyone. I've never heard him say a bad word about horses or people. I'd honestly think that was a British thing if I didn't know plenty of other Brits through riding and know that it's not.

"Where is Nebraska Sky?" I frown. The fact Matt didn't trust me to ride two horses today is a sore spot. He said he thought that I had all that I could handle but I also kind of suspect he didn't want me riding both—from his perspective, it would suck if Milton beat his horse while I was riding or if his horse did better with me on him when competing against Milton. Either way, a loss for him.

Anyway, Milton jogs sound. He's fine.

In addition to pulling rails in stadium, Lexi has one refusal cross-country. I know that Lisa's disappointed but again, the mare has done worse.

Third day. Lisa's done and stadium is a fairly uneventful experience for Milton. Milton spooks a bit at some of the spectators hanging and shouting but not enough to even slow down.

In the end, it's us that gets the blue ribbon. We get our picture taken with the shiny silver plate we've won. It will be on the event venue's Facebook page and Twitter feed by evening. Milton really spooks during the awards ceremony, and I don't blame him because the dish is reflective and while I stay on I can't help but think it's funny that getting the big prize is our least successful phase of the entire competition.

Blondie holds the scary tray after our moment in the sun and one of the kids from the barn that volunteered to help out with the scrub work takes more photos. "This is the first time I've ever seen you smiling so much," says Blondie.

"I smile," I say. "This is proof." This is proof of everything.

Lisa ultimately comes in fifth, which, while not great, still exceeds both of our expectations. "Best of the worst," she says, which is true. Even the winners had kind of crap records and it's definitely possible that the course designer kind of over-faced the lower levels.

We're exhausted by the end of the day when we arrive back at the barn, given how we've been on our own for so much of the competition and by the time we get all the horses put away and checked on the horses that didn't go with us, we can barely stand, we're so tired and hungry. We order a pizza sent to the barn and sit in the tack room to eat. It's cold now that the sun's going down and a slight mist is falling outside and we turn on the space heater. The barn is always colder than it is outside, it seems. Icebox.

"Milton's some horse," says Lisa. I've sometimes wondered if she wishes she were riding him but she sounds sincere.

I don't know what to say other than "thank you," so I do. When I compliment her on her riding she looks away.

"And thank you for helping me through that mini-meltdown."

"We all have them."

"Not you. Not Matt, that's why they call him the Iceman."

"I guess I manage to time my crises of confidence when I'm not competing. Usually at three in the morning."

"So what do you do then to talk yourself out of it?"

"I listen to the Killers and fall asleep and then I've forgotten about it by the time the sun's out. And usually just riding kind of gets me out of my funk."

"Why do you like the Killers so much?"

I shrug. "The lyrics. The music. Everything." Brandon Flowers, the hot lead singer, I think but don't say. Neither Lisa nor I talk have talked about our romantic lives with one another, and I don't feel like starting tonight. This is already too much thinking aloud for me, especially after a long day. I reach for another slice of pizza, and unlike Lisa, I don't blot the disks of pepperoni before I shove it in my mouth. I thought that gesture was sort of stupid and girly, but suddenly I realize I have oil all over the front of my light blue barn polo shirt.

"Shit."

"Oh, Simon. Here, let me take care of that for you." I take off my shirt and Lisa scrubs it in the sink, then puts it on a hanger; I pull on a sweatshirt from my tack box over my naked chest.

"Thanks, Mom," I say, and grin. "Although my actual mom would just say that was all my own damn fault and I can't have nice things."

Lisa's a good woman. I just wish there weren't such a river of bullshit running through this barn. I wish I could tell her, "I like you but I don't understand why you like Matt given his incredibly huge ego and incredibly small penis." Perhaps her standards got lowered after spending so long in the corporate world.

## CHAPTER 20

# STUCK ON YOU

Matt returns to the barn, grey and ragged as a rotten piece of meat, and even though he's weak and can't ride, he's his usual sarcastic self. I'd tried to forget him but his presence is impossible to ignore.

I call Daniel. I can't get it out of my head anymore. "Why don't you like Matt? I know you don't gossip but I need to know."

"I haven't known him for years."

"Yeah, but it must be pretty bad because you still remember."

"Matt brought a horse with him when he was a working student like you. And the horse, well, the horse had issues."

"Like my horse?"

"No, your horse can be a tricky ride, and the two of you couldn't do a good dressage together unless—well, except when—your lives depended upon it. This horse was also a good jumper, like Fortune, but every now and then he'd have multiple refusals. Mind you, when he was good, he was very, very good, but when he was bad, he was … No sense of self-preservation, which is not what you want in an event horse. Back then, we didn't have as much sophisticated chiropractic work and such to see if his issue was physical. Anyway, Matt sold him to a dumb junior a couple of states away who didn't know the horse's reputation—she was a showjumper, not an eventer so she didn't follow the sport—and of course he ended up dumping her the first time she showed him. The rider was fourteen. The parents knew nothing about horses. The horse wasn't really good for anything at that point—he was a dirty stopper and it had become a habit—certainly not something a kid could manage. Plus, I didn't like Matt's attitude. He wouldn't listen, always argued back. Wouldn't work unless he knew he was being watched and he thought it would get him something. Arrogant."

"I've been accused of being arrogant."

"You will never win any prizes for personality, Shaughnessy, but you're a hard worker. No one can take that away from you."

"I know Matt doesn't like me. Maybe he doesn't like anyone. He certainly wouldn't take the crap he pulled with you from me."

"Because you're a better rider than him and he knows it."

"Wow. Thank you. That means a lot."

"My real falling out with Matt came when I sold him a horse against my better judgement, a nice but kind of spooky warmblood. She was slow to develop, even when she was with me, but he moved her up the levels really quickly and she slowly became more and more unhinged, from what I saw of her. Eventually, she had a really nasty rotational fall with him and she had to be put down. He walked away from it. I didn't like the way he handled that mare. She was a nice horse. She deserved better. I still feel guilty about it."

"He did well with some horses, though. Like Geronimo, who is still at the barn, competing and sound after all those years."

"Some horses will do well under any program, others not so much."

"He's been pretty hands off with me and Milton."

"Thus far. Well, you've done a lot with that horse. He didn't have a good reputation, other than having good breeding and athleticism, before Matt imported him. I'm just saying to be careful and have your eyes open, Simon."

"If Matt would sell Milton to me, I'd leave in a minute."

"Sometimes it's good to cut your losses. You're a good rider, Simon. Find another horse, another situation."

"I've already been through too many horses, too many different situations in too short a period of time. I might not like everything, but I'm in this one for the long haul. Milton—" I almost catch myself saying something really stupid like I love the horse, but I know that Daniel would accuse me of having Black Stallion Syndrome (BSS). Even though Milton is a gelding.

# CHAPTER 21
# THE CRUELTY-FREE SADDLE

When I go visit Ben on my next day off, he opens the door to his sister lying sprawled out on the living room carpet. She's reading a textbook. "What are you doing here?" he asks.

"Nice to see you too, oh brother of mine." She looks quite a bit like Ben so I know she is his sister. She's got the same sandy hair (only hers hangs down her back) and slightly tanned skin and piercing eyes. But she doesn't look like I expected her to look. She's wearing a long skirt that looks like a flowered bedsheet, has tats all over her arms, a tight top that her boobs are hanging out of, and an ugly cardigan sweater with weird patterns all over it. She also has her forearms on the floor and is touching her skull with her toes.

"Studying hard?"

"I'm just doing some yoga to clear my mind."

"Clear your mind somewhere else. It freaks me out when you contort yourself like that."

"This is my house, too. I've been a transient for the last couple of days because my roommate's boyfriend is in town. You can't kick me out of my childhood home just because you want to sleep with *your* boyfriend."

I flinch. On one hand, she's so upfront, talking about her brother's boyfriend, so she's cool with me, on the other hand I feel like she's talking about me like I'm an object, as if I'm not there. I wonder if she would be so crass if I were a girl. I feel like she's making a show of the fact that, I don't know, she has a gay brother. It bugs me, regardless.

She unfolds herself from her pretzel shape, sizes me up, goes to the kitchen and returns with some weird green crap in a glass jar with a straw hanging out of it.

It occurs to me that, although Ben has mentioned his sister and the fact that she goes to school around here, I can't remember her name. He must have mentioned it to me but I only remember the names of their horses, Doxie and Larry.

She's got some piercings on her belly and she itches them as she looks at him and I look away as she practically hikes up her shirt so high I can see her bra. Seriously, I don't need to see that.

"Are you going riding later?" says Ben. "Did you bring your plastic saddle?"

"Cruelty-free saddle," she says. After delicately sipping the green gunk from the jar she puts it down and reaches behind her to grab her left foot in her two hands, kicking it back, then doing the same with her right. Why don't you just keep doing all that weird shit with your body, I think, eventually that should scare your roommate and her boyfriend away?

"You could come to my barn to ride Tess, take one of the horses I need to ride today off my hands," Ben says. I flinch a bit. Tess is mine. Well, not mine, but I really liked riding her. Doesn't he remember?

"Wait, I recognize you. You're Simon O'Shaughnessy. You ride Milton Keynes. I saw that on Facebook."

"Simon's won a bunch of stuff," says Ben.

"Milton Keynes is kind of a stupid name for a horse. Ben and I passed through Milton Keynes when our family was touring England years ago and it was just this nothing place."

"So I've been told," I say.

"Milton. *Better to reign in hell than to serve in heaven.*"

"Huh?" Better to rein in hell? Stupidly, an image of trying to get Milton going forward pops in my mind, versus reining him in, even though I know that's not what she's saying.

"That's like, a really famous quote. Milton. I read *Paradise Lost* for one of my English classes."

*Better to reign in hell than to serve in heaven.* I think about that for a second. On one hand, I totally disagree because I always thought of hell as a normal life and thought it was better to do the most menial thing around horses, as long as it was doing something that I loved. But that being said, I feel hell at Matt's is what I've chosen right now, all the same. I don't know how Ben's sister pulled that one out of her ass although she can evidently touch her head to said ass without really trying. As far as I can see, it's one of those riddles without an answer, a sentence designed to trip you up, which is what I always hated about studying English in a class, versus reading for pleasure to get to the end of a story on my own.

"My name is Sasha, btw. It's a boy's name in Russian." Well, I'd never mistake her for a boy, so no worries there, Ben. Especially after all the twisting around she's really hanging out of her shirt now, all over the place, and I just don't need to see this.

The music she is playing is this monotonous, Indian-sounding tone which wasn't so bad at first but is really getting to me. It's hypnotic and not in a good way. I walk over and turn it off. I really want to be alone with Ben and I'm angry.

A woman walks in and I assume it's Ben's mom because she says, "I'm just getting myself some juice before the next client comes. Ignore me and carry on with your friends." She's a tall, sandy-haired, athletic, healthy-looking woman wearing khakis and a long-sleeved polo. She doesn't look like a therapist to me. I only saw the school psychologist for a few sessions in high school because my school made me and I just stared at the table the entire time and wouldn't talk. I don't even remember what the guy looked like exactly, I just remember that I hated him and that he wore a tie. Ben's mom seems friendly enough and normal, despite her weird obsession with heritage breed chickens. "Ms. Hillard, I'm Simon," I say, trying to be polite.

I then remember what Ben said about the lupus and not being able to ride anymore. You really couldn't tell, I think, looking at her from the outside. I expected her to, I don't know, be shuffling around like she was in pain but then again how many times have I—and my brother too, to be fair—been able to cover that stuff up because if we didn't, we wouldn't be able to compete? I'd never do that to a horse of course; I'm not like Matt, but when it comes to humans, I figure it's cover up, hunker down, and don't let them know you're sick unless you need life support. There's a small part of me that wonders if I had something like that, if I could ignore pain. I don't know. Maybe it's harder if you're older and you're not a professional rider or whatever; the stakes are lower. That must be really hard to have your son compete and not be able to ride yourself or maybe she thinks it's better than nothing? I couldn't live vicariously through someone else. Though, if it was just Ben competing and not me, I don't know, I just still don't think I could deal with it.

Ms. Hillard goes to the kitchen and I hear her open the refrigerator. Unlike her daughter, she doesn't appear to know my face but she might not be that into social media and doesn't recognize me without a helmet on. Or maybe she doesn't go to that many events because of her health. Either way, I'm glad to be anonymous in her eyes.

"Are you one of Ben's friends from the barn? Are you staying for dinner? That reminds me, I need to defrost a London broil. Oh, Sasha, don't make a face like that."

"I can't help it when I see bloody, dead stuff like that, Mom."

"Just because you've made your diet such a big part of your identity doesn't mean you can control what the rest of us eat. And it's frozen and wrapped, hardly bleeding. Simon, we buy a share of a cow from a local farm. Isn't that wonderful? We also get raw milk from the farm, although don't tell anyone because that's illegal."

"I doubt the cow thinks it's so wonderful, being cut up and dead," says Sasha. "Or giving her milk for your cereal."

"We're a big believer in all natural foods here, for our health," says Ben's mom.

"Jesus, Sasha, you're like a dog wearing at a bone with that vegan thing," says Ben.

"That's not a very apt analogy." She grins. She sits back down on the floor and sticks her nose in her thick textbook.

"Actually, I thought it was a pretty appropriate one," says Ben. "Simon and I are going out for our own bloody dead stuff lunch, he doesn't have time to stay for dinner." His mother smiles, kisses him on the cheek and then descends to her basement office to do whatever she does to people down there.

"Are you really dating my brother?" says Sasha, not even looking up from the book.

"That's an interesting question. Ben, are we dating?" I try to sound as if I'm mocking her words, which I sort of am and sort of am not.

"Why yes, Simon, I think we are," he says, with exaggerated formality.

I laugh. "Ben said you ride hunters," I say. I vaguely remember him saying that to me. "And you did the Big Eq?"

"I'm not a *competitive* rider anymore." She kind of sneers that word, *competitive*. Like she's past that.

Ben says he has to go upstairs to change his shirt because he got some manure on it. I didn't even really notice it until he pointed it out and I follow him. We pass what I assume is his sister's room. The door is open so I can't help but stop and gawk. It's totally different from the rest of the house. There's a huge mural of galloping horses painted on the wall. It's kind of weird, abstract, and floaty, more like brushstrokes that look like horses. I was always good in art in school, and people told me I was talented but I haven't even doodled in ages. It almost looks like a cave painting, minus the guys in loincloths going after buffalo or whatever. But better than a cave painting, it's, I don't know. Different. Arresting.

"Sasha did that," says Ben. He doesn't sound proud, his tone is almost like *can you believe someone bothered to take the time to do that to a friggin' wall?*

But I'm impressed and annoyed because it means I can't totally hate her since there must be something good inside of her to be able to make something like that out of nothing. I almost say to Ben, *I used to be able to do stuff like that,* but I don't because he wouldn't care and that sounds kind of pathetic anyway. I don't do much other than ride now, I'm too tired half the time even to follow sports on TV. I'm so exhausted every day when I get home from the barn. And it's not the work, because honestly I did more physical labor at Daniel's and that was way more tiring and I still had enough energy to go and see Max every evening when I wasn't doing night checks. Just being around Matt drains me hollow.

"Cool room," I tell Sasha after Ben has carefully selected a new polo from his nine million Ralph Lauren polos hanging in his closet.

Sasha grunts at me. She now actually seems interested in what is in her textbook.

Even by my very low standards of sibling behavior, in my humble opinion Sasha is being really rude, which is surprising given how easy (going) Ben is with everyone, I can't imagine him treating one of her boyfriends like this.

But then again, I get a feeling she isn't really talking to me. I feel she's talking to her brother when she interacts with me, her perfect brother who everyone adores. I guess at least she can get at him with her bitchiness even though she can't compete against him on a horse.

At that point, the cat Sigmund comes running through the house, ringing his bell. And despite the bell, he has indeed caught a mouse, apparently, somewhere, because he runs over to Ben, who seems to be his favorite person, and lays it at his master's feet, purring. Sasha screams and we decide at that point to go.

Ben's whole family feels weird to me. I'm uncomfortable because his house is so different than my own. I think of my mom's messy home, the way she barely notices anything (sometimes she'd forget to feed us dinner) that doesn't have to do with horses. The way my brother and I would always be insulting each other and rough-housing as kids until she smacked one or both of us. That feels normal to me. The way Ben acts around his mom seems weird and fake. The way his mom seems so deferential to him, almost like she wants to serve him does as well. But then I remember it was she who used to be the horse person. I guess Ben's all she has left as a connection to all that. It's not like you can be competitive with heritage breed chickens. Or can you? And his sister is just ...

"What's up with your sister?" I ask. "With the whole *competition* thing?"

"She's never been the same since she did didn't make the Maclay finals her last year as a junior," he says, smiling.

"I never made it there, either."

"Really? That surprises me. Your eq is pretty good."

"Why thank you, I'm so honored you've noticed. Nah, on the rare occasions when I did anything but jumpers it was pretty much all on sale horses they wanted to move quickly, not horses that were remotely competitive on that level. I was never exactly popular at the barn with the trainers. Half the time they wouldn't let me ride in the qualifying classes. I'd be annoyed as hell with my brother if he were a better rider than I was so I can understand why she cops an attitude with you when the subject comes up," I grin. "But there was never any chance of my brother being better than me. He just didn't care." And he didn't have any nerve, I almost wanted to add, thinking of Sean's mediocre shuffling over 2'6 hunter courses, which was like a stab in the heart for my mother. Although he did do some barrel racing and stuff like that. But I always thought that was because girls liked that, not because he liked the horses. He actually wasn't half bad in dressage, but no way would Sean or I ever have the patience to succeed at any serious level in that world.

"Sasha got more passionate about how competing was beneath her the worse she did," says Ben. "But to be fair, we didn't know that much when we were starting out and I think she'd feel differently if she'd been with a different trainer. I went to her hunter barn a few times and the stalls rustled with empty tubes of Perfect Prep."

"Oh, I know that sound," I say. "It's not like I haven't seen bad things in eventing. I wish everyone could just treat their horses right and then we could compete from there." I think of Milton in my mind and if you can look away from a mental image, I do. Am I doing right by him? But I also feel warm because once again I sense that Ben gets me, he gets everything.

Of course, it's easy to say that competition is bad and that horses should just sit out in the field. But with some horses like Fortune, I could swear that they loved the novelty of a show or an event (dressage excepted with him, of course), the tension of a new course. And the plain fact is that, without competition, there wouldn't be horses like Fortune or my mare Damsel in Distress, or Milton, or Tess or anyone. And without competition, there wouldn't be me, because if I hadn't had that in high school, well, it was like oxygen for fire as far as I'm concerned. I try not to think what it would have been like, what I would have been like without horse shows to give me a reason to move forward, not just from jump to jump but simply getting out of my bed and getting to school every day.

Ben looks up at the sun and squints. "At Sasha's barn, the head trainer was eventually banned, and you have to be really, really sloppy to get banned, as you know. She was quiet about it with us when it was happening because whatever you see around you is normal. And she was never a very confident rider. She still rides but mostly just walk, trot, canter, occasionally pops over a low jump. I'm so lucky that I found a good barn, a good trainer, and a good horse. There is so much that's due to luck in this sport, no matter how good you are."

I'm a little surprised that even Ben appreciates this, although of course I agree. I was lucky to train under Daniel McAllister, not a bad trainer, to find Fortune's Fool. Sure, I had to have the talent, but without those opportunities, I wouldn't be where I am right now.

Today, Ben has to ride multiple horses so we really don't have that much time. We go back to the trails where we rode last time, this time on foot, and find another place where we're relatively sheltered and alone. "I wish you could have come back to my apartment," I say. I think it must suck royally being an adult and not having a place of your own. Even when my brother and I were teens, if we did bring anyone in the house, my mom wouldn't notice. She wasn't helicoptering around. But his parents don't seem to bother Ben. Living with his parents is part of the deal, so he can train and keep Jasper. So he can stay focused on winning.

I should be happy, now. That's what I should do now. Just be happy. Just keep focused on my career and not question things so much. My lips brush Ben's hair and my fingers weave in and out of his fingers like we're one, and for a moment I am, maybe, one mind, one body. I'm eating up our time together and his assurance and contentment because nothing has ever really gone bad for him. But our time together always ends and then I'm back to being me again. Always restless. Never content.

He drops me off at his home and before I get in my Subaru (which is already filthy with horse manure and littered with McDonald's and candy wrappers), I watch him get into his own car, watch him pull away. When he's not near me, I find myself digging my fingers into the steering wheel, frustrated that I'm going to have to wait to touch him again. The feeling subsides when I go back to my life at the barn but the coming down from the high is always hard.

I remember galloping around just for the hell of it, not caring if it mattered, saying fuck all to the slow optimum time of a hunter pace when I used to ride in them back at Mom's old barn. Better last and fastest than first. Even sometimes when I would reluctantly be given a horse to ride in a hunter class I couldn't stop myself from going too fast if I liked the horse. Just enjoying the ride. I can't do that now, anymore.

## CHAPTER 22

# LEXI

Matt has a buyer come in to look at Lexi. It's a kid and her parents. She's riding at Beginner Novice right now and while they seem well-heeled, I'm surprised they're buying a horse with Lexi's price tag and temperament for a kid who has just started eventing. Then again, some people at my old hunter-jumper barn would buy $25,000 ponies for kids who had been riding for a year competing in mini-stirrup so who am I to say what's weird?

I'm not really sure what this means for Lisa but Lisa shows Lexi off well enough. Then the girl Hannah gets on her—she's a leggy teenager, so tall that from a distance she looks like an adult and the kid gets Lexi around without dying even though she's not very strong with Lexi to balance the mare even over the little fences. She tries Lexi over a few jumps on our cross-country course. On this shrunken-down version of being in the outdoors, Lexi starts to pull.

Despite Lexi's lackluster record, the girl and her dad decide to take her on trial. I honestly don't think it's a great match, I'd think the kid needs more of a babysitter. Hannah doesn't seem like she grew up around horses. Even though her father knows some stuff about riding, it's not like he events and he's not a trainer. I'm a little surprised that they considered it a successful ride.

Dad tells me, "Hannah's quite a fan of yours." The girl grins at me, giggles and looks at the floor. Now that I'm even closer, I can tell she's probably not even old enough to drive. Fourteen? Fifteen? Of course, at that age, I was already riding really crazy horses but I'd grown up with it. It occurs to me that they might want Lexi just because she comes from Matt Stevenson's, which they assume must be good because of the Iceman's reputation. And my own.

"It's taken a lot of work with my current horse Milton," I say. "Even more than with some other horses I've had in the past. Milton's a tough horse." I look around to make sure Matt's out of earshot. "So is Lexi. In some ways, even tougher than Milton." I'm laying it on a bit thick but sometimes you have to.

"This is what I want to do," murmurs the girl and looks at the floor again, blushing. I don't know if she has a crush on me or eventing or whatever. I find it weird, almost disturbing that people would look up to me right now.

I show her Milton but he just stands there eating. He doesn't feel like coming over. He's not in a friendly mood today.

After they drive off, I ask Lisa if she'll miss Lexi and she just shrugs.

Matt and Lisa go out to dinner when we're done. After Matt came back from his operation, they've been more open about the fact that they're dating. Other than that, I can't see any change in him. I should have known he wasn't one of the types to, I don't know, find the horse version of Jesus just because he got sick.

A few days later, Matt goes to teach a clinic somewhere in Chicago. It's a place where I've never been but where I wouldn't mind going, but he's taking Lisa with him to help demo stuff, not me. I kind of mind that, given that my resume is more impressive than hers at this point, although I tell myself that obviously Lisa will be more entertaining to him for the two nights he'll be staying. The official line is that he needs me to teach when he's away.

But he takes Milton which I can't forgive him for.

Milton doesn't load at first. He was always great about loading, one of the few things he didn't suck at, behaviorally.

Today, with Blondie holding the rope, the big black horse just plants his feet in front of him and won't move. He snorts great lumps of snot, nose quivering, and I can see the whites of his eyes against his gleaming, show-sheened black coat. Lisa tries the lunge whip, tries to make him back up and then move forward, but he just stands there, throwing his head in the air. For the first time in a long time, I see his hooves leave the ground and Lisa gets scared, slacks the rope, and he yanks it away from her, turns and runs back into the barn.

I laugh a little bit since he seems so surprised by his newfound freedom. The gates are closed, so there really isn't anywhere exciting for him to flee. He goes back to his stall, sniffs where his grain bucket usually goes.

"Simon, get your horse on the trailer, we're going to be late," says Lisa.

He's not my horse, otherwise he wouldn't be going, I think. "How are you guys going to get him back on when I'm not there?"

"I'm sure he'll be different going home," says Lisa, helplessly. "He's never been like this before."

I grab him by the dangling lead rope. Feeling as if I'm betraying him, I lead him on without incident and clip him in; Blondie lowers the bar behind his butt. Damn you Milton, I guess you do trust me, because you seem to think I won't lead you anywhere bad. Geronimo's next, and that's it. They're only taking two horses.

"Ready to go," says Matt, striding over to us. It's 6:30 a.m. and his hair is still wet, I know he squeezed in a quick early session at the gym before having to sit driving for so many hours. He looks even more militaristic than usual with it all slicked back. "Call me if anything goes wrong," he says to me, brusquely. I nod as if to say, "Yes sir," and watch the two tails pull out of the yard, leaving me behind. I have a horse to ride before an early morning lesson with a client who comes every Tuesday before work. I'm already behind schedule thanks to Milton. No rest for the wicked, *jawohl*.

## CHAPTER 23

# BETTER TO SOMETHING IN HELL THAN TO SOMETHING IN HEAVEN

The next event comes up quickly, Lisa still doesn't have a horse of her own to compete. I ask her how Milton did at the clinic, and she just says, "Fine, but Matt mostly rode Geronimo," which I take to mean "terrible."

I read the write-up of the clinic and it's all about Geronimo. I kind of gather that Milton didn't even make it past the warm-up ring. Not ready for prime time, so to speak. I only get a real answer from Blondie, when I confront her. "Lisa told me he was wild from all that time he spent in the trailer, even after lunging and schooling on the flat. Fit to pop, they said. It was a weird ring. I don't know why they have riding stables in cities."

I remember what Daniel told me about Milton's previous behavior in Germany, before Matt purchased him. *Damn near ran through a fence.*

Milton's still not right when he comes back. He seems uneasy and unsettled when I'm schooling cross-country. He's uncooperative working in the sandbox, which isn't completely out-of-character but more so than usual. When he visibly tenses up as I put on my saddle one morning, I find Matt to ask him to get the vet to check him out.

Matt's in his office, which is rare, since it's just a little shoebox of a place near the center of the upper barn where he keeps paperwork and stuff. But I can hear him on his cellphone long before he can see my face, so I know he's there.

"What was that about?" I ask him. It's rare to hear the Iceman shout like that but I could hear the words 'stupid' and 'don't take me for a fool' and all the types of things people say when they're pissed off but are trying to be just professional enough not to swear.

"That kid who bought Lexi. She rode Lexi in some schooling show and Lexi started refusing every other jump. Now the father is blaming me. I can't be blamed for what owners do to their horses after they leave my barn, and every horse is going to take a transition period. That's why I don't allow horses to go out on a long trial. Anyway, kid got dumped at the last fence."

"Is she hurt?"

"The daughter or the mare?"

"Both."

"A lot of things can put a horse off. Oh well, at least the dad isn't a lawyer. I never sell to lawyers or the children of lawyers, and that's one of the reasons I'm still in business."

"Speaking of being off," I say. "I've been wanting to get Milton checked out. And I'd like to be there when he is."

Matt unleashes a long list of epithets at me but eventually agrees to have the vet look at Milton tomorrow and tells me not to ride the horse today. "You cost me, Simon," he says, which I know isn't a good thing. "A vet bill and a schooling day. If nothing is wrong with that horse, I expect you to make it up on your day off."

"Look, I know his ulcers have been better but remember he still has them. We don't want to wait for him to get sick. Better safe than sorry."

I know if nothing is wrong I lose my day with Ben, but if something is wrong I lose my ride while Milton recuperates, I think. Oh well, sucks to be me and had to be done. I shrug and make my face blank in front of Matt. Move on to the next horse, a client horse, which I have no attachment to after I surrender the reins. But of course, that is never really entirely true. Even if I only see this horse occasionally, even if his owner will never get past the lower levels so it's pointless to put too much effort into really improving his bravery and endurance, I still feel some sense of responsibility. It's still a horse to me. Maybe I'm really not cut out to be in this industry.

Milton checks out sound even though he's still tensing up whenever I tack him up. The vet suggests warming him up on the lunge line, maybe more turnout, but I know it's just what he's saying to justify his fee. He has no real solution. So on my usual day off, I just ride Milton and despite his initial edginess, he does manage to settle by the end of it all. He's not the same but he makes a convincing show of being the same. Good enough, I tell myself, even though it isn't.

Matt's office is empty when I go looking for him to tell him I'm done with Milton for the day. I'm not sure what to do with myself in the time I have left on my day off. Then I notice some paperwork on his desk. It's a bill of sale from that troublesome deal he made regarding Lexi.

I have an idea of where the kid lives. It's not totally in the middle of nowhere. I know the kid is keeping her horses at home and trailers out to a trainer so she might be there. I'll take the chance.

Given the fight they had with Matt, I'm not expecting a warm reception when I turn up. But for whatever reason, the girl doesn't seem to hold any problems she's having with Lexi against me. I guess to her I'm just a rider.

"Just wanted to see how the two of you were making out," I say. Hannah immediately runs over to call her father.

"I'm not here on behalf of Matt," I say, carefully. "Just was always fond of this horse." The father doesn't tell me to go to hell, fortunately, and asks Hannah to tack up Lexi.

"That's too harsh a bit for her," I say, since Hannah is still using the bit Lexi came with from Matt's. I flinch a little looking at it. It was bad enough with Lisa using it, since Lisa has pretty good hands, but in the grip of someone going BN? No wonder Lexi was going wild.

I try to cover for Matt a bit although in my opinion she should never have been in something like this. "No offense, but as a beginning eventer, there is just too much of a temptation to pull back if the mare gets a little bit strong, which invites a refusal. I have something that might work better in my car."

I watch Hannah ride Lexi. Hannah's nervous and she does tend to pull which makes Lexi pull harder.

"You do know Lexi is an OTTB," I say. "You can't get into a pulling contest to slow her down. Keep pulling like that and she'll just go faster. Pulling back with tension to her means something exciting is going to happen. Relax means that there is nothing to worry about, it's just a boring little jump."

At least now that Lexi is freed of the gag and her mouthful of wire her pace is steadier and eventually Hannah is able to properly half-halt.

"She looks better," agrees the father. "I guess Hannah *was* pulling and I couldn't even see that. But Matt said it's important to control her? Will she have enough control with a less strong bit?"

"There's more to working with a horse cross-country than just bitting up. I'm not saying every horse should go in a happy mouth but ... Look, for a girl that age, sane and sound is what is important, not fancy," I say. "Lexi is pretty, but if I were you, I'd put my money into training for now, not events."

"I understand what you're saying but Hannah is young and she has a competitive streak. Can't even stand to lose a race in gym class."

She should have gotten a packer, I think, based upon your experience and your daughter's riding. I feel a little bit sick that Matt sold them this horse, but I can't badmouth my employer. Christ, I feel dirty. "Well, given how she feels about the horse, you have to move on from here. They aren't ready to compete even at Beginner Novice. And I'm not saying get more training for my own pocketbook because I'm not freelancing right now. And Matt doesn't really handle beginner beginners. Your daughter needs a regular trainer, not just some sporadic coaching or advice."

It feels funny to be saying this, given that for years my Mom was my trainer. But then again even though she was my mom, she didn't treat me any different than her other riders—well, she was actually probably harder on me.

"We couldn't afford your barn anyway," admits the father.

Then why did you buy a horse from Matt's barn? Think it, don't say it, Simon.

I'm curious about something else. "Where's Hannah's mom?"

"I know. Usually it's the mom that's into horses. She likes them but she's scared of them." Oh well, no hope there, I think.

"My father couldn't stand horses," I say. "Hannah's lucky." I snort a bit, thinking of what he would think about using the money I inherited when he died to do what I've been doing. All of the money he made investing, in real estate and in the market, being frittered away so I could jump across manmade obstacles on animals he hated. I am my mother's son, no matter what else you might say about me.

"You're her idol," the guy says, nodding at his daughter. "She was kind of riding a bunch of different disciplines, not really settled on any, but when we were on vacation she saw you in Vermont on that grey horse of yours. She said, 'That's what I want to do.'"

"She's not a terrible rider," I say, not adding 'given that she's not really from a horsey family and doesn't have any real direction or professional coaching.' I guess people do what they can. "Keep the snaffle. I don't need it."

As I pull away in my car, I think about the money I still have in the bank. I could quit. Open up my own barn. I could get clients. Buy some young horses. Bring them up. Forget about chasing Ben in more ways than one. Take my time. I wouldn't feel so out of sorts like I do now. I made a bad gamble on a stock, Dad, I think, in a rare moment of prayer, and I don't know how to get out of this investment in myself, in this job at Matt's. In Milton. But I just can't bear to cut my losses, even if it is what a good person might advise. God knows where my prayer is going. What was it that Sasha said? *Better to reign in hell than to serve ...* I shake my head to clear it. It doesn't matter. I can't give up Milton. I just can't. Enough with the confusing riddles. Don't rein in, kick on, more leg.

I pull onto the highway just for the hell of it, and for an hour or so I just burn gas, going as fast as I can go, going nowhere. I only stop when my phone pings and I look over and I can see it's Ben.

Back in my apartment, it's another meal of fast food eaten with my phone in one hand, my eye on a baseball game. That keeps me too busy to think of what happened today, too busy to think of anything. Electric Slide is Lexi's show name. Hopefully the father will have good sense not to use it for at least a year or so. Patience, patience and practice? I'm such a hypocrite, I think. Again, I wish I had someone to talk this over with, but I don't, so I push it all away and just tell Ben what I'd like to do to him, over and over again.

## CHAPTER 24
# FRANGIBLE

I think we should skip the next event with Milton. He's constantly fretting and off his feed, and although I have finally gotten him to consistently focus when I'm schooling him, it's been taking more strength than I've needed in a long time—since I came here—to keep him forward. For a horse that wasn't in serious competition before he came here, he's had a lot thrown at him.

Matt isn't happy when I say this. "If you want, you can always hop on him, or Lisa," I say. I'm not always great at giving explanations, and maybe it's easier for him to understand on Milton's back. I have a feeling he might ride Milton anyway, when I'm not around, despite how badly it seemed to go the last time I spied him. But he won't do it, at least he won't with me watching and just says that I need to have more confidence in the progress we've made. That makes me less inclined to argue although when I step out of Matt's office, I get the uncomfortable sensation that I've just been bluffed in the same way Hannah and her father were. I've always loved playing cards. And I was always good at it, but I think I might have lost this game.

Milton pulls like a freight train through the dressage test, but I'm so used to that from all the horses I've known and loved in the past, we actually do manage to fake it ("faking the connection again," I can hear Matt's voice in my head as I salute at the end). The muscles bulging in my arms and abs aren't visible, and as always my face is a blank. I'm much more concerned about cross-country, though. The course is a long one, which means Milton has plenty of time to get distracted and to not be inclined to get to the end of all things. But he will get there, I know. I might not agree with Matt's training philosophy but as a rider I always finish what I set out to finish.

When the buzzer sounds, Milton's ears are at least forward. He looks interested with what's ahead and we spring forward into action. I use my stick anyway, though, given that we need more pace if we're going to make it under time. Fast and forward is what's safest for us now that we're committed. I know that the course gave the first few horse and rider combinations some problems—there's already been one fall. The ground's slippery, too, and Matt, Blondie, and I had a long debate about what kind of studs to use in Milton's shoes to navigate the turf.

This course is kind of notorious for poor footing. There're even two options on some of the wider fences—an outside and an inside track, to let the rider pick which one is optimal if things are really slick. Obviously, the inside track is the faster one, and over the first few fences that's the one I select. But during one of the long gallops Milton fusses—there's a series of puddles and he kicks up mud into his own face and begins to spook at that and starts to suck back.

"Shit, Milton," I mutter, "goddamn," and every other expletive I know and some I just make up on the spot. Is he really going to lose it for us here? Over mud that he himself is kicking up? I touch him with the stick, then use it hard, hard like I haven't had to use it on a horse for a long time since I rode some of the sleepier lesson horses back at Daniel's. Milton shoots forward. Damn straight you better go forward.

I try to balance him for the next obstacle but he resists. It's a corner fence, a type which hasn't given us problems for ages but as we go one, two, three ... instead of jumping he adds, ends up at the base and for a brief, sick second I'm convinced we're going to be hanging over it. I hear a crack, and Milton flies away. The jump's down but we aren't at least.

Automatic eleven penalties. Again, I hear myself spewing every curse word in the book but at least I didn't eat dirt. Hell, even worse, at least I wasn't eating Milton, with him laying on my leg. On the next question with an option, I take the longer, slower one. Even my confidence is shaken.

Milton's a mess by the end of it, frothing so much sweaty foam there's more white on his back than the grease on his legs. I should have retired after that, I thought. I was so in the zone I didn't even fully understand what had happened. I stay with him, don't give him to Blondie although I let her tag along as we go over to have him examined by the vet. I'm praying he's okay.

The vet looks dubious but Milton passes for now. Stick a fork in us and we're done, I think.

"Not bad," Matt says.

"What?"

Matt sounds pleased. "You're still in it, still competitive."

"How is that even possible? Breaking a frangible pin is an automatic eleven penalties."

Matt sounds proud, as if I've done something clever. "But it wasn't on the list of frangible obstacles. You took down the fence, but it wasn't designed to fall apart."

"Jesus, we were really lucky we didn't have a rotational fall if we smashed through a solid obstacle with no frangible pins."

"They thought it was a freak thing, that the jump fell down through no fault of your own. It wasn't designed to fall apart. Well, let's hope he's sound tomorrow. If he had to choose something to break, that was a good choice."

"Matt, he's not himself and you know it. Something's not right."

I think of the way Milton drove through the fence, as if it wasn't even there, spooked at every shadow being led back to his stall, and even though he was foaming sweat with exhaustion, wouldn't accept water from the bucket I offered him. I don't know if it's the acid in his stomach that's churning around, taking his mind away from his job, or something else.

"You're like a sentimental twelve-year-old girl the way you worry about that horse," says Matt, shaking his head and walks away. "It's like you're in love with him."

We finally get Milton to drink. I walk him out slowly, trying to get him to cool down, but he keeps sweating, fussing and starting. My legs are rubber and shaking by the time I leave, and I feel guilty doing that, rather than staying for him. I seriously contemplate sleeping by his stall, and if it weren't for the rules about staying in the stabling area after hours I might do it. I know I won't be able to rest. No rest for the wicked they say, and this time they're right.

The next day, I'm standing there in my usual suit, this time with a different pale blue shirt, a slightly darker one. Black and blue, I think. Like Milton. Unlike usual, I don't run fast to show off Milton's gaits. I just go through the motions. We get called into the holding box.

I stand there. I can feel Matt's eyes on us, watching from the rail. The vet and I make eye contact. I feel my head shake just a little bit, my eyes cast down.

As I lead him out, I hear the words "not accepted," the words I want to hear, yet they still sting. I know I've failed.

When Milton doesn't pass the soundness jog, Matt raises hell and files a complaint, of course. Given that he had a runout on Nebraska at that same jump we broke, this isn't going to be a banner day for his horses. Ben wins it all. I think of what Freddie calls him, bloody Ben Hillard, but this time I'm just jealous of how relaxed and happy Jasper looks when I watch him go clear during stadium. Breaking down a solid fence and nearly breaking my horse isn't how even I want to win.

Ben doesn't text me or communicate with me during the event, except for the occasional glance and smile as we cross paths. He doesn't even ask me how I am or Milton. Fuck you, Ben, I think, and no for once I don't mean I want to fuck you.

I feel bruised inside and out by the time I lead Milton off of the trailer. At the end of it all, I feel like I was the one that crashed through the fence, not him. It's somehow humiliating to me. I can't even find words to explain why.

My family has been texting me all weekend, though, which doesn't surprise me.
My mom:

*glad you are safe shame about the horse when you were ahead but people will understand it is not your fault*

My brother:

*U have 9 lives, catboy*

I know it's jerky, but I don't answer them until it's over, rationalizing they could see I'm not dead based upon the social media coverage.
What does surprise me is there is also a message from Max.
*Thank God. That could have been a rotational fall.*

Yes, I would know that it was Max, even without looking at the number because everything he texts has periods, just like he talks. Even when he's expressing his concern about my not being dead.

Christ, I know that it could have been a rotational fall. For some reason, his message really bugs me and I answer him first.

*wasn't so we are going to learn frame our mistakes*
*from I mean*

Stupid, stupid iPhone. It always corrects things wrong or doesn't correct what I want it to correct at all (granted, I am a super-lazy typist, and am usually just using one thumb with a horse in my other hand, but still, do your job iPhone). Like a bad trainer, I think, picking out all the wrong things.

Then the phone starts singing. It's my brother, an actual phone call.

"Look, I've always had my suspicions that what you do isn't a real sport but can you please explain to me how you can demolish a fence and not get penalties?"

I'm really not in the mood for his sarcasm. "Didn't have frangible pins. Frangible pin rule."

"Only an eventer uses the word 'frangible' in everyday conversation. Can you translate into English?"

"Because they were concerned about rotational falls—the horse getting caught over a solid obstacle and crushing his rider or himself"—I can feel Sean cringing, wimp that he is as I explain, "course designers have begun to use frangible pins so an obstacle will break apart when you hit it and you'll just get penalties. Not hurt. But the penalties are pretty severe. Eleven at present. Used to be twenty-one."

"Like jumpers."

"Basically only a lot more points. Anyway, this fence didn't have pins. It wasn't supposed to fall apart. It just did because he smashed into it so hard. It wasn't a refusal, though. He just smashed through the complete solid thing."

"Jeez, he must have been pulling like a train."
"I think some more schooling might be in order."
"Be careful, bro. Again, even a cat only has nine lives. "
"If I were careful, I wouldn't be doing this but you know I always manage to land on my feet."

# CHAPTER 25
# DOWNSIZED

Matt calls me into his office on Monday. I haven't heard from him about working any of the horses (Milton and Nebraska are off, of course, but there are still a few sale and client horses that should get out).

"I didn't like your little performance during the soundness jog, Simon."

I don't like the way you call it a performance, I think. This is like being confronted by one of my teachers after not doing bullshit homework. I shrug. "He wasn't sound. He just ran through a fence that wasn't even supposed to fall apart. And I can't think either of our reputations would be exactly enhanced by insisting he complete the competition. It would be a tainted victory, anyway."

"Goddamn it, Simon, I'm not asking for your opinion, just telling you that you should have done your job and tried to get him through it! We were lucky that he didn't break a frangible pin until you fucked up!"

"I think giving my opinion of whether a horse I am riding is sound or unsound is part of my job." I've been kind of expecting this so I also point out that this happened to a British eventer awhile back and he retired after cross-country even though he didn't get penalties for it and no one blamed him for that, and his crash into an un-frangible fence wasn't nearly as spectacular as Milton's. I talk and talk but I can tell Matt isn't buying it. His decision's already made.

"You're never getting on him again."

That hangs in the air for a moment. I'd like to say that I was numb to it, but I'm not, even though I should have expected it.

"You're fired."

What can I say to challenge those words? That we've never been friends but we got along as riders, that I'd even been mistaken for a younger version of him? I'm not sure if I expected this or not. I'm just numb. I've never been fired before. I've always been the hardest worker, wherever I've been, and even when the people who employed me hated me, they let me stay on because they couldn't do without me.

"Juan's waiting for you outside. He'll escort you to the tack room so you can get your things."

"That isn't necessary, Matt. Damn it, I'm not going to go shopping in the tack room if that's what you're concerned about. What do you take me for?"

"You know what I take you for."

"You're seriously mental, Matt. You need help."

"I don't care what you think. After leaving your last job before it ended in Germany with one of the world's top eventers and getting fired from this one, no one will hire you again. You're finished in this industry."

I know never say never and he's just talking big but even hearing those words hang in the air freezes me inside and makes me sick.

There's nothing more to say, so I turn to leave. I've never begged for anything in my life and I'm sure as hell not going to start now.

"Well, maybe Ben Hillard would hire you for something," he says to my back.

"What's that supposed to mean?" I say, whirling around.

He smiles and shrugs. I was hoping to get him to spell it out but even he's not that dumb. Although even if he did call me a faggot to my face it's not like I would what, sue him, or make a fuss. This is the horse world and that kind of stuff doesn't apply here. There's no HR to appeal to. Our HR is just SOL—shit out of luck—if your employer is an asshole.

I take my saddle, bridle, boots, and various bits, martingales, grooming stuff, and other things out of the tack room. The groom watches me in silence. I wonder what Juan thinks of all of this. I always liked him although we never really communicated and got to know one another. He only speaks Spanish. I did take Spanish in high school but I retained exactly none of it. "When am I going to use this?" I'd whine to my teacher, thinking about the horses I had to ride. Actually, I've discovered, I could have used Spanish quite a bit. Another stupid decision of mine.

"*Ayudame*," I say. I remember that much. The stuff obviously isn't heavy, but it's awkward to carry everything at once to my car. I take two of the saddles, bridles, and one boot in each hand on the first trip while Juan takes my third saddle and some of the lighter bits and pieces of leather. I throw my standing martingale over my own neck like a noose. Finally we have it all packed in my car, plus my tack trunk of grooming stuff, wraps, and all of the horse things I've been accumulating since forever.

"*Lo siento*," I say to him. I'd like to say good-bye to Milton but I know he's not supposed to allow me to do that. I mean, I'm much stronger than him, I could force my way past the guy. But that would be a shitty thing to do to all of us. But I am sorry, sorry for everything. Then I hear Matt's voice. He's walking with Lisa through the parking lot. He's striding across the ground. She's struggling to keep up on her stubby legs.

"God, I can't help it. He just got under my skin. The music he listens to all the time, the bitchiness. I've never liked …" I'm not sure if he's saying him or them. "I can't help it. It's just my nature. It's just nature."

Lisa's softer voice has a wheedling tone, good middle manager she is talking to her boss although I can't hear how she responds. Really, they never should have downsized her. I'm sure she was great massaging shitty decisions when she was working in a corporate job. She's only a decent rider, not a great one but she's an awesome diplomat, I can tell you that.

Juan disappears. Like all good stable staff he has a talent for making himself invisible when trouble might arise. I go to get in my SUV but I make eye contact with Matt and Lisa so I know that they know I heard what Matt said.

"What can't you help, disliking riders that put the welfare of the horse first?" Good fucking luck with a horse you can't ride, I think.

"You're so full of shit, Simon. You want to win just as much as I do," says Matt.

"But not like you, Matt. Not like you."

"Damn straight you're not like me."

"Behold the fields where I grow my fucks, Matty, and see that they are barren." I start the car.

"Honestly, you are the biggest fucking faggot I've seen in this business and I've seen a lot," he says.

*Behold the fields where I grow my fucks and see that they are barren*, I think. The statement feels very profound and very empty all at once.

## CHAPTER 26

# QUICK BRIGHT THINGS

At first, I just step on the gas, pull out to the nearest highway and go.

For the first couple of miles, it feels really good. I'm free, I think. I can do whatever the hell I want. The problem is, the only thing I've really ever wanted to do is ride. And ride well.

I've always prided myself on my sense of direction. I'm not like my brother who could get lost in a paper bag unless there was *this end up* written in crayon at the top. But to not get lost you need to know where you're going.

North. True North, I think. Because that's where he is.

Well, Matt is right about one thing.

I stop at my apartment, get some essentials because I plan on staying where I'm going for a while, I don't know how long.

I am going to Ben's right now because I have nowhere else to go. I can't think right now. I just need motion. Although I'm even more lost and lower than I was when I first spotted him from a distance in Germany all those months ago. Now I don't even have a position.

I push that out of my mind, I push that all away. It doesn't even feel real right now. It's not like a death or a sick horse where you can see the reality of what happens in front of you, feel the aching from standing all night or walking, the way your skin is rough and wrinkled to the point of no feeling from cool hosing a leg or the acid smell of medicine burning your sinuses. Milton's still there, still here with me in my mind, but gone.

I can pretend right now that it's just like it is on my day off, that I'm going to see Ben and everything is normal. I turn up the music really loud. "All These Things I've Done." Loud enough to make my ears feel like they want to bleed. I want something to hurt right now in my body to take away the pain from everywhere else. I want a fight, I wish I lived somewhere where I could go looking for one, but I can't, so I just drive. Who are you calling a faggot, I want to say to someone and then show him I can mess him up good. Just like I did in high school. But that was a long time ago.

After a certain point, I just feel numb again. *Behold the fields where I grow my fucks and see that they are barren.* All these years I've been giving fucks, not actually fucking but fucks in the sense of caring. And where has it got me? Nowhere.

I don't even know if Ben is home but his car is there so he might be. How can I break this to him? I'm unemployed and a complete loser now? That I'm going back to square one like that stupid kids' game Chutes and Ladders, which I always hated because it had nothing to do with skill, it was just spinning a wheel of chance? I'm still so hyped up on adrenaline right now I almost don't care. I'm breathing hard, like I do coming off a hard ride at an event. I feel like I'm in an altered state, my mind is racing.

Ben's car is in the driveway and so are three others. I assume one is his mother's, one is his father's, and the other is Sasha's. I don't want to go in at first so I just sit there for a second. Stare at the big paddock with the retired packers in it. Your perfect first horses, I think, looking at them serenely grazing together, the type of horses I never had. I go over and give them each a peppermint.

I've had those candies stuffed in my pockets at all times practically since I was born, I think. I've fed countless red-and-white circles to countless horses, picked out countless half-dissolved ones in their plastic wrappers from the washer after doing my laundry. Ben's kind to these old nags, but I know that they probably don't get much attention any more, given the family's schedule. Just an occasional ride by Ben's father. Maybe Sasha when she's home with her plastic saddle.

I can now enter the house. I feel calm enough again, like the horses were a drug that steadied my brain, like a swig from a flask if I drank. I ring the doorbell. Ben answers it and when he sees it's me he suddenly turns white.

Does he know I've been fired already? I'm stupid and illogical because I'm so messed up in the head. It just makes sense that everyone knows what's in my brain instantly. And then I see the guy behind him. Guy's not wearing a shirt.

Guy walks to the door. "Ben, do you need cash for the pizza?" Then he meets my gaze.

I almost laugh. From the latest up-and-coming eventer on a supposedly unrideable horse to the pizza delivery guy in less than a day.

I size the guy up. He's pretty hot. Bulging pecs. His face looks vaguely familiar from somewhere, maybe a horse trial somewhere. Or maybe he just has one of those generic faces. But it doesn't matter, I don't need to know his name. I can see everything I need to see already.

I turn away, taking the brick path two stones at a time with my strides and then I stop. There is a part of me that wants Ben to chase after me, to say, "It's not what you think, don't go," and all those stupid clichés. Fuck that part of me that wants that. Fuck that part of me that wants to believe lies. But he was right. I am such a fucking cliché.

I think of all the 'straight' guys I used to hook up with in high school. So was that it? Ben slowly being broken into his gayness, versus his vague 'sort of bisexual but I think the girls I sleep with are really meh' attitude he had when I first saw him banging that chick in the barn? Kind of like I used to break in the better horses until they were sane enough for the 'real' riders to place on. But:

*Behold the fields where I grow my fucks and see that they are barren.*
*Behold the fields where I grow my fucks and see that they are barren*
*Behold the fields where I grow my fucks and see that they are barren*

I keep saying that, over and over again until I can bring myself to turn the key in the ignition again, to leave for nowhere.

## CHAPTER 27
# BARREN

Boston. My brother is still in Boston, even though school has ended. He's renting a much nicer apartment than he could have afforded before he got his share of my father's inheritance and is doing another internship there, only having much more fun than he did at his last one, given that this time he has extra cash. It's home to Mom's in New Jersey or Sean's in Boston and honestly, I pick Boston more because it's closer to Connecticut more than any other reason. It's away from rather than to Maryland.

I can't even put all the crap that's happened into a text message. I park at the apartment complex, stumble out, and then wait in front of the place on a bench. It's a beautiful, warm day. Everyone looks happy. People are carrying their coats. Couples are walking hand-in-hand. I hate them all.

Clearly, I've been trying too hard all this time, nose pressed up against the glass. I'll never find the door in. I'm better off where I am on the outside, alone, watching, just like I'm watching people now.

I see my brother in the distance. It's past dark now. I've been driving all day. I'm exhausted. He's with a girl, a tall, willowy redhead (Sean has a thing for them, like some people have a thing for certain colored horses). Our eyes meet.

"Simon, what's wrong? Is somebody dead?"

"No. I just lost my job."

"Thank God. I mean, thank God it's only that but that's shitty. Why, because your horse ran through that jump? That wasn't your fault. He was crazy, right?"

If I don't have a job I might as well be dead, I think. I think about reading about Milton being ridden by Matt, or worse, by Lisa. I think about Ben and Jasper, who are still together. Honestly, the loss of the horse is worse. I could say *fuck you Ben, we'll beat your ass*, if I still had Milton. Maybe not the next time, but eventually.

"I've been driving around all day. Haven't eaten all day. I need rest. Sorry," I say. So much for his plans for a hot date. Maybe they can go back to her place, whoever she is. Christ, it's just like high school. Sean with a girl, me just there, stuck in the house or in his car before I could drive, me with nothing.

Sean lets me in, takes me up in the elevator. The apartment has a beautiful view of the Charles in the distance. Buildings are glittering with brightness. But I have nothing to do in the city. It has nothing to do with me.

I lay on the couch, close my eyes. I'm literally dead tired. I figure Sean can take the girl to his room or figure something out. I guess I'm being a jerk again, but at this point I don't even have the cognitive capacity to figure out getting a hotel room. I fall asleep in my barn boots, jeans, and shirt, right then and there. I hear hushed whispering. Like they're talking about someone dead even though I have assured them that no one has died.

I wake up the next morning at 4:30 a.m. Sean's door is closed and the girl's coat is still there so I guess she's his regular girlfriend and has stayed here before. I'm glad in the sense that I won't be blamed for scaring her away—not that he'd say anything, but I'd feel bad if she thought he was this weirdo with a weirdo brother who just turned up at random times. I realize I have no reason to be up this early. For the first time in my life, I have no horses to take care of. But I can't help it. The schedule is in the marrow of my bones. I take off my manure-encrusted boots because I realize that Sean might not appreciate them lying where he might be sitting to watch TV later on.

I pull out my phone and read quietly for a little while. Put my iPhone earbuds in and listen to music. Numb myself out. My stomach is acid and empty but I have no interest in food. I feel like I'm observing the hunger from a distance, like I'm observing myself and the wreck of my life. Everything is just too messed up and it's pointless to care. *Behold the fields where I grow my fucks and see that they are barren.*

There are messages on my phone, including one from Lisa. It's really long and I honestly don't feel like reading it. But I see the word 'love' written many times. She loves Matt. She loves Milton. Love, love, love. Over and over again. Whatever.

Another message from Max asking me if it's okay to ride Fortune in a hunter pace coming up and telling me stuff about my horse's worming schedule and how much grain Fortune's getting. I answer that, yes, yes, yes, of course it's fine. No 'love' in that one. Then I turn up the Killers and slide back into oblivion. Max used to call me 'killer' when we were first dating, a nickname based on my favorite band. How inappropriate, I think. How ineffectual I feel right now.

Sean's girl comes out quietly, her wet hair red as blood from the shower. She's dressed for an office job. I close my eyes and I'm aware she's looking at me really closely. I wonder what Sean told her. I wait until she clanks out of there in her fashion boots. Then I do kind of fall asleep, despite the loudness of my tunes until Sean sits next to me. His dark, curly hair is wet and slicked back and his blue eyes seem to take up his whole pale face. Everything is weird and surreal-looking, even my own brother.

"I told work I'm coming in late. What the fuck happened? I've never seen you like this."

So I tell my brother everything. In all the gory graphic detail. Starting with Germany and seeing Milton for the first time. Step by step. And about Ben, too. Because all of this is important so he understands my thinking or lack thereof.

And he listens. Which is kind of cool about my brother. I mean, say what you will about him, he listens. But then he says, "It was good you got out of there. That guy Matt was an asshole."

"But the horse wasn't."

"Actually, the horse does sound like kind of an asshole, too."

"No, no he wasn't. Matt made him that way."

"Okay, fine, but you can't deny Matt was."

"I'll never make it in this profession if I can't learn to deal with people like Matt, and I don't seem to have that capacity."

"And that Ben guy was an asshole, too. But I'm sorry, Simon, that shit happens to everyone. It's happened to me."

"I know."

"You move on. No offense, but you haven't had that many relationships in your life."

"Are you saying I'm immature?"

"You're ... inexperienced, not your fault."

Jesus, I've dated real people with jobs and lives, unlike you, I think. I don't know about his current girlfriend but Sean's never dated a girl like Max, I think. And it's different ... I mean, Ben's the best young eventer, everyone says. It's totally different from some college girl cheating on Sean. Or Sean cheating on girls, I think but I don't say.

Ben's schooling Jasper at this very minute and I'm on my brother's couch, flopped on God knows what. There are piles of unwashed clothes, some protein bar wrappers, and all the usual crap you'd expect in a guy's room with no time or inclination to clean, not that I'm complaining because my place was the same. Dirty dishes are in the sink, a half-empty pizza box is on the coffee table, and more clothes—nice ones, like suits and stuff—lie on the chairs. Don't get me wrong, like I said, I have horse manure on my boots and jeans. But I'm just a different kind of filthy. I'm different than Sean, I always have been. I belong in a barn, not here, and I'm proud of it. And what Ben did to me, because of Jasper and because of Milton, is different than anything Sean has ever experienced. Don't give me that *because you're gay and didn't date in high school you're immature.* I've had to wrestle with this issue since I was fourteen years old and people were asking me to catch ride ponies drugged to the gills, Sean.

I know Sean's trying to be nice, so I just shrug. "Look, go to work. I'm still figuring stuff out." I am thinking of what Matt's going to be saying to people about me. It feels pointless even to apply to a job somewhere else.

But then again, I have enough money in my savings account to last me for a while. Without horses especially I don't need to get a job to survive like a normal person, not right away. I could lie here forever. No commitments, no nothing. I really don't feel like moving at all. I turn away from Sean and look at the view in front of me from the picture window. "I'll find somewhere to stay."

"Nah, Simon, stay here."

"No, no, I don't want to cramp your style."

"This apartment is as much as yours as mine. You know what I mean."

"I told you not to bring that up," I say. I know he means the money.

Technically, Sean didn't get an inheritance when my dad died. My father left it all to me, I guess because I was the only one who visited him after he got sick. Sean couldn't stomach seeing him again. I mean, my father was an abusive asshole when we were growing up, and Sean remembers it better than I do so I can't blame him for that, but our dad did. Anyway, I split the money three ways—myself, Sean, and my mom—but I don't like to talk about it. It makes me feel weird, and I don't want things to be weird between us.

Thinking of money makes me feel really lonely and sad. Mom worried about Sean wasting it all. She said maybe I should just keep it and give bits and pieces to my brother when he really needed it. I feel that I've been the one to waste it now, not him. He looks so together in his nice apartment, with his job, with his tie.

"I want to keep an eye on you," Sean says. I laugh. "Seriously, I'm worried about you."

"Go to work," I say. "I'm fine. I'm just tired," I say. Tired of the fuckery that is my life.

"Take a shower. Get out. There's a great bagel place on the corner. Take a walk."

"Bagels taste like shit here. I haven't had a bagel since I was last in New Jersey."

"Get a doughnut then. Take a walk. Just enjoy yourself for a change."

I don't know what the fuck he's talking about but just to make him feel better, I follow him out, get my clothes and stuff from the trunk of my car, make sure my saddles are still there (not that it matters).

But I don't go out. I go back to the apartment with my bag, throw the bag on the floor, get out the science fiction novel I started a million years ago before shit started to really go down with Milton, and just read for the rest of the day. Fuck going out. Fuck it all. I live in the world of *Divergent* instead.

## CHAPTER 28

## SLEEPING LIKE THE DEAD

I waste the rest of the day reading with ESPN on in the background. I know Sean goes to his gym after work (which he calls a box, which I find quite ironic, given that he's already working in a box of a cubicle). I spend the day entirely alone and I guess Sean crashes at the redhead's because I don't see him until he stops by in the morning for some extra clothes and some stuff he needs for a work presentation.

"You haven't even moved from the couch," he says. "Have you eaten anything? Or drank?"

I shrug.

"Do you want anything? I know you don't drink coffee. Uh, would you like a green juice?" I hear him whirring whatever he's making for himself for breakfast in the kitchen. I remember Max had one of those things, whatever they're called. They sound like they're going to take off for outer space when they're just blending crap for a milkshake. "Maybe a protein shake?"

The idea of a protein shake fixing how I feel sounds so totally ridiculous I actually smile. But I don't say anything nasty because I know Sean means well, and finally he leaves me.

Mainly to take away the acid taste of hunger in my mouth and the fact that the smell of Milton on my clothes makes me sad, I get up, shower, put on a clean Clash t-shirt, and then tug on the pair of jeans that smell least like horse. I look around for some real shoes, find my Doc Martins, remember that Max gave me those as a Christmas gift, put them away, and then put on my nicest pair of barn work boots. I even brush my teeth and shave. I'm not one of those guys that can pull off hipster stubble.

I wander around outside in the beautiful spring day, find a grocery store, get a Mountain Dew and some junk food that I can eat versus the weird powders, bars, and half-eaten fancy takeout Sean has growing in his fridge. I considered stealing a slice from the pizza box in the living room, looked at the pizza, then decided against it.

I grab a silver packet of Pop Tarts straight from the box and sit on a rock in what passes for a park on a city corner. Even Pop Tarts don't taste good right now. At first I wonder if they're stale because they taste like sand and I could always rely upon them to taste the same before it all happened.

It's wall-to-wall cars and people around me. Either people rushing to get somewhere, tourists gawking, or one of ninety million college kids giggling, studying, flirting, or generally wasting time. I'm the only person in the entire city thinking about horses right now, I realize, and the mess I've made of my life. There's no place for me here in any of this. I mean, what am I going to do, take the college tour of MIT? It's a little late for that now.

So I go back to the apartment, the TV and my phone.

## CHAPTER 29
# THE EXTRA MILE

This pattern repeats itself for the next few days ... until Saturday morning. I discover it is the weekend not because I have any sense of time anymore (I don't), but because Sean is up early, saying he's going to run a 5K. "I'll be back in a few hours," he says.

"You mean like a race?"

"Yeah."

I get up and dig in my bag for my sneakers. This intrigues me. "Can I still enter?"

"Simon, you haven't run in like, years, since high school gym class, and that was just sprinting around the basketball court."

"This is a 5K, right, not a marathon?"

"Yeah."

"I can still beat you at that."

"What? You are so full of shit."

I pull on cargo shorts (which are of a muddy and indeterminate color), leave my favorite KNOW YOUR RIGHTS Clash t-shirt on (which I slept in), and tie my Converse sneakers over my bare feet. Sean's decked out in neon yellow sneakers, neon yellow and grey socks, neon yellow and grey shorts, and a grey t-shirt with upside down neon yellow letters on it. I know what it says from seeing it before he put it on, it reads THIS IS MY HANDSTAND PUSHUP T-SHIRT.

"You're really going to stand out wearing that," says Sean, looking at me disapprovingly. "You're going to get blisters all over your feet in those, too. You do realize that you have to like, train for this. This isn't like running to catch some stupid horse in the paddock."

I shrug, stick my wallet in my shorts to pay for whatever this thing is, and follow him out. I feel like driving, but he insists on taking his car, a tiny VW SUV that I admit handles really nicely. At least the Germans are good for some things. I open up the window and breathe heavily like a dog with my nose hanging out. I like the feeling of air and motion rushing past my face. God, I've missed that.

"You do realize you're gonna die."

"What?"

"People train for months for this. Even a little 5K. And I'm a Division I cross-country and track athlete. I know you don't have any respect for running as a sport but it is a sport. You have as much chance of doing well at this as I do of succeeding at Rolex."

I don't really listen to him because what he's saying is dumb. Yes, that would be true if I weren't moving around putting one foot in front of another in my daily life. But Lisa, who was obsessed with her weight, used to wear a Fitbit on her wrist, and just walking around the barn, even she'd log miles and miles, and I always ended up doing more running around than her because if there was any extra help that needed doing by anyone, they'd usually get me. I don't say this to Sean, though, because it's typical of him to try to psych me out, just like he did when we were kids, competing to see who could dive off the highest rock into the ocean or when we were playing hoops one-on-one. Sports psychology, my ass.

The whole atmosphere when we get there is like a carnival or one of the cheap horse shows Sean and I used to go to when Mom really had no money. There are tents all over the place. Bad music is blaring in the background and the sound system's rigged up so poorly all you can hear is bass. There are tons of people milling about, all dressed like Sean in stupid puffy neon shoes and shirts. The only difference between this and a carnival or team penning is that instead of selling fair food, all of the food is apparently free and it's stuff like bananas and bagels.

I sit down on some grass, lay back, and close my eyes. Sean's talking and laughing with people from his gym or box or whatever and he knows to leave me alone, although I see him keep an eye on me. Maybe he's afraid I'll get scared and walk away.

When we line up, the field is huge. It's well past the 9 a.m. start time, more like the hurry-up-and-wait of the hunter ring than an event, I think. I find out that the 5K's supposed to be in honor of some charity or another since someone makes a long speech I don't much listen to. Maybe that's bad but no one cares, I can tell. Everyone, even the people with strollers and the fat people and the lazy moms in yoga pants with strollers, wants to get going.

When the starting gun goes off I leap forward. There are people ahead of me but I easily thread through them, like weaving poles. I didn't realize it but it feels really good to move again. I feel light and empty from all the not-moving and not-eating and my muscles are fresh. For a bit, I'm not even conscious I'm in a race. I'm just flying and that's all that matters.

I am dimly aware of the fact that in another kind of race, a long race, it would matter if I went out too fast, too soon, but not in this one. After the first mile marker I'm acutely conscious that it's just me, Sean, and two other dudes who are really competing—one lanky white kid and one short, tightly muscled black kid—in a four-man pack. Sean is pacing himself because he always talks about pacing but I figure I best blaze ahead as fast as I can go. It's not like I need to slow down to make the striding on any upcoming water complex or avoid a bad distance at a table with weird ground lines. People who know nothing about horses always ask me if I'm a jockey when I say that I ride, and this is as close to a plain old honest Thoroughbred horse race without tricky traps as I'll ever get.

There are water stations filled with cups after the second mile, but none of us bother with them since they are obviously not for us. They're for the slow people, the mere mortals dogging away at their ten-or even twelve-minute miles who will start to feel heat at this point.

I notice the black guy is starting to flag. He looks like a sprinter, from what I've seen of runners. My brother always excelled at the longer events in high school. No one could touch him cross-country or at the 800m during track events, which was part of the reason of why he got a scholarship in the first place. The tall lanky white dude is close enough for me to hear his breathing so I step on my gas a little bit mainly to get away from the gross sound of his heaving. Honestly, he's kind of hot, I can see that he has a nice ass even though he's wearing baggy shorts but in my current state I'm too amped up to feel any desire.

Halfway through the last mile, Sean pulls away from the pack and I do the same. I must admit, my brother is faster than I gave him credit for—as a kid, I was faster than him at short sprints, and as soon as I started to get some muscle I could always beat him down to the ground with my fists, even though I was younger. But I'm not just cruising, I'm really working myself beyond what I thought I was capable of. I know I have to save a few dregs of energy for the end even though I've spent quite a bit of myself already. I can feel all the muscles I've honed mucking, throwing hay, riding bareback and with no stirrups over the years crying out and I am summoning them up, like a magic incantation or something.

Sean's a little ahead of me, then a stride or two more. I can see the finish line. For a split second, I think I just can't, that's it, this is me at full gear. Then I catch a glimpse of the white of his eye and the soles of his yellow shoes, and I know my brother as well as I know myself—he's a little bit scared. He's surprised. He didn't expect me to do this well. He really thought he would beat me *easily*, the bastard.

And I think of Matt and Milton and the big black horse I put so much into, so much thought and energy and heart and love, the horse I'll never lay my hands on again. Because there is so much I can't control. And bloody Ben Hillard. Bloody, slippery Ben Hillard who, even when I beat him on Milton, was still the darling of the eventing world. Who I loved, I guess, and who clearly didn't love me. Enough. Just sent stupid messages about love, love, love. Although I thought he did. Again, I couldn't control that. But I can control this and I dig deep down in a dark place of my soul and with six or seven easy strides I leap ahead of Sean, pass him, and win the entire fucking thing in my beat-up old Converse shoes. I can practically feel the pavement bruise my soles, I'm pumping so hard and my sneakers are so worn.

I hear people cheering and stuff. I know it's not official; they have to check the time on the stupid chip that's on the number pinned to my shirt. But I don't care about that, I just love turning around and seeing the expression on Sean's face as he crosses the line second.

"Motherfucker," he spits at me as we walk to the side to let the other runners pass the line and not get in their way.

I start laughing hysterically, so much that my heaving ribs hurt. Whenever I beat him as kids, Sean would get all cool. Like when he'd get his usual handful of white, pink, and green ribbons in the hunter ring, he'd grin at my mom like that's what he meant to do, as if my caring about such a silly sport was evidence of my general weirdness and stupidity and gayness. But he cares about this, God help him, and there is no way to conceal it.

"Now, now, that's no way for a Division I athlete who is in *training* to talk," I say, smiling. I try to act all cool but then I have to go to some grass and puke up the contents of my stomach. Fortunately, there isn't much there so it's mostly bile. I look around, find some free water at one of the nearby tables and wash out my mouth. I rinse my teeth, spit the first swig out and then I drink. I grab two more cups, pour one down my throat, the rest over my head to cool down.

"Motherfucker," Sean says. "Motherfucker. Mother. Fucker."

I know if our actual mother were here, she'd say, "Language, Sean." She hates cursing which is probably why Sean and I have mouths like sailors when she isn't around.

We have to stick around for some prizes and a ceremony, I guess, but that won't be for a while because some people are going to take almost an hour to finish the damn thing, including some of the old guys from Sean's box whatever. So I get a banana, a crappy bagel, and some iced tea in a bottle now that I can finally eat to wait it out. There's no Mountain Dew or soda of any kind to be found. Motherfucker, indeed.

"What type of shoes do you have on?" It's another guy who has crossed the finish line. I look at my beat up, ratty old Converse which have anarchy signs and FIGHT THE POWER written on them in magic markers and 'fuck,' among some other choice phrases. "Are those barefoot or minimalist shoes?"

"I have no idea," I say.

"I was just wondering because I've tried so many different kinds."

It occurs to me that some people take this really, really seriously, the way I do riding. It was $35 to enter. They charge you $35 just for breathing the air even at a cheap horse show. I mean, I care because I had to beat my brother, but it suddenly occurs to me that entering stuff like this, getting the right gear, and as Sean would say *training* is people's thing, out in the city and out in the suburbs, just like our thing was horses. Honestly, it seems kind of sad and pathetic.

I feel bad for the guy and I just say, "I wear what's comfortable for me," which is true, not that this is farther than I've ever raced at one time in my life. And that I still don't care about or respect running, but that as competitive as my older brother might be, I will always want to win the most. I will always want to win more than anybody. And that is why I will stick around, pull myself out of bed tomorrow and move forward, wherever the hell forward might be at this point.

Sean is still so mad he can barely talk to me. I mean, like really mad. This is so awesome I don't even have words. He doesn't even try to hide it! *Behold the fields where I grow my fucks and see that they are barren.* Well, a little bit less barren today. I can't stop smiling. This almost makes everything that it took me to get here worth it.

After a few hours Sean is able to speak to me again, and then that's only in halting sentences. We're back to normal by dinnertime which is spent at a sports bar getting wings and beer and watching multiple sports simultaneously on multiple screens. We don't speak about what happened. I'm not a jerk. But it will always be there, between us, and that is glorious.

## CHAPTER 30

# THE BOX

Sean drags me with him to go to his gym or box or whatever he calls it on Sunday. I'd always been able to successfully get out of working out with him in the past given my 24-7 barn schedule, but one of the other, unfortunate effects of unemployment is that I have absolutely no excuse now.

I'm a little bit surprised at what I see when we arrive there. A bunch of about five or seven people are standing around a rope hanging from the ceiling. I'd guess the end's about fourteen, fifteen feet up (I'm just over six foot, so that's how I'm estimating). One person is climbing up it, knees to chest.

Other than the ropes, there are a bunch of medicine balls, weight racks and plates, bars hung from hooks, pull-up bars, and some other stuff—I don't know what you're supposed to do with it all, but no treadmills or bikes or anything. It's not like the gym Matt took me to.

"Killing it!" one of them shouts to the guy finishing the climb before he slides down. The climber's got bulging muscles on his calves and thighs and a tight ass (although I'm sure he's gripping with everything he's got with all the pressure of being watched). After the guy slides to the ground and turns around, I suddenly see it's not a guy at all but a girl with short hair and a really flat chest.

Well, this feels all weird.

The rest of them go. Some of them are people with tats and piercings, others look like normal pencil-pushers and mini-van moms wearing baggy shorts. Everyone is wearing some kind of neon, just like Sean. Most of them make it up, but some just go halfway, yet everyone gets cheered on. Another girl who I guess is in charge of everything—she's got long black hair in two braids tied with neon bands and they keep calling her Missy—then talks about the workout everyone's going to be doing which involves doing five deadlifts, five handstand pushups, and one rope climb as many times as possible for nine minutes. The guys lift heavier weights than the girls.

"This is Simon, Tara," Sean says, introducing me. "He's the brother I told you about."

"You ride horses," says the girl-who-is-not-a-guy whose name is Tara. She's got a really childish, squeaky voice. Nope, definitely any attraction I felt for you while you were hanging up there on the rope is so not happening on the ground.

"What else has he told you guys about me?" I ask, warily.

"Oh, nothing but *nice* things," says Missy, the girl with braids. "That you've won all sorts of stuff riding things. Are you like a jockey?"

"Even you would be too big to be a jockey," I say. Actually, she's short, but way too heavy. I don't say, "And too fat," because she'd take that the wrong way. She's not fat fat, just muscular and not jockey thin. A little perky block of a woman.

"We'll go easy on you since it is your first time. I guess you're not afraid of heights since you're a rider."

Rope climb was one of my favorite things in gym class. It was impressive yet involved no interactions with asshole jocks on a team. My muscle memory kicks in as I press down on my shoes to get up the rope and slide down carefully and manage to avoid ripping apart my hands. I was always careful about that so they wouldn't bother me when riding later. But I'm not riding later. Oh well, fuck it.

    Missy asks if I can do a handstand because she says it's another of the skills that are needed for the workout. This is another thing I was always good at as a kid and although I haven't done one in a while, I bang one out. She explains that a handstand pushup is lowering your head to the ground and then pushing it up while pressing your legs against a wall while upside-down. I'm beginning to gather that this new fitness thing of Sean's involves doing stuff that comes easily to most people when they're kids and fearless and then relearning it after they can't move around really well from sitting all day in an office job. Finally, she goes through good form on deadlifting and I kind of zone out on that because it's just picking up heavy things and putting them down. I figure I can stand anything for nine minutes.

Despite my confidence, I admit I'm sweating, breathing hard at the end of it. Nine minutes is about what it takes me to get through some long cross-country trips, and I thought it wouldn't feel so bad. I sit down, just like I did at the end of the race but fortunately this time I don't puke. Everyone looks pretty rough but they tell me I did okay.

    "This WOD is just right up his alley," I hear Sean say to Missy, who seems impressed by my ability to keep up on my first day. "He doesn't have any real lifting experience; he's just freakishly strong." He says that dismissively. "Even though he doesn't look it."

    Some of the guys, including Sean, who are preparing for some kind of competition do some more deadlifting stuff, and I hang around and do what I can, mimicking them. They correct my form but they aren't nasty about it. Some of the beefier ex-football player types actually pat my back and say stuff like, "Nice work bro, hope you'll come again." In gym class, even members of my own team would try to hit me with the ball like a missile and every team captain would pick me last even though I was the best shooter in basketball. I'm kind of surprised by this reception, but maybe it's because they like Sean. I know lots of them are stronger than me (there's a big chalkboard where all the weights of the people in the gym write down their PRs of their lifts which naturally I look at to compare myself against). But even flying blind I can still kind of hang in there, and I guess that's enough. I do manage to rip open my hand with all the climbing and the bar work and I learn that it's good to chalk up beforehand for next time. But like I said, what does it matter if my hands bleed? It's not like I'm going to have some green horse pulling at them any time soon.

"She's very upbeat," I say about Missy to Sean later, "for a gym teacher."

"Trainer not teacher. Box not gym." Pause. "She's been through hell and you wouldn't know it, would you?"

"What do you mean?"

"She was addicted to drugs really badly before she started CrossFit. Now she owns her own box. There are more success stories like hers than you would expect," and I know he doesn't mean the financial success of the box.

"Whenever I hear someone called Missy I can't help thinking of Missy Clark, the famous Big Eq trainer. When you say 'Missy' without a last name, everyone in the hunter-jumper world knows who you're talking about," I say, thinking of my old barn.

"Jesus, you're a weirdo," says Sean.

I stare at my bloody hand. It feels good in a way. Like I've done something important and strong for a change.

I go out with Sean's friends afterward—five guys and squeaky-voiced Tara—and most of them are actually pretty nice. They talk about lifting and running and things like that. They're kind of obsessed with it. But it's better than the usual stupid shit people talk about. Everyone except me orders wings and ribs but no fries. Protein, they say. They need their carb portions for beer.

"I knew you would like it," Sean said. "I hope next time we work on some of the Olympic lifts so you'll understand this stuff takes skill. That was an easy day for you but every day is different. What do you think of Tara? She's divorced, you know. Starter marriage gone bad."

"She hardly sounds old enough to drive."

"She's older than me, actually, but not by much. I've been trying to get to know her better but she's kinda burned by that I think." It's almost unheard of for a girl to say 'no' to Sean so I can tell by his voice he's both frustrated and intrigued. I'm sure she'll crack soon; though, they always do.

"What about the red-headed girl I see you with?"

"Oh, that's just a friends-with-benefits thing."

"You're such a shit to women, Sean."

"She knows where we stand. Look, I'm sorry I mentioned it."

"You do know that Tara looks like a guy. I was attracted to her myself when I saw her from a distance."

"That's so not true. You're just saying that to be annoying, like usual."

## CHAPTER 31

# SNATCHED AWAY

"Get under the bar," I say, but he drops it. "Charlie, seriously. It's not even heavy. This is the girl weight." I grew up in a barn with trainers that didn't mollycoddle you and I can't help but bring that up. This isn't an official class or anything like that and no one is there to hear me except this pimply, wussy seventeen-year-old kid I can't stand.

It's been two months since I first walked in the box but it feels like two years, a lifetime ago. After that first day, I guess I kind of got hooked. And really, I have nothing better to do. I have no desperate financial pressure to get a job. I have a place to stay—Sean kind of likes having me around (although I carefully avoid contact with his redheaded friends-with-benefits girl, even though he says she is cool with everything). Of course, he did manage to get in Tara's pants, but he seems to go more over to her place, so I only have to put up with her voice in the box. She seems nice enough.

Charlie is one of those hopeless cases. He's already had a lot of private one-on-one coaching from Missy and a bunch of the other people that are certified coaches at the box but by now they've kind of accepted that he sucks. He's struggled to keep up with everyone in the teen classes even with extra help. The coaches just sort of ignore him and congratulate him for not dying every day at the end of WODs.

His dad's a member and kind of my friend and the dad took me aside and asked me if I could give his son some tips today. I know the dad's desperate because everyone else has given up on Charlie. Charlie is one of those people who hates CrossFit but his dad has him doing it so the kid will "toughen up" and stand up to all of the kids that give him shit in school. So I said okay.

It really is kind of funny that his dad is mad that kids call Charlie a faggot even if Charlie happens to be straight. I couldn't say to his dad that Charlie is just the kind of kid I hate more than anything because he's a total wuss and he fears even seeming like what I am. I look at the kid's face. It's pocketed with acne scars. He has even worse skin than pale Irish, freckled me (I already have lines beneath my eyes, I've noticed in the bright fluorescent light of Sean's bathroom). He must be a moving, living target.

Charlie drops the relatively light bar again. I'm also kind of annoyed with him because my snatch isn't great, either. I mean, better than Charlie's or even Charlie's dad but still ... not good. Sean was kind of right that it's not the same thing as lifting stuff up and putting it down. It's a technical lift. You have to jerk it up explosively, extending your hips, rocking up on your ankles, and using your whole body to power it overhead.

I've been telling myself, okay, I'll do this fitness stuff, but only if I can do it without seeming like I'm trying, just like math in high school. I don't know why. In high school I always made such a show of how little effort I needed because mainly I was tired and I really didn't find it very hard and I needed the extra sleep in the back of class. With this, I feel that if people find out I suck at anything (even if sucking by my definition is just being ordinary and having to work hard at it to just be normal) then Sean's won, somehow, and this fitness stuff is just as hard as the horses. My background has helped me with some things requiring agility and brute force but not with others.

Charlie tugs the bar up, drops it. We go down more in weight and he gets it overhead and then falls down on his ass. He won't even make eye contact with me at this point. I know he's not trying. He just doesn't think he can go forward, he's made that decision. If he was a horse, I'd use leg but of course with a human you can't.

Even I, with a field barren of fucks, even I am trying more than you, Charlie. At least I've tried at something in the past. Jesus, Charlie, put your heart into something I think. His dad says Charlie doesn't have friends, spends most of the day in his room, playing video games. He's not doing well in school. I guess Dad thinks this will fix his kid.

"Look, your dad just asked me to help you, I'm not getting on your case or anything to be a—to be mean." But he's not buying it.

"I really don't care about this stuff," he says. "My dad cares. Hell, you care more than me."

He's probably right. It pisses me off to see someone give up at anything. "So what do you care about?"

He shrugs. "Dunno."

The bored, flat toneless quality of his voice grates on me worse than Tara's squeaking. Then I think of my own new mantra: *Behold the fields where I grow my fucks and see that they are barren.* The one that's helped me forget about my old dreams and push aside everything that used to make me feel alive. Because as much as I can get a momentary high from lifting heavy or zoning out my brain in overdrive to bang out reps on a speed rope, I know that as soon as the motion stops, I feel sort of dead. Take apart the bar, put away the jump rope. They're all just inanimate objects.

"I get it, Charlie," I say. "But sometimes pushing yourself, even just in the gym, even if it's not your thing, can make you feel better about the things that do matter to you." I have a feeling these things involve hot girls he has no chance with and getting to the next level of whatever video game he plays online.

Charlie nods and I show him where to put his hands on the bar, wider than they are right now. I explain where he's not powering through his legs enough, try to use different language than I have before so he might get it. And this time he does get it overhead and sticks the lift. "Fifty percent bodyweight. That's way better than you've done before, right?" Then I stand up, look at the clock, I still need to work on my own stuff before the next class begins.

"Thanks," says Charlie in a way that makes me I feel I should say something.

"You okay?"

"Yeah." But he doesn't move.

"Your dad said the kids at school were giving you ... problems." I don't say "giving you shit," my first instinct.

"They were messing with me."

"They used to mess with me too in high school."

"I assume you beat the crap out of them."

I laugh. "Well, yes. I did."

He laughs as well and seems to relax. "I would never be able to do that, though."

"Just don't let them touch you inside," I say. He smiles and nods and he goes. I'm such a fucking hypocrite.

After class, I go home, shower, and get ready for a first date I set up. I need to look somewhat presentable so the guy isn't like, "Oh, look what the Internet dragged in."

I know I should be happy. I have a new hobby. I look at myself in the lone mirror in Sean's bathroom. I can see how my body has changed. My biceps and triceps are popping out of my shirt. My stomach, always muscular, is now seriously cut. My chest isn't all bone and clavicle and my leg muscles look more solid. I look like what I am now, a gym rat, versus the useful invisible muscles I had when I was just at the barn every day, riding horse after horse. I look like the kind of guy you'd want to pick up and guys do. What I'm saying is, I have money in the bank, I have a social life and time to enjoy it, and I should be happy. But:

*Behold the fields where I grow my fucks and see that they are barren.*

"Sometimes I think of sending in my resume to an eventing barn," I say casually, strolling out of the bathroom. "If there is anyone who will still have me. I can't imagine what Matt's said about me since I've left horses." I'm convinced that I'm a pariah in the sport. I've tried not to look at Eventing Nation and Eventing Connect in my newsfeed but I flop down on the couch and do just that. *What do you care about*, I asked Charlie today. I still have time before I leave on my date.

Sean looks shocked. "I thought you gave up the horse thing."

"Maybe I just need to ride." My car still smells like horses as do some of my oldest clothes, the odor of barn and manure and hay can't be washed out. My saddles and bridles and bits are all in my closet here and even when I get into my gym clothes, I am reminded of Milton.

"Christ, don't you ever learn? You have a good thing going here, bro. Don't fuck it up."

"I'm not saying that I don't."

Pause.

I'm still getting over Milton is the truth. And while I've gotten over the loss of Ben as a boyfriend, his image still haunts me as a rider. But I can't talk about that with Sean. He'd never understand.

"Max emailed me about Fortune this morning—just checking in and I guess I got to missing it all."

"Simon,"—I jerk my head up because my brother so rarely calls me by my name, "the truest definition of insanity is to do the same thing and expect a different result. Horses have done nothing but break your heart."

Or given me their hearts, I think. But again, I know what Sean is saying would make sense to a normal person so I don't respond.

There's another thing, too. "Matt and Lisa are getting married."

"No way—that other girl that rode at your old job?"

"I don't expect to be invited to the wedding." I look at my Facebook newsfeed. There's a photo of Matt and Lisa holding hands, dressed in their stadium gear. Lisa is grinning, Matt has as close to a smile as he can manage on his thin lips. Well, she won't have to go back to corporate life now, I think. I really don't care. All I want to know is who will be riding Milton at the next event and how he is going. Has he colicked again? How are his ulcers? Have they worked through the issues he was having, his refusing and resisting?

My phone pings with a text message. It's first-date guy. I just hope this one looks like his photo. I've been with more guys over the past couple of weeks than I've been with in my whole life, and I've been a quick study. I know there's no way you can count on what you see on a screen to be the truth. Then again, maybe some of them have though the same thing of me.

## CHAPTER 32
# BLAST FROM THE PAST

So I signed up for some kind of stupid trail run through the woods and mud. I did it because of a couple at the gym—Ed and Zack—these two nice, middle-aged guys who invited me over to dinner one night. Over salmon (which, like all members of the box, they identify as "clean protein") and sweet potatoes and broccoli, they told me all about the different Iron Mans and marathons and trail runs they'd done together, and they suggested I get my feet wet trying out a 15K.

I didn't want to seem wussy, and it seemed like a good idea at the time. Basically three miles with an extra six tacked on, right? When I woke up on the morning of the race it was pouring rain but I've ridden in the rain so that didn't faze me.

The first couple of miles were great but then around mile six or seven my legs started to feel weird and dead. I'd never felt this before but then again, I'd never run at a consistent pace for that many miles before. It's like they were buckling, and as hard as I was breathing, my breath did nothing to propel me forward like it did those last few steps of the 5K. Dig in and press on I thought. Move forward. I did but the sight of other people moving ahead, some of them older dudes who evidently had trained for this damn thing made me want to go even slower. I felt like I was being sucked back into the earth, into the mud and gunk.

A fifteen-year-old won the whole stupid race. His thighs were convex. At least I didn't tell Sean I was doing this. That was the only good thing about all of it. Definitely would taint my 5K victory.

I don't want to admit to myself that Sean, given that he has run a marathon (he even wears the stupid shirt he got from running it) could have smoked me. He runs 15K all the time. This really eats into me, as does my relative lack of a decent snatch, even though I can deadlift almost as much as the really big guys at the gym. Technique, Sean would say. What you need beyond something coming easy to you. Something beyond going fast, hard, heavy, and unthinking. Caring.

I started riding so early and it did come easier to me than some, so I've practically forgotten how to accept being bad at something to learn it, especially physical things. I suddenly feel very tired, realizing that, if I want to do anything, it's going to take work.

With riding as well, lots of the work that people praised me for way back when—the willingness to muck stalls, the riding greenies—were things that I enjoyed, even though other people didn't so much. And I actually do love that stuff, provided I'm treated with respect for it, which I wasn't at Mr. F's.

I step on the gas of the car, harder and harder. After resting and scarfing some bananas and bagels I feel fine again. I'm angry at my body for that. I mean, it couldn't be that bad if I don't feel like hell. Damn it, if you're going to fail me, at least mean it. No matter how much I hate myself right now my body feels resilient and strong again, even more than usual because I haven't punished it lately staying out in the heat and cold or being stepped on and bitten by horses. I've just been focusing on myself in the gym.

It doesn't make sense to feel like I do inside right now, like I've hit a dead end and still my body is mocking me by not feeling worse, almost like people used to mock me at school and Matt did at the barn. Speed, speed is the only answer to feeling empty. Race your way out of it. For the first time in my life I long, I want to feel pain because I don't know when it's going to find me again. I want to feel risk and danger but this desire is all bottled up inside me like a knot.

The sun's out, cheerful, laughing at me. Sun's out, guns out? I feel mad enough to shoot something right now, that's for sure.

I know it's dangerous to drive seventy, eighty, ninety, over all these winding country roads. I'm not that familiar with them and although the rain has stopped there are still slippery piles of leaves that I skid on. Whatever, I think, whatever.

And then I see on a straightway, in the distance … this woman wearing a neon crossing guard jacket. It says VOLUNTEER.

"Wait!" she shouts, waving her arms. As much as I'm in my own zone, in my bubble of motion and loss, she penetrates it, and I don't want to scare her, I don't want to take anyone down with me.

"Horse coming through!" I think she's shouting, but I must be hallucinating that.

I slow down, stop the car and what do you know? There's a girl on horseback decked out in a cross-country air vest and skull cap, who canters across the road. VOLUNTEER tells me I can pass but I don't move, I just stare at the bay mare galloping away.

I realize suddenly that it's an event. Probably a schooling thing because I've never heard of one taking place in this location before but an event all the same. The VOLUNTEER is holding up a thin neon rope strung across the road, to alert cars that the course passes through the real world, the normal world for a brief sweet second. "Please go slow. The horses get scared," she says. Patronizing as hell, VOLUNTEER.

I think of all the times I rode Fortune through Vermont and how some cars would come careening by and try to almost hit me; others with more well-meaning drivers would slow down, honk, and shout "Horse!" with joy. Suddenly, I realize that she thinks I'm one of those types, the type of person who doesn't know anything about horses. I look down at myself. I refuse to wear yellow runner's clothes, but I'm in my favorite camo shorts, my Killers t-shirt, and the real trail sneakers I finally broke down and bought for the 15K. I'm spattered in mud. I realize I look like a civilian, one of the great, vast numbers of people to whom horses are just creatures to pet by the roadside and then leave.

I don't know why, but that stabs me in the guts. I look at her and think ... can't you see my whole life just by looking at me? Isn't every single horse I've ever ridden written on my face? Every second, every other thought I've ever had has been about horses since as long as I've been alive it seems. And as soon as I step away, it's lost and gone? I can still feel the echoes of the galloping in my chest of that strange horse, a horse that's probably just getting through its first Training level cross-country course.

My sucky trail run is gone, forgotten. It cost me so much less, just my own bitter pride. But this small cruelty she doesn't even mean, the words of this VOLUNTEER, is the worst blow of all. Don't scare, don't hurt the horses? I tried to protect Milton and Lexi from Matt, really I did. In some ways, I even sacrificed myself. Fat lot of good that did.

"Excuse me ... Where is parking for the event?" I ask instead. "I'd like to watch." VOLUNTEER looks annoyed but points me to a nearby lot which is packed with trailers and SUVs. I see a guy walking by with his horse, talking with his friend. Mostly Pony Club types, and when I walk by the jumps after leaving my car, I notice that the highest-level flags are white on black background (Training).

But still, that bay horse I saw was beautiful. Maybe I wouldn't have noticed her before but it's been so long since I was close to a horse at a gallop. I can still feel the rhythm of her movement pounding against my chest. I just ran almost ten miles and even that didn't stir me like seeing a horse.

I stand where I can see a good number of the jumps. The riders are capable. Amateurs and kids that they are, there are no spectacular refusals. But what does stick in my mind is that a specific rider looks very familiar, a girl walking with her horse.

I go back to the trailer section after a reasonable length of time and go looking for her.

"Karen!" I shout. She's changing into her stadium jacket, whirls around and looks at me like I'm a ghost.

"Simon?"

Karen used to ride at the old barn where I was a working student in high school. She was one of the hunter-jumper girls but a good one. Not a hunter princess.

"You've gone over to the dark side?" I ask.

"Simon, this is so weird. I've been thinking of you, with all the success you've had recently. I've wanted to get in touch to tell you I'd been eventing as well, that you'd be so proud of me. But what are you doing at this little baby event? Not riding," she says, looking me up and down. I'm not even wearing boots.

"Nah, I was literally driving through and I had to stop and look."

"This is Twister," she says, introducing me to her little chestnut gelding.

"What is he, a Morgan? Wouldn't have cut it back in your high school days at Angel Heart," I said.

She laughs. "I want to have *fun*. After all, I'm not a professional. I don't have the money or the patience anymore for the hunter world."

"I never did," I said, "even in high school."

"Oh, I had the biggest crush on you back then. All of us used to talk about how you'd go cruising around a jump school with punk music blasting in your ears. We'd have never dared to act like that, and you only got away with it because you were you. I'm so glad you made it."

I look at my trail running shoes. "Well, there's never anything like making it in the horse world. It's always a struggle to stay on top."

"Of course, of course."

"I'm not riding—Milton, anymore," I said. "I lost that ride."

"Why?"

"Usual shit. Even the eventing world has it. Barn drama. Politics."

"I'm sorry to hear that but you'll find another one," she says, brightly. "You were so talented. I always said that we'd say we know you when, and now we do."

"You actually went farther in the Big Eq than I did," I remind her.

"Well, you never had a consistent horse to ride, and certainly never a packer." I'm surprised and kind of touched that this was even noticed by some people. I always felt sort of invisible at that barn. Karen had a lot more friends than I did.

"Yeah, they always put me on the sale horses and the crazy ones at Angel Heart."

"But you cleaned up doing the jumpers and you certainly found your niche afterward."

"Here, let me hold Twister while you finish getting changed," I say. I walk over with her as she prepares for stadium, give her a leg up so she can school.

Karen's a good rider. Not a particularly bold one but she has a great position, always did, and her Morgan's a steady kind of guy. They make a good team. She was always in the ribbons at the top shows. I know she went to a really, really great college. Again, another person who did things right, sensibly, unlike me. Someone who, after aging out, keeps horses in the correct place in in her life: weeknights after work, on weekends, holidays.

She gets third at Training level and she's very proud. So am I. She tries to explain to me what she does when she's not eventing, something called a bond trader in the city but I sort of glaze over. We get burgers from the grease truck for lunch afterward while Twister munches hay in the trailer. It's a relief to eat with someone who doesn't talk about carb portions for a change.

We exchange numbers, promising to keep in touch. I don't have the heart, angelic or otherwise, to tell her I'm not in horses anymore.

I told myself I wouldn't but later I check to see how Milton's been doing on my phone. Record-wise, I mean. He placed eighteenth at his last not-particularly-prestigious event with Matt on his back. I feel a sense of relief, which I know is mean to the horse but what can I say? Time faults, a refusal, and pulled a rail.

## CHAPTER 33

# WORKING OUT

Normally, when my phone rings I assume someone has like, died or something, because people usually text. So I'm wary when I get the call while I'm working out at the box at 7 a.m.

At first, because of the accent, I can hardly register someone is talking. British. "Simon? Simon O'Shaughnessy? I hope you don't mind me tracking you down like this. It's Freddie Whitechapel."

Christ on a cracker. Someone drops a barbell and grunts. Their form is crappy but I can't breathe enough to even care or feel superior.

"I was wondering if you knew of anyone, perhaps at Daniel's, that might be interested in a working student position at my barn? I've had an advertisement"—he pronounces it AT-ver-tis-MINT—in *Yard and Groom* for ages and no one suitable has responded."

"That surprises me," I say.

"I've had people offer their resume, of course, but no one with experience with young horses and who have moved sufficiently high up the levels. And of course, I want someone with strong horsemanship skills as well as someone who can ride. And good references. It shouldn't be so much to ask. But apparently it is. You wouldn't believe some of the CVs that have been delivered to my inbox."

"Killin' it," says one beefy guy, approvingly, as a girl thrusts up a bar from her chest. I know it's a PR for her on the bench press, based upon his reaction. He's been spotting her and cheering her on.

"The fact is, I've been out of horses for a bit. Since Matt took me off Milton," I say to Freddie. "So I'm not sure who to suggest."

"You mean you haven't found another position?" says Freddie.

"I assumed that I had become a pariah in the eventing community," I say, dryly. I look at my hands. They're still getting calloused but in different places, from pull ups and rope climbs now. But the ones from grabbing a pitchfork and from the reins between my fingers are there as well. My hand is just one big callous, I think. Impenetrable, dead, scaly.

"Oh, please, Simon. It was Matt Stevenson who fired you. Everyone knows he's a complete tosser."

I laugh. I thought Freddie liked Matt but it could just be his way. He seems to accept everything and everyone. "Is that like a complete and utter bastard in British or something? But I feel like I should be able to get along with complete tossers to work in the horse world."

"No one holds it against you, Simon. At least, I don't. Nor does anyone I know worth respecting."

"Thank you Freddie," I say. I actually feel a bit misty although I can't let that show in my voice.

"What have you been doing with yourself, if not riding?"

"Lifting weights, jumping rope, running, getting fit without a horse."

"Good God and God bless you for that. I know I shouldn't but my main aerobic activity in the morning is having a fag and a cup of coffee. I'm down to one fag a day, and that's quite an accomplishment for me." Pause. "Fag as in cigarettes." But I knew that slang from Germany, since some of the Germans I met had learned their English in Britain.

"I needed something to keep me busy." I know Freddie has a lot to do in the morning, and as kind as he is to talk to me the connection will be extinguished like a light in the next few seconds. And we'll probably never speak again unless …

"Look Freddie, why don't you take me as your working student?"

"What? Simon, you aren't serious."

"Why not? I don't have a job right now." Hell I don't have a life. I have a gym membership, I have some random hookups with guys I barely know, I have another race scheduled I'm not really bothering to train for seriously. What I have is a false life. It's a life of fields barren of fucks.

"This is an unpaid position, first of all, and second of all, to say you are over-qualified would be the understatement of the year."

"I have savings. I was actually going to spend a year in Germany doing another working studentship, but that didn't work out and I got a job at Matt's. But what I'm saying is that I could afford to do another one."

"I would have to pay you. I can't afford to pay you what you're worth. But I would pay you."

"When would you need me by?" And then I think of Fortune. This time, it might make sense to bring him. "Could I bring a horse, my old horse?" I stand up, too excited to sit still. Finally, things are falling into place, again.

Sean doesn't agree. "You do realize you're crazy to leave every guy's dream of working out all day in a nice city and hooking up at night to doing shit work just to ride horses again for free."

"Well, Freddie said he'd pay me a little."

"A working student again?"

"You're still a student."

"And you're going to take your horse away from Max?" That is admittedly the one part of my plan that I think might not work. And this time I don't have a trailer to borrow from a barn. But I'm going to go up all the same. I need a horse to ride sometime on my own, a horse that is all my own, and I need to get my life back as it was because that's the only thing that makes sense right now. "I thought we could share an apartment until I finish up with school. Maybe even after if I stay in Boston." Sean has just a few more classes to take in his major. Then he gets his degree and he's finished. I'm pretty sure they'll ask him to stay on where he's interning. He's a likeable guy, everyone likes having him around—unlike me.

"I'm sorry," I say, and shrug.

As if to get back at me, Sean says, "You know I'm selling Camera Shy."

"What?" Camera Shy was Sean's Quarter Horse. He competed in Western events throughout high school, team penning, barrel racing. I even rode Cam English a couple of times.

"He's a nice horse," I protest.

"I know. That's why I'm selling him to the high school girl who is leasing him. I won't have time to deal with him once I'm working full time. What am I going to do, bring him up to Boston?"

"There are boarding barns here."

"And they're a pain in the ass to get to in Boston traffic. Besides, how am I going to fit driving to the barn with CrossFit and something of a social life? It's just not worth it to me, Simon. Look, I'm finding him a good home."

"What and when will you ride, then?"

"God, you're so dumb, Simon. You have such a one-track mind."

"Is Mom okay with this?"

"It's not like she can really use him. He hasn't been jumped over anything of serious size since you left for Vermont. Her exact reaction was, 'Well, at least now we've shed ourselves of all of our useless animals.'" Sean imitates Mom really well, and I know by the language he uses that what he's saying is true. "C'mon, Simon, she's finally going to be able to afford a real horse, now, one she can ride in some serious amateur-owner classes. She doesn't need to worry about an extra mouth to feed, or even worrying about a lease that might go bad."

"Well, when she does get a horse I hope she has me try him out first," I say.

Sean laughs. "Any nice, fancy hunter Mom would like you'd say was too slow."

I don't respond because he's probably right. I'm glad that Mom and Sean are doing what they want, I guess, pursuing their dreams, but I just don't understand them. I have to let it drop. I know this is what happens to horses and Sean's found Cam a soft landing and will do right by him. But I still feel like my childhood is being sold. Even the fact that Mom won't be riding the usual horses she rode with her old barn and is moving up to something more suitable feels weird, just like it will feel weird to see her competing again, bobbing over fences while I watch from the rail. I need to stop so many things being weird, I decide.

Later that night, Sean and I meet up with my friend and Sean's former girlfriend Heather. Heather's stopping in Boston to see both of us since she's just finished her internship at a magazine. She's still in college, majoring in English, doing IHSA (Intercollegiate Horse Show Association) stuff. Also doing all the right things. I feel a little bit bad because I was so close with her in high school, I always said she was one of the few people who got made fun of as much as me, although she wasn't gay, just weird and nerdy. But I hardly think about her now, although when I do all my thoughts are good.

I mention my new working student job to Heather and she's impressed but then again she's never evented in her life, never had the money or a horse to do anything but nice schooling shows, so pretty much anything I do is impressive to Heather. Still, my ego is bruised enough I'll take all the adulation I can get at this point.

"You'll never guess who I got to meet," says Heather. "It was just taking him around the office but still …" She waits a beat. "Brandon Flowers." Heather is a plain-looking girl, with a white circular face like you'd draw with a pencil, framed by two lines of dark straight hair, but her face turns pink as she says this, and I can kind of tell that she's been waiting to talk about this for a long, long time.

"What?" I admit I'm taken aback. I don't expect things like this to happen to Heather.

"Yes, they were interviewing him for the upcoming issue. I even got to copyedit it."

"What? What did he say when you met him?"

She laughs. "I can't tell you. It's an exclusive interview. You'll have to wait."

"What is he like?" I'm so jealous I can hardly spit out the words.

"I just led him through the office. It wasn't that exciting. But he's just as cute in person as he is in pictures."

I'm annoyed and disappointed with her. If I had that opportunity, I swear, I would have pinned him to the wall with all the questions I have about his lyrics. I wouldn't be satisfied with just making sure all the exclamation points were right on someone else's article. "Damn, Heather, how are you ever going to be a writer if you don't take advantage of opportunities like that?"

She looks hurt. "I can't help the fact I'm shy, Simon. Besides, it wasn't part of my job. If I had been really aggressive they wouldn't have been happy. I've met other famous people through this internship and you can't be in their face."

It's not about shy, I think. It's about settling. Settling for just getting someone amazing a cup of coffee (or whatever Brandon Flowers drinks, since I know he is a Mormon and doesn't drink coffee) versus talking to them. Just like I refused to settle in my current life of not riding. Even if I'm just hanging by the first rung of the ladder by going to Freddie's, at least I'm pulling myself up again. It annoys me when even people I like and respect like Heather can be so passive.

Sean tells me afterward that I was a real jerk. "You know Heather worships you, Simon. Hell, you taught her how to post the trot, you're like her riding idol."
    "C'mon, she used to date you, Sean, not me."
    "Just because she had a crush on my younger brother."
    "That's so dumb I'm not gonna even respond to it."
    "You're so blind when it comes to people, it's not even funny. Maybe you should go back to horses because those are the only people that will tolerate you."

## CHAPTER 34

# STILL GREEN

Vermont always takes me by surprise. To go from the industrial highway—with the trucks carrying God knows what and the cars stuffed with tourists and college kids—to the sight of green hills and farms seriously makes me feel like I've driven into another country, but this time one where I am welcome, where they speak my language.

I don't make a dramatic entrance with a trailer this outing at Daniel's. Instead, I drive over to Max's house and wait there. I feel he's had my horse long enough it's practically his by now. I figure I'll ride Fortune this weekend, talk things out with him. Arrange to have Fortune shipped back when he's ready. Ease him away from Max, slowly. In short, not be a jerk.

I know it's very unlikely Max isn't working today but he's usually done by 7 p.m. or so, which it is now. Unless he's had an emergency. And if he has, well, I have nothing better to do. For the moment. But sure enough, I see his battered SUV pull up to the condo around dusk and he gets out. Limping.

"Holy shit, Max, did Fortune do that to you?"

He jumps. It takes a second for him to compose himself. "Simon, one of these days, you'll be the death of me, I swear. What are you doing here?"

"Are you okay?"

"If you must know, I got kicked in the leg—not by your horse though. I'm fine. Just sore. Unlike you, I do get my injuries checked out." He sizes me up. "If you don't mind my saying—you look ... different."

I laugh a bit, knowing I've put on quite a bit of muscle in a short time. If only he knew. And I begin to talk. I backtrack a bit. Because he doesn't really know what I've been doing with myself since Milton and I broke the non-frangible obstacle, doesn't know *how* I left Matt's. As I talk I help Max unload his stuff from the car, although he says it isn't necessary and he's on the mend.

"I've missed being able to talk about stuff like this," I tell him. "Sean has been really decent to me but he doesn't understand."

"Your brother's a nice guy," says Max. He always liked Sean. I look around for signs of someone else, like that guy that was there one night, but his place is just the same as always.

"I better go and let you have dinner, I'm going to grab something in town," I say.

"You mean, you're inviting yourself over for dinner because you know I won't let you do that," says Max.

"Yeah," I say.

"Since I didn't know that you were coming, I should warn you that I'm making fish, which I know you hate."

"I'll live." But Max makes me a grilled cheese sandwich to have instead when he sees my face at the fish smell.

"You're such a child," he says as he watches me dig in. I know he's not just talking about my taste in food.

I know why he says that, and I can't even deny that from his perspective it's true. "I feel a million years old right now," I say.

"At least you can walk properly. To add insult to injury, it was a Shetland pony that got me. Thank goodness he was kind enough not to kick me in the kneecap."

"Of course he was. Closer to the ground ..."

"Closer to hell," Max finishes the phrase.

"Can you still ride with it?"

"I actually have been but no jumping. Just dressage because the longer stirrup doesn't bother it as much. It's healing though."

"So we can still go riding together tomorrow?"

"I thought you were going to Freddie's?"

"I'm going to talk to Daniel and arrange for Fortune to be sent down in two weeks, after I've settled in there. I'm sorry to take him away from you."

"I knew it was coming," he says, stoically.

After we clear the table, I put my arms around him and start to kiss him. "Don't," he says at first, annoyed, and I know why, I've been kind of an asshole to him but I keep kissing him and he doesn't push me away for long. And then I know that this is the real reason I drove all this way, both of us know this.

Max has to get up early tomorrow but we still don't sleep for most of the night. He says it's so late, it's pointless to try to rest. I can tell he's a little bit high from the fact that I am here.

Over breakfast, I notice that the chess set we used to play on is still set up in the corner. "Have you been cheating on me, playing against someone all these months I've been gone?" I ask.

"Well, based on your assessment of my skills, I know you'd say it would be impossible to find someone worse than me at the game."

"If only you'd listen to me, you could get better."

"You'll just have to accept that it isn't my forte, Simon. No matter how much we played, I never met your standards."

"It's not enough just to play. As God, i.e., George Morris, would say, 'Practice doesn't make perfect. Perfect practice makes perfect.' Experience alone doesn't cut it."

"Well, you've gotten more experienced at some things since I saw you last, that's for sure."

Max has got me there. I met him right out of high school, and I'd really just messed around with guys before we started dating. "Are you complaining" I ask. "That I'm not as pure and innocent as before? That the student as surpassed the master?"

"I wouldn't go so far as to say that, and no, I'm not complaining. Just don't ask me to play chess with you. You know, not everyone cares about winning everything all the time like you. Some people do like to have fun. Even at games."

I grin. "Yes, but winning makes games more fun."

"I've seen you mess up a dressage test because you got too caught up in the fun of going fast to collect your horse, so don't give me that, Simon."

"Yes, but that was when I was schooling. Okay, maybe at a schooling show, not at a horse trial that meant anything to me."

"To be honest, Simon, although I've taken your horse to a couple of little shows and we've had fun together, I really don't understand why competition is so important at all when it comes to horses."

Now he sounds like Sasha, I think. "You haven't become one of those people who thinks that all horses should just be out in fields all day and not ridden?"

"Of course not, it's not that I think it's wrong to compete a horse that's happy doing his job and Fortune certainly seems to love the atmosphere of a show or an event—likes it a little bit too much, frankly, when we're going cross-country, even with a stronger bit which is why I prefer just competing in a ring. But I don't think anything's wrong with lower-level eventing. You know my issue with showjumping-like obstacles at Advanced level, but we've agreed to disagree on that one." I shrug. Of course, now they are making jumps that fall apart, something I have personally encountered but I don't fight Max, I've learned to pick my battles. "I just mean that it's a handful of seconds that usually separates the top competitors. It's hard for me to think that a horse is really better or worse because he was a few seconds or so ahead of another horse."

"Seconds mean knowing when to gallop faster rather than half-halt, when to take a tighter turn to save time, how to set up the horse right. Maybe you're right, that winning one event doesn't mean much, but when you're Boyd Martin and can bang out win after win on different horses, week after week, that means something. And there's more than just seconds on the clock that separates Michael Jung from just about every rider in the world, period. Just watch him ride."

"But what does that all mean? Well, I guess that's why I always liked Pony Club rather than showing." Max got pretty high up the levels in PC, to B-level, which is very impressive. I know professional eventers that still put that they got up to A-level on their resume, getting to the top levels in Pony Club is that hard. But it's more about proving what you can do, like navigating a tricky course or horsemanship skills, versus beating people. I never had a desire to do Pony Club. "I like competing with myself," says Max.

"Competing with yourself? Everyone always says that," I mutter, although what I really mean is that 'everyone who loses at stuff always says that.' "I'm not sure what competing with yourself even means. Is that like playing with yourself? Surely not as fun."

"You always manage to drag me down to your level when we argue," says Max, grinning.

"I live to drag you down to my level, Max. That's one of my favorite hobbies. And I always win at that, too."

"Bring the horses up the levels and the humans down them?"

"Pretty much."

When Max is finished working that evening we go riding, nothing crazy, just trail riding up into the mountains. I take Fortune, and Max takes a horse that Daniel loans him, a Morgan whose owner is away and needs to be worked. Max's leg already looks better but maybe it's because he's trying hard to keep up with me.

We stop where we always stop, what used to be my favorite place when I was working at Daniel's. As much as I'm looking forward to Freddie's, I know there is no place like this anywhere in Maryland, no place that lets me see so far and wide yet is removed from everything in the world except me and Max and the two horses we are riding. And that gives me the courage to say to Max, "Come with me."

"What?"

"To Maryland. There's nothing here to hold you, Max. You've said yourself that the old guy you work for isn't going to die anytime soon and you're not paid what you're worth, and you always let them give you the crappiest cases and crappiest hours at the practice. I'm sure you could find another job in Maryland. The state's full of horses."

I look out at the greenness in front of us, the hills that seem to go on forever in Vermont. It's always felt to me like another world. Green fields, I think. *Behold the fields where I ... .*

Max doesn't respond. He just changes the subject but I can see on his face that he's thinking about it. That he doesn't want to think about it but that he is. Fortune stomps and snorts. He wants to go. He wants to move.

*Behold the fields where I grow my fucks and see that they are barren.* That phrase sounded so deep and meaningful to me for so long, like a prayer—almost—but looking at real green fields in front of me with Max by my side, the words just seem like words again, and all words are meaningless and empty. All I can see is greenness and ground that is anything but barren.

When I go see Daniel the next day, he says, after hearing my story, most of which he already knows from the eventing grapevine, "Maybe a better man wouldn't say 'I told you so,' Shaughnessy, but 'I told you so.' I also told you, you didn't have to go to Europe to learn to ride."

"I should have just gone to Freddie in the first place," I say.

"Freddie's a good horseman," says Daniel. "I guess you had to find it out yourself," he says. "People don't change."

I flinch. I hope I can change. I like to think I have. Become more realistic. Gone back to how I was when I first came here, which was thinking, as long as I had a career riding, it didn't matter so much how and why and where. But then again, I know I'll never be satisfied unless I'm the very best. It just might be a longer slog than I hoped for or planned. And I want to do it the right way this time.

## CHAPTER 35

# SALT ON MY WOUNDS

Freddie watches me as I lead the mare off the trailer. Pearl's our newest addition and I'm guessing I'll be riding her at the next event. She's done one Intermediate and had a great dressage score and a monster cross-country time, just pulled a rail in stadium. Kicked it out of the cups with her enthusiastic little hoof.

Freddie's operation is a bit smaller and rougher than Matt's. Things are more worn around the edges, but it's more relaxed and friendly. Even the barn help seems happy. Technically I'm a working student but unless things are really overwhelming, I don't have to muck stalls or clean tack. Freddie treats me like a trainer, which is what I am, I guess, what I've fought so long and hard to become in my meandering sort of way.

We're taking Pearl on a cross-country school this morning in the nearby horse park, just so she can look at some different jumps for a change. Freddie will be on Jazz, his main Advanced horse.

I like Jazz, even though I think it's kind of a weird name for a British guy's horse—well, technically Freddie's half-American. His parents divorced when he was really young and he grew up in the UK and moved over here. His American wife Cheryl is actually one of the top-ranked showjumpers in the country, above Freddie in her own niche but that doesn't seem to bother him. Honestly, that would bother me and I don't totally get it but if it works for them, whatever.

Pearl is a grey but was actually born a chestnut. Fun fact—Gem Twist, one of the most famous showjumpers of the twentieth century was also born a pure chestnut. Pearl still has a lot of red in her mane and tail and some orangey dapples. Her show name is Fleur De Sal, which I thought was a flower until Max explained to me it's some kind of fancy salt.

Pearl's ears prick up out of curiosity and she whinnies as she looks around. There are a few other horses passing by on the way to the jumps. I tie her to the trailer to tack her up. She's not super-experienced but very level-headed. Everyone's already excited about her, and she has financial backing, the horse is already syndicated, which means that lots of people own little pieces of her, including me. I joke that I want to own only the chestnut mare parts of her, the red dapples on her ass. There's plenty to work on but she's eager, not spooky, and responsive. I like all of the horses I ride at Freddie's so far, even the ones I'm just working for lower-level clients.

At Freddie's, I actually don't find a need to plug in music into my ears all day long and I don't mind talking to people. Even though Freddie's not up in everyone's business all the time, things still get done because people like to come to work every day.

It's early Sunday morning, which means more schooling and lessons for me when I return with Pearl. I work all day and by the time I'm finished I look at my phone and I realize I'm almost late for dinner with Max and his friends. I have no time to change. I also realize I didn't even bring a pair of driving moccasins for the car, so tall boots it is. Maybe he won't notice or at least won't mind.

"Simon, you didn't," says Max when I walk in with my stained breeches and boots. Since the temperature has gotten chillier, at least by the standards of Maryland in fall, I've thrown a sweater on over my polo shirt. And I took off my spurs.

"Sorry, I had no time," I said.

"You could have at least brought other things to the barn."

"Yes, but that would have required foresight and planning," I say, grinning.

Parker and Cole seem to find it funny, however. "Well, supposedly riding boots are fashionable even for the general population, nowadays," says Parker. Everyone else at the table is already deep in wine and appetizers. I order a beer which I probably shouldn't at such a nice restaurant but at this point I guess it really doesn't matter.

"These are custom-made boots, and they cost more than the shoes anyone in here is wearing, I can tell you that." I look around to ask for a menu, but Max tells me he's already ordered me steak frites, which is the one thing he knows I'd like here, and I trust him. Since no one else is eating the bread, and I haven't eaten anything all day (Freddie and I left with Pearl at 6am to get back in time for lessons), I pull the basket near me, slather on the butter (which has been sculpted into snails or something like that) and dig in.

"Simon, you know, was actually born in a barn," says Max, dryly.

"It's true. My parents did have a stable on the property when I was a kid and I spent most of my time there," I grin. The bread is the tough, weird kind of bread I ate in Germany, but either I'm so hungry it tastes good, or a couple of weeks of Max's cooking has increased my tolerance, however slightly, for fancy food.

"Born in a manger like Jesus," says Cole.

"My mother would never have wasted good hay on me like that," I say.

It occurs to me that this is the first time I've had real non-horse friends. Before it was always riding friends, and we would do things like grab a pizza because we were all too tired to go anywhere after a day of work or showing, maybe go to a movie or watch TV together. If it weren't for Max, I certainly wouldn't know how to do this, exactly, which I feel is sort of like what they mean when they say "adulting." Or just having a life. I sometimes feel that he's my interpreter, since he seems to pass between the horse world and the civilian world so easily. That's a talent I've never had. It's all or nothing for me and even sitting here, chatting, I'm thinking of who I'm going to be riding tomorrow, what my schedule is. But I'm happy and relaxed and it's not from the beer the (cute) waiter finally brought. I remember now what that's like, to relax. Even though I've technically taken a step back in terms of the level I'm riding at, I feel like I've taken a step forward as well.

## CHAPTER 36
# FADE TO GREY

Max's schedule at the new practice is more human but he's still on call for emergencies on specific nights and one Friday, after a long day, I hear his phone ring beside our bed. He doesn't wake up so I elbow him and hand it to him.

"Mmpf. I've got to go." He switches on the light and I squint at him. "This horse," he mutters, shaking his head. "It's the second time he's colicked in the middle of the night. Don't wait up for me."

I pull the covers over my head to shield myself from the light.

"Then again, maybe you should. The owner's some crazy Russian guy named Jerry that bought the horse for his daughter to do lower-level eventing. The rumor is that he's mobbed up to his eyeballs. Hopefully, I'll be able to resolve this successfully or else I might not return."

I'm kind of intrigued since it sounds like a movie. Next to science fiction, really violent Quentin Tarantino films are my favorites. "Why mobbed up?"

"Lots of money with no apparent source, I think, and he just makes some vague claims about 'investments.' Plus, this barn's one of our best clients. They're very careful to call the vet every time a horse takes a wrong step. I don't want them to raise holy hell if anything happens on my watch."

"I'll send out the search party if I don't hear from you by noon. Hopefully, I won't wake up with a horse's head in the bed. Or yours."

"Very funny."

"I love you," I say after I hear the door to our house slam shut.

It's weird, but in the past couple of weeks, it's not so hard for me to say that. I used to feel a violent jerk even when I saw the word 'love' on my phone.

I have trouble going to sleep, not because I'm worried about Max but because my mind is busy. I look around at the walls, the furniture. It's hard to believe I'm here and this is mine. The house is pretty small because frankly neither of us have the time or inclination to take care of a big property. But Max has chosen with great care every single mirror, dresser, and painting (including his prized collection of classic LPs mounted on the wall). His Vermont condo always looked like a motel, completely organized but undecorated and without character. I guess he figures we're staying here for a while.

I get out of bed at 5 a.m., more restless than ever from lying down for so long awake. Since Max isn't here, I go to the garage and grab a Coke (he won't have the bottles cluttering up the refrigerator, which is full of his ingredients) and two of the Snickers bars I have stashed in the freezer. He tolerates my bad habits as long as I keep them hidden and segmented away from his idea of order and I'm okay with that.

I wait for Pearl to digest her breakfast. Freddie's already there, in a good mood as always. He mentions to me that someone called him, looking for me last night. I don't recognize the name—Mr. Yost—at first and then after a minute of slugging down the last of my Coke and eating my second candy bar, I suddenly place the name. It's Hannah's father, the guy we sold Lexi.

"I'm sorry I called your new employer, I lost your number," he says apologetically.

"No prob. How's Hannah?"

"That's what I was calling you about. We were wondering if you knew anyone that might be interested in buying Lexi. Hannah's—Hannah's not having fun. She's afraid to ride Lexi. The mare's just too much horse for her. The horse's not bad; we've been working with a trainer like you suggested, but we can't afford full training board and it's just not enough."

Even though it wasn't me who sold her, I think of how Hannah looked at me and I feel terrible. "She's not really a kid's horse, at least not now." Especially after Matt's questionable selection of bits, her soundness issues, and God knows what else he did to her when I wasn't around, I add in my mind. "Unfortunately, I don't know anyone that might be interested." Not much of a record to speak of, not easy, nothing particularly special to recommend her. I go over my schedule in my head. "I have a day off in two weeks and I could give you guys a short lesson. No charge."

This weekend we're taking Pearl and a few of the other horses to a combined test, just a schooling event to get them ready for the next major event. But the weekend after that ...

"No, I don't think a lesson every few weeks with you is enough. But thank you. We need to sell her," says Mr. Yost. "And if we can't, we'll see if Mr. Stevenson might take her back. At least then we won't have a feed bill."

That bad, I think. "Well, you can try," I say, trying to keep my voice as emotionless as possible. I hate just hearing Matt's name, especially as Mr. Stevenson, since the guy is trying to sound respectful and all.

"But thank you again for the offer. You've been very kind."

"Don't thank me, I didn't do anything."

After I hang up, I reflect on the fact I never had push-button ponies when I was really young—in fact, Sean's pony, who I also liked to ride, had a nasty habit of bucking if you tightened its girth just a hole too much and long ago my mom had a stallion that acted, well, like a typical stallion when there was a mare around in heat. I was on a horse before I even knew there was anything to fear, so nothing fazed me. I never needed something easy to give me confidence. I had, if anything, too much of that. And I never needed a trainer to tell me I could or couldn't ride. I think of Lisa who must be married to Matt by now. She might be riding Milton right this very second for all I care.

I push the confused rush of memories of Matt and Lisa and Milton and Lexi all out of my mind. Pearl shoves her muzzle over her stall and I touch it. Her nose, ears, hooves, mane, and tail are all shining slightly gold in the sun, a stark contrast against her pearl, pale grey. Just the faintest memories of the chestnut she was. Who knows what we can become? I get my saddle.

When I get home, Max is waiting for me. It took all night but he was able to save the crazy Russian guy's horse. "He kissed me," he says, dryly, "After the horse pulled through. "Nice horse, though."

"Should I be jealous? Well, his daughter events, even if it is just at a baby Beginner Novice level, rather than doing the hunters or the Big Eq, so the family must have some balls as well as money."

"Your mother largely did hunters if I remember correctly and having met her, I would definitely say that she has more balls than either of us put together." I can't deny that. "Jerry invited me to dinner afterwards, he was so happy, which I said was not necessary."

"Oh, Max, you should have accepted. I've never met anyone in the Russian mafia before. It would have been so much fun."

"It's not fun, hoping that a horse will live so you'll see another day, Simon. How did things go with your new crush?"

"Pearl went like a dream."

I feel like I've finally recovered from Matt's barn, like I had some kind of trainer PTSD, only I didn't know it at the time.

A few days later, on a rare weekday night when we're both free, Max and I go out to dinner together to some semi-fancy Italian restaurant. Before we even get our menus, a short guy with a heavy accent calls out to Max. He's accompanied by an even shorter blonde woman plastered with jewelry, and a very, very tall girl wearing some weird, deconstructed strappy dress that must be fashionable. When he says to the girl (who I assume is his daughter), "This is the man that saved your horse's life, Masha," I know it's the crazy Russian Max was talking about. Do all Russian names end with an 'a' for both boys and girls? Max calls the guy Jerry, but I'm assuming that's an English version of something completely unpronounceable.

Masha looks like something out of a fashion magazine. It's hard to imagine her in a barn at all, much less getting her hands dirty on a horse.

"You really must come to dinner," Jerry says, and squeezes Max's shoulder.

"I'm Simon," I say, offering my hand, since Max oh-so rudely hasn't introduced us. Jerry shakes it.

"Isn't this restaurant lovely?" says the wife. "I make Jerry take me here at least every week just for the Chicken Milanese." We've finally gotten our menus and looking at the prices, I decide that if they can afford this weekly plus horses, they must be doing something right, money-wise, through fair or foul means. "But I'm a very good cook myself. Max must come to try some of my traditional Russian food."

"We'd love to," I'd say.

"Good. This weekend?"

"I'll be at a combined test all next weekend but I'm free Saturday night the weekend after that. I think Max is free as well."

"Very well, it's settled," says Jerry.

Max looks pale after they leave. "Why did you do that?"

"I thought it would be fun. Like I said, I've never met anyone in the Russian mafia before. What are you so worried about? He seems to like you. After all, you saved his kid's horse's life."

"He likes me now. Wait until he figures out we're gay."

"Figures out? If he's managed to stay alive in the Russian mafia for all these years, I think he is probably already smart enough to figure out that we're gay, I hate to disappoint you."

"This is real, Simon, it's not one of those crime films you're so obsessed with."

The waitress comes and I order the one thing that sounds good to me on the menu, which is pizza.

"I really can't take you anywhere," says Max.

## CHAPTER 37
# PEARL OF A GREAT PRICE

A combined test is just a combination of show jumping and dressage, but I kind of like having this safe space to make mistakes, a dry run before I begin to enter the full heat of competition with Pearl. This is very much a schooling venture but there are a few big name eventers here with their top prospects.

I'm feeling pretty good until I see Lisa. She's riding a young horse I don't recognize. Maybe it's the next Milton? I cut her dead with my eyes as I walk past her. She's Matt's wife now, so for my purposes, as far as I'm concerned, she's part of him.

I've never given Freddie the full rundown of the really bad stuff that happened at Matt's in terms of what they said to me and what I said to them but he knows something's bothering me and maybe he just guesses who it is because he comes over to me and says, "Put him out of your mind," and then walks away whistling again.

Pearl is great during dressage. Her changes in tempo come easy and unforced. She doesn't resist reining back, like she sometimes does. She's calm and willing and we end up in the low 40s. The top scores were in the high 30s.

I'm getting Pearl ready for stadium when Lisa approaches me. "Simon," she says. She's still in her shadbelly, her coat hanging open and I can see she's wearing something to flatten herself beneath her shirt. It's ugly. I turn away from her. What does Matt see in her? What does she see in him? "I'm sorry it ended like it did."

"I'm not. I'm in a better place," I say. "Look, Lisa, what are you looking for, me to say I'm sorry and what happened didn't matter? Just take care of Milton."

"I'm sorry Matt said all those things he didn't mean."

Whatever, I'm bored with this and I'm not going to make her feel better. Maybe I should give in since I'll be seeing both of them in the future whether I like it or not but I just don't care to say something that isn't true. "He meant them," I say. "Don't bullshit me, Lisa."

At first I think it's my imagination when I hear shots but Freddie walks over and says, "It's the military base miles away doing some testing."

"Why do they have to schedule this when horses are competing?" I mutter.

"I suppose we should be grateful they aren't shooting at one another in the middle of the horse park. Since horses were ridden into battle, they think they should be fine," says Freddie, dryly. "I've seen people take both six and seven from one to two and both decisions have led to a pulled rail."

"I was planning on opening her up and going for the six," I say, but my words are drowned out by a low-lying plane zooming overhead. I whirl and look at Pearl, since the sound spooked even me, but although her ears prick and she tenses, she relaxes as soon as it is gone. She trusts me. Milton would be plastered to one of the trees by now, I think. Or I would be.

At least the sound of the planes are more like white noise, they aren't percussive and explosive. Still, "If all the horses make it through this, they'll be certified bombproof. Like, literally," I say.

After all the military noise, the buzzer in the stadium ring sounds muted to my ears but Pearl springs to action nonetheless. She gets excited and quick after the first fence and I do need to slow her down a bit to keep her careful, I take the seven despite what I planned but with a sharp inside turn I make up the time … The course concludes with three fences with a one stride between them, followed up with an easy vertical and we go clear, with no time faults at the end.

As I stroke the blue ribbon around my horse's neck, I reflect that life is good. I feel calm, peaceful, and I realize I've forgotten about Lisa. She's not around to see me anywhere, and I can't see her. Out of sight, out of mind. Hear no evil, speak no evil. Not in my division, not at my level. There's another plane in the distance but it's soft whizzing, gently mechanical, then a muffled boom. Pearl jerks but nothing crazy, no more than a normal horse would spook at a bag. I scratch her withers, hum a song. Silence.

Some of my competition didn't make it through the course thanks to spooking at the wargames. So the field was a bit thinned out. I know I won't be able to count on that next time but it's still a victory.

## CHAPTER 38
# THE RUSSIANS HAVE A WORD FOR IT

Jerry's house is modest on the outside, and at first I'm disappointed and think that the evening's going to be pretty dull. Inside is another story. He makes us take our shoes off (apologizing profusely) because the floors are all imported marble and the carpeting is antique. Every wall on the house is covered in art. There are also these huge glass windows looking out into the backyard when we sit down in the living room although there isn't that much to see other than grass and a kidney-shaped pool. The fence is just a boring plastic fence like you'd see on every other suburban mini-mansion but the pool has some kind of fancy tile at the bottom, shimmering in the darkness of the porch lights. Jerry offers us wine, shows us the vintage, and then goes on and on about the history of the bottle like it's one of his dearest friends.

"This is really not necessary," says Max, who turns slightly pale when he hears how old the wine he's been drinking is. "I was just doing my job. I don't want you to put yourself out for us." Jerry tuts him and goes to pour a glass for me. I explain that I don't drink wine.

"Wine is good for your health," says Jerry. "And your soul."

"Yes, but I don't like it. Max says I can't appreciate good things."

I look over at Max who is gazing at his glass of wine. I know him well enough to see that he's debating whether drinking will make him too uninhibited on one hand but on the other hand he might not be able to survive the night with me if he doesn't drink. He takes a swig.

Masha strolls by, sipping a Coke. She says she hates wine too, and offers to get me a soda. I accept a Mountain Dew gratefully but refuse the caviar and sturgeon Jerry presses on Max. "But your friend doesn't like caviar?" she asks, reaching over and cramming some of the little disks loaded with fishy-smelling stuff in her mouth. She brushes past and I can feel her half-exposed breasts pressing into my arm. I would have never thought she was a teenager, if I didn't know better.

"I'm hopeless," I say, grinning up at her past her breasts. "Now tell me about the horse Max saved."

From what I gather the horse is a retired, very successful jumper. Jerry shows me a YouTube video of Masha's gelding with his last rider. He's a beautiful Hanoverian Thoroughbred cross and he literally pilots his shaking, timid teenage rider over a stadium course like he knows the way better than she does.

"Wow," I say. "I'd buy that for my kid too after seeing the video. Glad he is still with us."

"When I move up the levels I'll need a better horse," says Masha, lazily. "We're looking for a second one as well."

"Why eventing and not the hunters or the equitation like your friends?"

Masha giggles. "It's more exciting. I'm easily bored." Even just for dinner with her mom and dad and us, she's wearing a really low cut dress and a pair of sparkly flip-flops. Her nails glitter in the light so blindingly I have to avert my eyes. "My father took us to see Badminton a few years ago and I loved it. Have you ever ridden it?"

"Badminton is one of a handful of CCI**** in the world and probably the most difficult of them all. So the answer to that would be no."

"My Masha is a thrill-seeker," says Jerry, proudly. "She's only been riding for two years. However, there is a long and proud tradition of riding in my family. My father learned to ride in the old Cossack style. *Dzhigitovka*." He points to one of the paintings which I've just noticed that depicts a man hanging off of a horse upside down, with only one leg cast across the saddle.

"Wow, that's amazing! That makes skijoring look like something for wussies," I say, remembering the rollerblading over fences I saw in Germany, something I'd still like to try but haven't. I turn to Masha. "Can you train me to do that? I think you should do your next dressage test just like that." She giggles and bats her long, mascaraed eyes at me.

Max pushes his glasses up his nose and looks closer at the little painting. "That's beautiful," he says, somewhat reluctantly.

"It's inlaid with real gold," explains Jerry.

I look at the horse more closely. It's somewhat crude in its proportions but there is a kind of weird, compelling quality to it. It looks almost alive the way the gold sparkles.

"The relationship of man and horse, one of the inspirations for great art through the ages," says Jerry.

"Oh, Dad," says Masha, groaning, as if he's about to spout off a lecture she doesn't feel like hearing.

Then Jerry takes us upstairs to show us some other paintings in gold, which he calls icons. I don't like those as much, not just because they don't contain horses, but also because most of them have strange, weird eyes that look almost human, like they can look back at me. Religion or whatever. Better to serve in hell and all those sorts of questions that annoy me when people start talking about them. Jerry doesn't strike me as religious but the objects do look extremely expensive because of all the gold.

Max asks to use the bathroom before dinner, and he says there's a gold icon in there as well.

"I love art and beautiful things," says Jerry. "I like my house to reflect that in every corner. Let us eat now, my wife tells us everything is ready."

Max hisses in my ear. "You do realize that all of this is real art. These icons should be hanging in a museum. There is a small fortune just in the bathroom alone."

I'm too preoccupied wondering where I can learn to do that *dzhigitovka* stuff. "Relax, Max. This has been very entertaining so far. And you saved his daughter's horse's life. We have nothing to worry about."

"Dear God, that caviar and wine alone was probably worth the vet bill twice over and the very bill wasn't cheap," mutters Max. "Make sure you eat whatever his wife serves you."

I'm worried it will be fish, but it's actually some sort of breaded chicken, ham, and cheese thing that tastes really good. I consider the evening pretty successful, especially after Jerry moves from wine to vodka and starts talking about how Masha's science project in high school is so impressive it's going to be the basis of some life-saving therapy for cancer as well as how she plans to go to the Olympics someday. I don't ask whether that's before or after Badminton.

"That was *more* entertaining than a film," I say, as Max and I pull away in his SUV. "They just never stopped. Riding for two years and going to the Olympics soon. Upside-down on horseback like the Cossacks. The curing cancer part was like the cherry on top."

"That was *not* entertaining, Simon, that was terrifying. I just hope we're not questioned at some point about if we ever saw something missing from the Met or the Hermitage or whatever."

"Did he pay for the vet bill in cash in a brown paper bag? Or a suitcase?"

"I honestly don't want to know."

## CHAPTER 39

# ALL THE KING'S HORSES AND ALL THE KING'S MEN

Back in the real, i.e. non-Russian world, I go to my first full event with Freddie several weeks later. Milton and Matt will also be there I know. There's part of me that is still afraid I will be a pariah, based upon what happened last time. I plan to shut myself out from everyone, but Freddie keeps up a running line of commentary and chatter and I find it hard to withdraw into my usual shell. I manage to forget everything and Pearl and I have one of our best dressage tests ever. After it's over I can't stop grinning. But our score doesn't reflect how well we did—53.7, a fairly terrible score for what was one of our best efforts. The top finisher gets a 39.6 so it's not like the judges are being stingy with the points (quite the opposite, I'd say). I picture the offending judge that really dinged us as some stuffy DQ who wears a hairnet to bed. Blah, blah, only competing with myself, a sign of better things to come, it's a subjective phase. I could say all those things to myself but I don't. Stuff it, forget about it.

I almost do until I see Mr. Yost and his daughter Hannah approach us. "That was amazing," says Hannah. She's gotten even taller since I remember her when I saw her last. Her arms are so long and lanky the cuffs of her sweatshirt don't even cover her wrists.

"When she heard you were riding here she had to go and watch," her father says.

I remain touched by Hannah's unwavering fandom in the face of the fact that my previous employer screwed her over by selling her an unrideable horse for an amateur. "Unfortunately, you weren't judging."

"That was SO unfair," she says, when she hears my score.

"It's fine, I'm still not out of it," I say, and shrug. Time to put it out of my mind. "How is Lexi?" I ask, changing the subject.

"Lexi is no longer with us. We took her back to Matt's," her father says apologetically. "So if you know a nice *quiet* and *reliable* horse that would suit Hannah, please tell us."

Quiet and reliable? Maybe a rocking horse? I think but don't speak.

I see Ben and his family. We're not competing against Jasper, of course. He's favored to win Advanced, but he's not riding anything from his barn at Intermediate today. I see Ben in his usual sparkling clean white breeches, his lawyer dad following behind, and then Sasha trailing them all in a bright orange pea coat and rubber, flowered boots to match, sticking out like a sore thumb among all the muted earth tones of the other competitors and spectators. With her hands stuffed in her pockets she looks like a little kid being dragged to go to the supermarket. His mom's not there, I notice. Maybe she's having one of her bad pain days which is a shame because I'm sure she would want to watch her son if she could. I still kind of hate-love Ben at the sight of him, but I feel bad for anyone like Ben's mom who legit can't ride anymore even though I know that could never happen to me.

I put on a pair of Dubarry boots to preserve my show boots while I wait, and when I bend over I'm conscious of someone watching me. I jerk my head up and see bright orange.

I don't know what to say to Sasha but she blurts out, "I'm sorry about what my brother did to you."

I laugh. "Oh, that was a million years ago, I've forgotten about it." Which I have—and I haven't because it does eat me a little bit that Golden Boy might win this thing. I hope Freddie can beat him with Jazz, but I know with my objective mind's eye it is unlikely. "I'm sure Ben hardly remembers my name."

"Oh, he talks about you. He even said today he was glad to see you here. He'd been worried you'd dropped off the face of the earth. He thought you were hurt or something …"

"I've been doing some other stuff, taking some time off." I want to make that clear.

For a brief second, a vision of Ben flickers in my head. Not the public Ben who appears so many times in photos on Eventing Nation and Eventing Connect's websites and Facebook feeds. The Ben I trail rode with, that time I felt I had stepped outside of this ugly world, somehow. And I remember Tess, the horse I liked, who looked like my old dead mare. I guess I'll probably never see her again. Then I push all memories away. I shrug and remind myself that particular Ben is gone, even though Ben still exists in the world. Maybe the Ben I cared about was never really real.

I consider saying, "You don't need to apologize, I never apologized when my brother cheated on his girlfriends in high school," but I think that might sound really harsh.

"Pretty horse," says Sasha, looking at Pearl.

"Pearl? Pretty enough to be a hunter, right? Well, not fat enough, though."

Sasha laughs. "I don't do that stuff anymore. I told you."

"I know. I'm surprised to see you here at all."

"I still ride. I just didn't like what I saw in that world."

"Neither did I."

"I thought you left eventing because of my brother."

"I meant when I was at a hunter barn a billion years ago. No, no, I'd never leave riding for a guy. Not like that."

Sasha seems less angry than when she was doing yoga on the floor and saying "I don't *compete*." I wonder if something's happened to her or between her and her brother. Maybe she just misses riding and was in a bad mood that day because she's in college with a big question mark of what she'll be doing after and Ben's future seems so bright. I get that.

She looks at Pearl with a kind of longing and I say, "She doesn't bite. I'm lucky to be riding her." And today I do feel lucky, completely the opposite of how I felt with Milton, despite him technically being the better horse. Sasha strokes Pearl's nose.

The Intermediate cross-country course is relatively uncomplicated compared with the ones I've ridden before and is one of those rare courses that has a minimum of skinnies and questions designed to trick the horse. The facility where it's located has plenty of land and although there is a lot of up-and-down, I actually enjoy riding it. After she ignored the booms and zooming planes during the combined test and just zeroed in on me, her rider, I have a lot of confidence in Pearl.

There is no one here to watch me, unlike Ben. Other than Freddie of course. It's been a long time since I've had an audience. Max is working and he hates watching me cross-country anyway. Even if they were living nearby, my brother and mother couldn't come. Sean has some Olympic lifting competition so he hasn't even texted me to tell me not to fall off, like he usually does. Mom's trying out some new horses for one of her riders.

Then I hear, almost like a ghost from the past, "Loose horse, loose horse," and without even looking around somehow I *know*. The big black gelding goes galloping past the spectators I see in the distance and I tense up for a second and Pearl does too even though he's far, far away and even if he were mine, there would be no way I could catch him where I am now. Fortunately, the area where he is running is pretty well fenced-off. Can't surprise a driver by running across the road like a chicken.

They catch Milton, eventually.

Freddie comes off the Advanced elated, clear and with the fastest time yet. Both Jasper and Ben and Milton and Matt still have to go. The loudspeaker tells me Matt's on course. I feel torn. As much as I'd like to, I can't wish him ill without wishing his horse the same.

I have a few moments to watch so I station myself near the big water complex. There's a drop into it and the Advanced course takes the rider through a series of one-stride skinnies on the way out. It's very steep, the path is narrow and it takes a great deal of trust in the rider on the horse's part to navigate the way. And yet, as difficult as it reads. Ben and Jasper hop through it, like it was a crossrail on flat ground through a puddle. Ben makes it look so casual and easy there isn't even much oohing and aahing from the crowd. As careless and casual as Ben may be with his body outside of riding, I remain jealous of the connection and partnership he and Jasper have forged. Bloody Ben Hillard, as Freddie says. Jasper's ears are pricked forward. The horse almost looks like he's skipping and smiling.

I notice Sasha is standing there across from me, her hands still balled up in fists in her coat. She looks like she's clutching something even though her hands are probably empty. I try to look away, but we make eye contact before I can help it. Damn, that stupid coat and those flowered boots of hers keep catching my eye in the sea of sensible brown and green. I just can't get away from either of the Hillards.

Her brother's going to win this, my gut tells me. It's his day. Freddie's on his A-game but Ben's riding effortlessly. He's riding like someone who doesn't even know he can lose.

The next horse refuses the drop, as if to underline Ben's general awesomeness. I walk forward a few jumps on the course. It's getting crowded and my tolerance for the crush around me and their non-riding chatter is at its breaking point. I look up at the sky as I walk. The sun is stronger now, I'm glad I rode earlier. For once the scheduling was in my favor. Listening to the announcer, I know that Milton's on course. The time allowed for the Advanced course is over nine minutes. Even if the questions aren't complicated it's a test of endurance as well as jumping ability and agility. I remember Milton's great heaving breaths, his great heart. Once he got going there was no stopping him. The problem was finding the right buttons to push to get him in that gear.

I hear, "Hold on course." I hear the ambulance in the distance. People or vet, it doesn't matter. The hairs bristle on my neck and somehow I know once again, who it is for, even before I hear Milton's and Matt's name. Some of the other onlookers go to see what's happened. My feet remain planted in the ground. What can I do?

I wait and I wait until I can't anymore. Then I run over to one of the spectators nearby. "Did you see what happened?" I ask her strained face.

"Cracked his hind legs on the jump. They think he hurt his stifle from what I heard. They took him away in a trailer. He couldn't put weight on the leg."

"And the rider?"

"Oh, you can see why they call him the Iceman—I think he got the wind knocked out of him, but he walked away. They're getting the medic to give him the once-over but he seems okay."

I don't even pretend to look relieved. Fuck him, fucking Iceman indeed.

I can't stop myself. Like texting an ex or whatever, I guess, I call up Lisa later that night.

"How is Milton?"

"You know, it would have been nice if you asked about Matt. He is after all the human in the partnership."

Pause.

"They've checked Matt out and he's fine. He's going to ride Nebraska for stadium," she says.

"You owe it to me to tell me how *Milton* is. I don't trust whatever Matt's going to say to the press."

I can hear her thinking over the phone, weighing our former friendship with her relationship with her ... husband. I can hardly even say the word in my mind. "It's bad, Simon. They think Milton fractured his patella."

"What happened?"

"Matty says it was touch and go over the whole course. Milton was spooking at every third shadow. Matt had leg on him the whole time. Milton cracked his knee on the jump because he wasn't picking his feet up; he was more focused on whatever was rustling in the bushes. Stall rest for three to five months because at least it's a simple break, although surgery might be needed if that doesn't work. Of course, his personality won't help, I can't think that Milton will be Mr. Sunshine without turnout time. Matt's saying it might be time to cut our losses."

"He wouldn't—look Lisa, I'd take him off your hands before it came to that."

"Simon, you know he'd never sell him to you. Or anyone he knew was associated with you like Freddie. He hates you."

"Your husband is a psychopath, you know?" I say.

"You just don't understand him," says Lisa.

"You mean he'd rather put him down than sell him to me? Really?"

"We're not putting him down. Stall rest and then see what happens. Look, Matt's very shaken up with what happened. It could have been a very serious injury."

"But it was a very serious injury, Lisa!"

"I mean to Matt! He could have been hurt. He could have had a career-ending injury."

"Well, wouldn't that have been a fucking shame!" I hang up on her. I hate my species today. I really, really do. Hate it with a blind and burning passion.

I have to get myself together for stadium tomorrow. Don't lose it this late in the game. Put it all out of your mind. I'm miserable and don't eat throughout dinner and Freddie knows why. He tries to tell jokes, tells me to have a pint but when I can't even smile he leaves me alone, leaves me to stew. I know that once I'm out there, I'll be fine and focused, I'll be in the happy place where nothing matters but the bell and the course for a little while. It's the day after tomorrow that I'm actually worried about, when the darkness will really settle in.

Pearl and I end up fifth, not because of any major errors—we go double clear but our crappy dressage score sets us back. A rider I haven't seen much of before had blisteringly fast clean cross-country and stadium rounds on a small, pony-like little critter (a warmblood but a weirdly stunted one). That pony thing could turn on a dime like a barrel racer, made us look slow. The crowd is really wild for Matt, even though he and Nebraska end up tenth. I don't understand it, like it's some sort of a miracle that he ends up only breaking one horse, not two?

Relatively speaking, my performance isn't horrible, I should be happy, but something in me has to strain to praise Freddie, who is second behind Ben at Advanced when I talk to him afterward. I expected better and when you expect better you're always disappointed, no matter what the ribbon. The fact that Milton's going to be locked in a stall for the next few months still preys upon my mind even though I know I should tell myself he's not my responsibility, not anymore, and I have enough to worry me.

On our ride home in what Freddie calls the "float" and I call the "trailer," I notice Freddie doesn't go over the event much with me. I can feel he's keeping his distance, that he knows I'm just holding it all in. I'm trying to keep things together and not unravel at myself and others. I feel angry at myself that we did, in my estimation, badly and I feel guilty as hell about Milton. He's a good horse. He deserved better than what he got from us humans.

As he makes small talk, Freddie cheerfully mentions that there's talk of making the Olympics into a CIC, mainly for time's sake. "Dressage and stadium one day, cross-country the next. Easier to fit in between commercial breaks and such."

I don't envision myself riding at the next Olympics but I did picture myself in my head doing that plenty of times as a kid and now I realize that even the ability to live that vision might be dead. It's a strange feeling. But then I remember Daniel saying that when they did away with roads and tracks and steeplechase in the long format, he felt weird, that the sport he trained for, for just about his whole life, was gone. I want competition but I want it to be fair, I want them to keep things the same, at least when I'm around, so that eventing if nothing else feels secure. It's like racing a 5K and then drawing a line in the sand only two miles in rather than three, I think.

Everything has gone wrong today. Everything. I'm trying to be normal and make conversation but after a while it's too hard and I just look at the window. "All those in the know who saw your dressage test said they thought you were judged unfairly, Simon. Don't hold it against yourself as a rider."

I don't want to whine (or "whinge") to Freddie but I'm still angry. The weight that's put on dressage is such b.s., I think. No matter how hard I try, I can't find a way to escape bad judgement. My own and other people's.

When I get home, I can't keep up the act anymore, plus I know that Max knows me too well. As much as I love living with him, I've come to realize that it's hard to hide things when he sees me every day. Plus there's his sixth vet's sense that enables him to pick up when something's off with a horse or a human. I get home late, but he's still up, doing some kind of paperwork.

"How did it go?" he asks. I'm kind of irrationally annoyed he didn't text me even though I probably wouldn't have answered him.

"Didn't you read? Didn't you see?" And I tell him all about Milton. Milton who for once was the main story, not Ben. Milton whose injury has now been played over and over again on countless iPhones and iPads by people who just hack their horses over a few lower-level courses now and then or worse, people who don't event at all and like to say, "See I told you so," before they do whatever godawful things they do to their own horses in whatever discipline they ride.

Max looks shaken. "I've had a hard weekend, Simon. Honestly, I just checked your division to make sure you were okay. It's not that I don't care. I did see that you placed."

"Fifth," I say. I throw my bag on the floor and flop on the couch, close my eyes. "Do you think Milton will be okay?"

"Simon, I can't diagnose a horse without seeing him. The stifle is a very complex joint. I'm sure he's in competent hands. You'll just have to put it out of your mind. You did well today. Focus on what you can control."

"Fifth. Christ, I wish you were caring for him," I say. I can't move. I'm not even tired. It's just that getting up requires thought and I'm not capable of that right now.

"I wouldn't say that, Simon." Pause. "I had to put a young horse down today. It was very hard."

"I'm sorry, Max." And I suddenly realize that I've been tone deaf, that although Max can pick up when something is bugging the crap out of me, I can't with him. If I'm thinking about my job or a horse or whatever, the connection between us breaks and he's lost for a moment to me.

"What was particularly hard is that the horse was treatable. With surgery and stall rest. But the owner couldn't afford it." Max takes off his glasses and rubs his eyes, cleans his lenses with his shirt, puts his glasses back on again. "I wish people would think twice before buying horses when they don't have any money. Horses get sick."

I don't say anything. After Mom got divorced, we always had horses. It was just who we were and what we did. Sometimes our horses did get sick, more sick than we could afford, like my OTTB with her floating bone chip. Mom just put that one on the credit card. The horses always came first with us, Sean and I never had the nice clothes or even the decent used cars that our middle-class friends had. Even as a dumb kid, I knew that sensible people would say we didn't have the money to have horses, certainly not two of them, and certainly not enough to even go to the lower-level shows we did before I got a job as a working student at Angel Heart and could trade labor for rides. But we had them. I always said that Damsel in Distress saved my life freshman year, even though we didn't have her long, because if I didn't know that I could ride her better than anyone else, I know I couldn't have survived all of the crap the kids shoved at me. I mean, I'm not saying I would have jumped off a building but there is only so much you can take before something dies inside of you for good.

"People with money can do pretty awful things to their horses, too," I say, thinking of Milton again. "I'm not sure what's worse."

"I think what I saw is worse," says Max. But that's only because that's what's in his mind's eye right now. I know he's looked at some jumps I've gone over and said that's bad too, that could hurt the horse.

I think back to when I was working at that hunter barn in high school, all the stuff I saw when I was still working there. I'd sneer at the clients that needed their horses LUD (lunged until dead) or stuffed with Perfect Prep, but I stayed there because I told myself I needed the experience riding horses for my career. They always rationalized it that it was better to drug a horse quiet than it was to have a useless horse that would go to no good place at all because he was dangerous. I told myself that if I rode well I wouldn't need that stuff, that somehow I'd rise above it but … there's always a rationalization until someone screws up like what happened with Milton and they go too far.

I know that I need competition like I need oxygen and competition takes money and if it weren't for that brief, sweet sense of cheating death together, then what's the point of riding horses at all? But there's got to be a better way. I'd like to think where I am right now is better and Freddie's certainly not doing badly. Hell, even Ben seems to be treating his horses right. It's not like everyone in the industry is an asshole like Matt. But it's still always a business if you're a professional, no matter what.

"Money and lack of money both make people do horrible things and horses take money," I say, shrugging. "Horses may bring out the best in us but needing money brings out the worst and that's how it will always be. It's not going to change."

Max puts his glasses back on. His eyes are red. "Oh well, there's plenty of people with real problems who would love to change places with either of us right now, I guess. Real problems, not horses."

I go over and put my arms around him. Both of us stink of horse and Matt also smells of antiseptic and piss and blood from his work and standing in a stable for so long. I don't care. I just don't care.

CHAPTER 40

# OUT OF THE JAWS OF DARKNESS

The next day, I sleep in late for me—8:30 a.m. since I don't have anything going on at Freddie's until 10 a.m. and even then it's a quiet day. I don't really sleep in, I guess. My eyes are still open at 5:30 a.m., but since Max is still there I don't move. I just kind of lie around and think even though this really isn't rest. I get up when he starts making coffee.

The news is on. There's some guy with an accent talking about how his wife's gone missing. "Irina, she go out walking the dog. Now she will never come home." They're showing this picture of a pretty blonde lady with some fluffy white stuff at the end of a leash.

"Well, there is always hope," says the TV reporter, who I can see is a young, carefully manicured African-American woman with a soothing tone of voice when they cut back to her.

"No. Irina not coming home," says the man, very definitely. He looks more scared than sad.

"Must be one of Jerry's friends," says Max. I laugh for the first time in what feels like ages. "You think it's funny, but I'm hoping I won't be called on for his next colic. I hope his horses stay healthy, otherwise you'll be the one going, 'Max not coming home' in front of the camera."

"Don't be silly Max, if you didn't come home, I'd just assume it was because you'd been kicked by another pony, not that you'd had a mob hit on you. Besides, Jerry seems to like you. *Love you*," I add, imitating Jerry's accent.

"Thanks a bunch."

I'm kind of grateful that Max and I have something to joke about, however morbidly, because I feel like hell. I know he is still hurting about the horse he put down, and I'm hurting about that as well, in addition to the fact I don't know what's going to happen to Milton. Even the quasi-victory I had with Pearl yesterday doesn't fill the hollow.

"You don't really think this woman is the victim of some mob deal gone wrong? She's probably with her boyfriend somewhere," I say.

"I don't know. Her husband seems pretty nervous, not mad, and pretty certain she's not coming back if that's the case."

"I feel bad for the dog, either way," I say.

I go to the garage for a Snickers and soda. Max fires up his juicer. We try to be normal.

I go to the barn. Freddie's in street clothes, talking to one of the grooms. His three kids are hovering around him. Two boys and a girl. They're good riders and while they mostly speak in an American accent, they can switch between a British and American voice so easily it kinda unnerves me. It's like they have two different people living in the same little bodies. Like Freddie, I know the older ones also speak French pretty fluently (they go to a really intensive prep school with a European-style curriculum). Only, while Freddie sounds like a British guy saying French words, the kids actually sound French.

The older ones are in their uniforms. "I'm going to a reading at Winnie and Harry's school today," says Freddie. The youngest, Tristan, goes to a nursery school. They're seven, six and four, respectively, and the ponies they ride are too small for me to school so they're not that much on my radar (one of Freddie's older and smaller high school-age riders gets on them if they need a school). Still, nice, polite kids. I remember how I was so disappointed when I found out Freddie was married with kids when I first saw him riding. But although I can usually take or leave them, especially kids this young, I can tolerate his because they have to be pretty adult around the horses.

Freddie really has this riding thing all figured out, I think. He's married to a showjumper, so she's still in the industry but they aren't competing with each other. They seem to juggle the family thing pretty well—she's away competing so the children are his responsibility now. (I think they were with their grandparents the weekend of the last event). He's not the best in the world, but he's in the top U.S. rankings and although I know he wants to go further, it doesn't eat him alive with single-minded desire like it does me. At least he hasn't left an ugly trail in his wake, like I already have—leaving Mr. F, pissing off Matt, and now Milton.

"Simon, you look like hell, not like someone who has won something. Don't let what happened to Milton preoccupy you," says Freddie. "I know you were fond of that horse and you put quite a bit of work into him. It's sad but it happens. And he might be back. Lots of horses injure their stifles, and it takes patience, but they do heal." I nod. I don't feel like speaking.

"But not everyone has patience," I say. Freddie pats my shoulder. The children are whining, saying they want to go. They're talking in their British accents because their father's here, but I bet as soon as they are in school they'll switch back to American. I wish I could change the way I talk and feel so easily, like switching a light on or off.

And yet ... when I get on the horse I'm giving a quick schooling, not a horse that's going anywhere, just a training ride for one of Freddie's older riders, I can forget everything. All that matters is the reins, bending the gelding around my leg, getting him off the forehand. Simple stuff but the rest of me, the unimportant part of me, ebbs away in my singular focus into something, however briefly, that I can experience that is clean and good. A little ah-ha of delight as he finally understands what I want and need after struggling with the confused and mixed signals of his owner all week. This I can do, I repeat to myself. This I can do. This is when I am truly myself, a feeling that all the money in the world can't buy.

## CHAPTER 41

# CLEAN CUT

Pearl and I win the next event, as Freddie predicts we will. Since I did qualify for Advanced with Milton, I can already compete at that level, as soon as Pearl gets her last needed NQRs and we're sure she's got her head screwed on straight (and she seems like a pretty sensible horse), we can move up together.

Chutes and Ladders. Move up to Advanced, spin the wheel, crash down again to nothing, go up a few rungs to Intermediate but the ladders for me are always shorter than the long slides.

Milton seems to have dropped off the face of the earth. No one knows what's happened to him. There is no news. I hear a rumor he's been moved to another facility to recuperate. At times I think about calling up Lisa to see how he's doing where he is. For whatever reason, she doesn't seem to hate me, despite Matt. But I can't lower myself to ask and eventually I think of Milton less, even though I see Matt on Nebraska here and there. Lisa I see less frequently, Matt has her on some younger horses that are just getting their feet (hooves?) wet. We're in different orbits.

It's pretty clear by now that Ben's not going back to school. Not only are he and Jasper winning consistently, he is now going to be riding that chestnut mare Patty at Intermediate all the time. She's become one of his regular rides as well.

I kind of settle into a routine at Freddie's, I start teaching some of his lower-level people and some of them even ask to lesson with me specifically which means I must be doing something right.

What's the most remarkable thing of all, though, is that when I see that girl Masha, Jerry's daughter, she's not as terrible as I anticipate. She's athletic in kind of a generalized way and gets it done for the most part. Although she has some scary moments flopping on her horse's neck, he's enough of a saint that he doesn't get fazed and she just rights herself and keeps going. I was seriously expecting the worst but she's not over-horsed despite all the talk about going to the Olympics and stuff. Still, I'm glad I'm not responsible. Freddie's younger riders and ammies are all doing well, even though most of them aren't riding much higher than Training right now.

Mom's no longer at the old, ratty barn we boarded at and now she's training kids who, while not in top contention for the Maclay, at least are going to A-rated day shows and stuff on a regular basis as well as the occasional away show in Florida or Vermont, depending on the season. The junior trainer at the barn quit, so it's just her and the main trainer who owns the place and she feels like she's under a lot of pressure.

"I don't suppose you could spare a weekend, Simon?"

"Ma, I could coach the jumpers, but I haven't ridden in the hunters for ages. Haven't even done an eq class since my senior year."

"You could sort out a horse or two if necessary."

"I thought you always said I just revved them up. I don't suppose I could make a crazy suggestion and say, let the kids sort it out for themselves?"

"Don't be ridiculous, Simon."

"Of course, this is the hunters."

"Simon, you know it's a completely different discipline. This is about perfection. You need another pair of eyes. Adding a stride in the wrong place can cost a girl a ribbon, a championship she needs for points. Adding a stride in eventing is just, well, nothing, if you make the fastest time. " So that's what she thinks about the kids I teach at Freddie's.

"You have to do a course correctly to make that fastest time. You have to do what you need to do. If that isn't perfect, I don't know what is. My kids aren't flopping around to get through a cross-country course. Honestly, I'd like to see some hunter princess get an OTTB fresh off the track through the easiest starter course without crashing."

"These are very expensive horses at my barn."

"And the ones I'm riding are cheap?"

"Not the horses you ride, Simon. I'm talking about the horses my clients ride."

"So just the horses my kids ride are cheap?"

"My point is that this is a different thing."

"You would have slapped me silly if I asked you to sort out my pony when I was a kid. You bought me an OTTB."

"That's different. You're my son. I expected you to really learn how to ride before you could walk."

"Yes, I'm grateful you wanted me to learn how to really ride, versus just pilot something around."

"These girls live in a different world than you do, Simon. We had horses at home when you were growing up. We always had horses. They're different."

Different. Civilians. It's all getting shipped off to SAT prep courses, squeezing horses in between social stuff and extracurriculars to pad the resume for college. Learning to really ride takes time. Milton flashes before my eyes once again. I didn't see him crack open, never watched the video, but I can see it in my mind's eye still, as if I had been there. "I'll see what I can do about getting off, I'll talk to Freddie." I can hear a tension, a worry in my mom's voice I never heard at the other barn.

Ben goes back to Germany to his old trainer, the one where he was a working student and for a lark, rides a young horse at a small German horse trial. He beats Mr. F's Ingrid though. I'm not sure why, even though I want Ingrid to lose, but that pisses me off again, so much so that Max asks if I'd like to go riding with him, since he's free for the afternoon, just to break me out of my funk. That's a sign I must be really unbearable to be around; he knows I'll be less awful if we're doing something involving horses together. I have a few hours between early morning and evening lessons so I agree.

It's Max who is riding Fortune the most now, so I let him ride my horse and I take Pearl. Some easy cantering will be good for her brain and she has the day off from real work.

"Are you okay," is all Max asks as we ride.

"Not really, not one hundred percent, but better than I was, so I'll live," I say. I pick up a trot and Max follows suit. He breaks ahead of me a couple of times as Fortune roots down and pulls into a canter, but he manages to sit back and get the big white horse listening to him again.

"Don't let him get away with too much," I say. "I don't want to have to deal with a hot mess next time I get on him."

He laughs. "By the way, you know that Jerry bought his daughter another horse."

"Something she can ride in the traditional Cossack style, I assume."

"No, a pretty chestnut mare, actually. Lexi. Anyway, the vet who examined her said she was nice. Fortunately I wasn't available for the PPE."

"A chestnut named Lexi? Christ, Jerry must have bought her from Matt. The last kid he sold her to, the father had to send the horse back."

Matt whoas Fortune and looks at me, one hand on the reins, one hand on Fortune's broad back. He'd never have done that a few months ago, have such an easy confidence in my horse. "Is Lexi dangerous?"

"It's not like she's some crazy killer horse but she can get strong, refuse if you get nervous and don't ask her things correctly. She's very, very sensitive. She's not a kid's horse, not really an amateur's horse. Lisa, Matt's … wife … had a lot of trouble with her. And Lisa's not a bad rider."

"Well, I hope she behaves for Masha. I wouldn't want to get on Jerry's bad side."

"Lexi doesn't have any major health issues, although she can get sore if you overwork her. She can just get stupid if you don't ride her right, that's all. Masha's not a terrible rider given she hasn't been riding that long but, Jesus, she is so not up to Lexi."

"Well, what's done can't be undone, as they say, she's bought," says Max.

We grow silent and without words we pick up a canter, than a controlled gallop, more like a hunter ring hand gallop than anything too crazy as there are so many branches hanging in our way. But I still have the knife in my pocket that Ben gave me long ago. I keep it for when I trail ride just in case we get caught in something really tangled. It has come in handy every now and then. I don't use it always.

Without consulting with one another Max and I stop to look at the view. There's a rainstorm coming in the far distance, I don't know this from the weather report but the air feels clammy and I can see the clouds advancing. It smells like a thunderstorm and we should head back. Honestly, if I were on my own I wouldn't bother or care but Max is with me so I will.

I lead us back on a shortcut and this time I do have to cut back a few vines so we can pass. Pearl stands there quietly but I hear Fortune stomping behind us, not sure why we aren't going forward. There's hay in the trailer and he's probably hungry.

"Swiss army knife?" says Max, watching me.

"Yeah," I say, not mentioning how I got it. Ben's in Germany probably drinking beer with his old friends from his working studentship right now. I doubt he's missing his spare knife.

## CHAPTER 42

# SICK AT HEART

They say everyone's winning streak eventually ends; Ben's doesn't end with a loss at an event but rather with one of those freak things that sometimes hits all of us who work with horses. There's an EHV-1 epidemic up in the Mid-Atlantic states and his area's affected the worst. Mom's show gets bumped up a few weeks because it's in New Jersey but Ben's really SOL with EHV-1 because the next major horse trial is in Georgia and Maryland's not affected so we can go but he can't. At least with Mom, most of her major competitors in the region are affected by the ban for the shows coming up.

EHV-1 stands for *equine herpesvirus* and it's extremely, extremely contagious. It can be spread by drinking from a sick horse's bucket or sniffing noses or on the hands of someone who pets a sick and then a healthy horse. Some horses recover just fine from it and don't have more than a fever while others can have permanent neurological damage. Or die.

Freddie's kind of distracted with family stuff right now. He tells me, "My father seems to have fallen into the pond again." At first, I think this is some weird British slang for something I don't understand, something rude, but then I get the idea that

Freddie's elderly, half-blind father did indeed walk straight into a pond when walking his dog and Freddie needs to go home back to England to sort out his father's long-term care. "Mind's sharp as a tack. He just needs a bit more help since Mum died. She was his eyes. Fortunately, driving's not as necessary there as it is here."

Freddie says that he'll pull back on the competition schedule for his horses while he's away because he thinks they've been somewhat overstretched anyway and can use the break but I can still take Pearl down to Georgia myself with a couple of the grooms and one or two of the more competent high school kids at the barn.

I'm not entirely surprised when Max tells me he had to see "Our old friend Jerry" again. Although Lexi passed her PPE, the horse has been acting up and naturally in the Hail Mary pass of everyone being given hell by their horses, Jerry wants to see if there was some vet issue which had arisen. Of course there isn't, Max informs me.

"Did you tell her that she used to be at my barn and she was always a sensitive ride?" I persist.

"I really try to keep my relationship with Jerry as professional as possible. Just like you predicted, the horse keeps refusing, running out and away with Masha. Despite her inexperience the other horse seems to be doing fine in the sense that Masha does make it from point A to point B every time without falling off but they haven't won anything. Which disappoints her father although honestly for someone who just started eventing, just not getting disqualified is a major victory."

"I'm sure Jerry informed the Olympic selection committee of this."

"Anyway, obviously Lexi's a bit different."

"Poor Lexi, if she weren't so pretty, girls that need packers wouldn't love her so much," I say, dryly.

I like Jerry so I call him up, tell him I know the horse and I need to talk to him. He tells me I'm the most wonderful rider in the world, blah blah blah.

"I don't know why you like Jerry," says Max.

I laugh. "I'm not as nervous as you. I don't know, I like the fact he's scrappy and full of himself and came over here without a pot to piss in and now can buy his daughter horses like they're shoes and lives in a suburban mini-mansion filled with gold."

"I don't dislike him, I'd just feel more comfortable around him if he'd come into the money legitimately," says Max. But who really gets their victories perfectly legitimately? So much is up to chance. Even Ben's lucky to have his loving, stable family and to have had a nice trainer practically since birth. I'm going to be lucky to ride Jazz regularly for a bit when Freddie's away. Chutes and ladders, I think, as well as poker, that's eventing, a game of pure luck and skill all at once.

Max is watching a Red Sox game on TV. I watch over his shoulder and then sit down next to him. During the commercial, I take off his glasses and put them on my face.

"God, you are blind," I say, looking at the smear of colors around me. Our living room looks suddenly like one of those blotchy paintings of flowers I remember from high school art classes.

"Not everyone has perfect vision like you," says Max. "You look cute with them on, actually, even though you'll never be able to see yourself clearly like that."

"Given what I see right now, I'm not sure I'd trust your opinion on how I look at any time." I hand them back.

Watching Masha on Lexi is actually kind of funny. She giggles when Lexi starts acting up, and she won't use her crop forcefully but ends up yanking on Lexi's mouth when Lexi does obey because her original refusals have made Masha nervous. Fortunately, Lexi's appropriately-bitted now but the memory of what Matt had her in is obviously strong with the mare.

Jerry is mad, both reasonably so and unreasonably so, when I tell him what I know about Lexi. I go over everything, from her first days at Matt's, to my losing that ride, to how she was trained, to how Lisa rode her. For once he sounds like a real father, not like Masha's PR guy for her Olympic bid. "This horse was sold to me as a safe horse for Masha," he says.

I decide to call up Lisa and talk to her. I consider texting but I'm not sure how to put into words the idea that some Russian guy Matt sold a horse to is most likely mobbed up and since the daughter's only been riding for like two years she better have something safe.

"Jerry seems like a nice guy," I rehearse in my head. "But even though the trial period has ended, I'd consider accepting Lexi if he wants to send her back." As much as I'm fond of the crazy Russian, even I wouldn't want to get on his bad side with a horse deal gone wrong. (I joke with Max about him, but I'd never sell him anything and unlike with Hannah I don't bend over backwards to offer any training to him).

"Hello." My heart freezes slightly. It's Matt. "Hello?" I hang up but Matt redials, the fucker.

"Simon, I know it's you."

"I was trying to speak with Lisa."

"Lisa's riding right now. She apparently left her phone on a bale of hay. Anything you have to say to her you can say to me."

"I doubt that." Pause. "Look, I was only calling because ... I know the guy that you sold Lexi to and I just wanted to say, I wouldn't cross him. There are rumors about him."

"Oh, really?" Matt sounds like he's smirking, what passes for a smile on the Iceman.

"He's probably mobbed up."

"Not every Russian person is in the mafia, Simon."

"The fact that he's Russian is not the only reason. Look, I happen to know him and know he's not happy with the horse. I'm just suggesting you try to make him happy. Honestly, Matt, I don't give two fucks about you, but Lisa's a nice woman and she doesn't deserve trouble." She's better than you deserve, for all her faults, I think.

Matt laughs at me (not with me). "I'll tell her you're concerned."

Oh well, for fuck's sake, I tried. "How is Milton?" I ask.

"Well, you haven't seen him competing, have you? Still not sound. That was a bad investment I made, two of them, in Germany that day. *Enjoy* Freddie, Simon."

I'm gripping my phone in my right hand so hard I'm surprised it hasn't cracked the screen. Yeah, Freddie's pretty hot and yeah, I noticed that at first. But it's not like that's why I think he's a great guy or why I took the job. Hell, if people weren't taken in by the sight of beautiful things Matt certainly wouldn't have sold poor Lexi twice. Everything seen through Matt's eyes somehow becomes sick and dirty, just like Max's glasses help him see everything clear.

## CHAPTER 43
# THE DEVIL WENT DOWN TO GEORGIA

The Fair Ridge horse trials down in Georgia are sparsely populated. Freddie's barn is actually the biggest name there. Freddie's still back with his dad in the UK, sorting things out. This horse trial doesn't offer anything above Intermediate. There are a couple of BN (big name) Canadian riders looking to get away from the chronic cold.

I haven't seen Daniel much lately, although I do expect to run into him at some point, but I don't think his working students this year are competing at a very advanced level, so perhaps he hasn't bothered even to show up and watch at many events. He tells me the last time one of his riders came to Fair Ridge it was hell—trappy and confusing. So the course designer might be my worst enemy, my fiercest competition here.

One of our teenage riders, a girl named Franny, has come down to help out and watch. She follows me as I do the course walk after Pearl has settled in. I try to be helpful and give Franny a little lecture as I go because I remember how much I hated being treated like a nonperson as a working student in Germany. "So, I could take the preferred option here and save seconds but will I risk a run-out? You have to know the horse, of course. There was one horse I rode ... for example, I wouldn't take the quicker option on this skinny with him. I know it would melt his mind and he'd refuse. With Pearl, I'll see how she's handled the earlier, less complicated questions."

The truth is, even I don't like the set up for some of these jumps and the ground lines and I hope I don't have to jerk Pearl's face to avoid a runout despite her relatively better brain.

The next morning, after Franny wishes me luck for dressage. I feel good and in the zone. Pearl doesn't have sweeping, impressive extended gaits like Milton at his best but hell, we're not being compared to him. 43.48.

I run into Frank Stroller, an older guy and a friend of Daniel's from way back when who is still competing. Frank's not quite as old as Daniel but he's up there. "It's like a graveyard here, EHV, scary stuff," he greets me.

"Where do they think it came from?" I ask.

"They're thinking racehorses from Florida that got shipped up to some barn in Jersey and it spread from there. Florida, where all scary shit comes from. Alligators. Disney."

I laugh. "Well, it sure makes things easier for us all, since it happened to hit a pretty competitive area."

"True, it's an ill wind that blows nobody any good, they say. Or it's an ill wind that blows Ben Hillard away. You guys weren't affected in Maryland? Matt Stevenson's not here, and he's near you guys."

"Nah, no one in our state yet. Not sure why Matt isn't here."

"He was your old boss?"

"Yes, yes he was." I change the subject. "Where's your son?" Frank's son Reggie Stroller is older than me, but still a young guy.

The Strollers are known as one of those dynasties of several generations of horse people.

"Reggie's switched over to show-jumping entirely. He's horse-shopping in Europe right now."

"Really? I knew he did jumpers to keep his skills sharp for stadium but he's given up eventing?" That makes me kind of sad even though I should be happy that one of my main competitors has been eliminated in a different way.

"He just thinks the sport of eventing isn't going anywhere. Too many changes in recent years. Plus, he's better at jumping the colored sticks," says Frank, grinning. "Me, I'm too old to switch at this point."

"Me too," I say.

"Shaughnessy, you're not even old enough to drink." That was what Daniel used to call me and I smile.

"I am—just," I say, and I remember with a start that when I first began to work with Daniel, I wasn't, I'd just turned eighteen. It's been years. "Sometimes I feel very old."

"I still feel young. Isn't that the damnedest thing?"

I go clear with a good time at stadium, and Pearl is still sound and fresh. Stroller congratulates me, and I stick around, uncharacteristically social, to have a few beers with him, sitting on a cooler with some of the other guys, old and young, in one of the stabling areas. I think of Stroller's son, building his future show-jumping career. Even at this level of eventing, this type of setup's not gonna pass on a hunter-jumper circuit of any kind, I think, looking around me.

I feel I've been eventing for ages, but the truth is, I could make the switch, too, to show-jumping. It might be easier. I have more of a financial base than I did before. But I need the nervous burn of energy before cross-country, I know, and nothing can replace that. What's coming up cross-country, particularly for an Intermediate is not really to my liking, but that's part of the breaks, right? You can only prepare, visualize, and hope for the best.

"Hold on course." Damn it, I think, and pull Pearl up. My chest is heaving. I keep Pearl moving, turning around my leg until they let us go again. But the wait is long. I wonder what it was. A fall? Someone seriously hurt? It doesn't matter from my perspective. I've learned not to think of such things. I just focus on Pearl, riding forward in my mind over the next obstacles. Finally, we get the go-ahead.

I can see that the footing is torn up—it's a series of three small skinnies, the A to the B is a short two-stride; the third requires a sharp veer left and invites a run-off. Perhaps the horse I was waiting for spooked his rider off. Anyway, I'm on edge enough from all the waiting that we make it over easily. Pearl's listening to me, at least.

I can feel that Pearl is getting tired with all the split second movement and I have to keep my mind awake and agile. Finally, we come to the end, and as the tables get wider and farther apart it's like a breath of fresh air. The only difficulty is making sure she's collected enough to make the striding on the final combinations. She's just happy to be done with all the narrow complications and so am I. It's a hanging log to a keyhole and I have to sit back and rebalance her with a Pony Club-size tug because she's so anxious to get through. Thank goodness Mom isn't here to see that, I think, or any of my hunter princess friends.

Only four riders including myself go clear cross-country without time faults but given that the field doesn't have much depth, that's not surprising. Pearl and I and Frank Stroller and his mount are the only two double-clears when all is said and done.

"That was a hell of a course," I think, proudly. A year ago I couldn't have ridden it like I just did. I mean, yeah, I would have gotten to the end but I would have been all strung out over it and likely would have had a run-out in some of the trickier places if I was on Milton. It seems like course designers nowadays are in love with skinnies, even though in the real world, no horse would jump through a series of tiny things like that, no matter how much they loved jumping.

But as Max pointed out to me once, showing horses is not the real world. And yet, this victory feels so real. Freddie is the first person I call, even before mom, even before Max. He sounds tired and I remember that the UK is ahead of us time-wise, stupid me. It's just like me to forget the rest of the world and feel as if nothing else matters when I'm competing. There could be an invasion, a war, a major celebrity death, who knows but if it doesn't happen on course then I don't care.

"Odd about Matt Stevenson not showing up," says Freddie. "You don't think something is wrong with Nebraska or he's being overly cautious with the EHV scare?"

My natural instinct is to assume that something is up with Nebraska Sky—maybe Matt worked him too hard and couldn't patch him up enough to take him. Then I forget about him until Monday morning.

I drag myself to work, exhausted from the weekend and getting all the horses settled back home. Even though it's a light day, there are still a few lessons and horses I have to train, and I have to make sure things are running smoothly until Freddie returns mid-week. I'm already on my second Mountain Dew when Lisa shows up.

It's rare for me to jump out of my skin—but I do at the sight of her, like a horse at damn plastic bag—even though distance-wise, Freddie's not all that far from Matt's barn, maybe forty minutes or so if I'm driving. Lisa looks like hell. She's pale and there are bags under her eyes.

"Simon, Matt went missing the day before we were supposed to go down to Georgia."

"Shit," I say. "Have you called the police?"

"Yes, they've issued a missing person report. At first they wondered if he might be at a girlfriend's place or something but I explained to him that ... even if he were, he'd never miss Fair Ridge."

I know this sounds totally weird but there's something about Lisa's honesty in that moment, when she acknowledges her husband's potential to be an asshole to her by cheating on her along with the fact that competition is more important to him than anything, that makes me like her again and want to help her. This is the old Lisa, the Lisa I knew. My first thought is Jerry, of course, but I don't say it.

"The police wanted to know if there was any bad blood between Matt and anyone else." She looks at me meaningfully, and then I harden to her again.

"Don't finger me, Lisa. Things have actually worked out much better than when I was there. He did me a favor if anything." Lisa starts to cry. I don't know what to do because patting her shoulder or whatever, much less hugging her, feels wrong, like Matt's here and watching us. I grabbed some doughnuts for breakfast and there are some napkins stuffed in my breech pockets, so I give them to her so she can dab her eyes and blow her nose. The napkins aren't really designed for this purpose so they rub her skin raw.

I'm even more exhausted when I get home and fall asleep on the couch. Max isn't home yet. We hardly even spoke last night, I got home so late.

I don't wake from my nap or whatever you want to call sleeping for several hours in the early evening is. I rise around 8 p.m., mainly from the sound of Max loading the dishwasher after his own solitary dinner.

When he's done, he sits beside me. "Well, now I finally get to see you. We'll have to celebrate your victory by going out when we get a chance."

I smile.

"I watched some of the footage. That was quite a maze of obstacles." I can tell by his tone of voice he doesn't mean it in a good way. But he's happy for me.

"Yes, that was a tricky one." I know he wants to tell me to be careful and I know he remembers I've told him that you can't think about being careful when you're riding cross-country at a certain level, so I say nothing.

I shift gears to tell him about Matt. Max looks worried. He says, "You don't think Jerry would—?"

"Something's up," I agree. "I mean, Matt might cheat on Lisa but he wouldn't not show up for an event, especially one without Ben and Jasper."

I think of the guy whose wife disappeared, the woman who went walking her dog and just vanished into thin air. Evaporated. There's something almost cool about that idea, like a superhero turning into mist in one of the sci-fi novels I still read when I'm bored. I still haven't let the ruining of Milton go. It's the one bad thing I hold onto and can't seem to shake.

"Do you think we should say anything to the police?" asks Max.

"What can we say? We only suspect." Besides, I have so much to do at Freddie's, the hard truth is I can't be bothered. It won't fit into my schedule, being questioned by the police.

Fortunately, they find Matt the next day. They don't specify how, other than he was found wandering on the highway. Some superficial cuts and bruises, but nothing bad. He seemed calm and lucid, all things considering. They're still investigating.

They show a picture of Matt riding, a really old photo, from Geronimo's glory days. The newscaster looks very serious. She says that Matt says he can't remember anything but that it wasn't a robbery.

The story drops, and I can stop wondering if Matt was in the same place with the woman with the little dog. Whatever happened,

I guess it was just to scare him. I wonder if even the Iceman is rattled by this.

Max and I drive to D.C. to belatedly celebrate my twenty-first birthday and my most recent victory on Pearl. It takes us awhile to find parking and it's a nice night so we stroll slowly through the dusk. "There's still snow on the ground back in Vermont," I joke, even though that's not quite true. "Poor Daniel. Do you miss that?" It's so much easier to find a decent place to go out here within driving distance, some release from the grind of our lives. I feel grateful as I stare at the setting sun. The place we're going to hit first is called Dacha, where I've never been, but I gather it's some kind of a craft beer bar or whatever.

On our way we see a familiar face. It's Jerry, with his two women in tow, getting out of a taxi in front of a restaurant. Max tries to pull me into a nearby store, any store, but it's too late, he's already seen us.

"It's been awhile," I greet Jerry.

"Too long, too long," says Jerry and embraces us both. I can feel Max tense up next to me. "But then Masha has gotten out of horses."

"Entirely out of horses? I didn't know that."

"Masha's new horse … with some discussion, we had to send her back to where we bought her. She was not suitable for Masha. A dangerous horse."

Ah, I see. There was a discussion with Matty, I think. "But what happened to the first horse? The one Max saved?"

"Masha, yes, she loved that horse but the horse was still not winning. We have sold the first one as well. Horses, they are not reliable. Masha is now taking fencing classes, aren't you?"

"Well, you can't hope to win everything in your first year of eventing," I say. I'm glad I can add, honestly, "Given her lack of experience, Masha had a good position. Why not just stick with the first nice packer—?"

"Packer?"

I try to think of how to explain this without seeming to be offensive. "First nice horse that really, really takes care of Masha; that's a packer."

"In a few years Masha will be in college so what good will that do us? Masha's fencing instructor was on the Ukrainian Olympic Team for the saber! She says that Masha has great potential." Masha is looking at her beautifully manicured nails. They're a dull, dark blue today.

"Well, other than fighting with my brother pretending that broomsticks and pitchforks were light sabers in the barn, I don't know much about fencing, but I'm sure you'll do well," I say. God help Masha's instructor if she doesn't do well. Fortunately, Masha seems pretty coordinated.

"I'm hungry. Can we go eat now?" Masha asks, peering into the restaurant where they were headed. Jerry's wife shushes her.

Jerry invites us to eat with him, "Unless you know of some place better. Where are you going?"

"It's called Dacha," I say.

"A Russian restaurant?"

"Not exactly," says Max. "A bar, I'm afraid Masha's not old enough."

Masha makes a face.

After we leave, I say, "So much for *dzhigitovka* and Russian trick riding."

"That's a huge relief," says Max. "They've moved on, and the health of their horses is not my responsibility anymore."

"I guess it was inevitable. Hard to get to the Olympics before college and maintain your manicure. Didn't you do fencing as part of the Pony Club Tetrathlon?"

"Nope, that's the Pentathlon. Tet just has shooting. And if you see Jerry again, don't bring that up in case Masha decides that saber isn't her thing and she wants to take up guns. Although I will add I was extremely good at all phases and shooting's the weakest phase of most Pony Clubbers in the Tet."

"Surgeon's hands even back then."

"Oh, stop. I suppose if I had any sense that's the sport I would have pursued, or running or swimming. What does it say about us that even a crazy Russian with money to burn like Jerry thinks that horses are too much trouble?"

"It says that even you're a little bit crazy and I like that."

We sit down at the bar. The guys here are hot but it's not too crowded or loud. There's a place to sit out in the open and it's just cool enough now that night is falling that it's not wall-to-wall guys but it's not dead, either. It's not really a scene, and we decide to fortify ourselves with food for the rest of the evening. I know what I want within seconds of looking at the menu, which is typical of me. Burger and a dark beer, something German (okay, cars *and* beer, I give the Germans credit for that). Max orders a chicken thing and a cocktail with mint called the Lamb of God, which I find amusing. "Is that like a sacrifice?" I ask. I'm curious to taste it even though I doubt I'd want to drink the whole thing myself.

"A toast to Matt being found," I say, picking up my beer and clinking Max's glass. He doesn't clink back.

"Really, Simon? Really?" I figure since Matt's safe I can joke about it and I can't resist. I reach over and take a sip of the Lamb of God. It's fine but nothing special, just a taste is enough, and I'm happy with what's mine.

## CHAPTER 44

# YOU CAN GO HOME AGAIN (BUT IS THAT A GOOD THING?)

In a movie, I guess, Matt would, I don't know, find religion and apologize to me, Hannah and her dad, and Milton, but Lexi's posted for sale again the next week and that's that. There's lots of speculation, of course, in the eventing community about what happened. The news just says that they're investigating the abduction but they don't have much to go on. It's hard to imagine the Iceman wandering around, dirty and broken and I assume scared on the highway after being threatened by some crazy Russian dudes for screwing Jerry over. But the next photos of him I see are him at some clinic and he looks the same again.

EHV doesn't go away but it's contained enough that they start to have shows and trials in the Northeast, and Mom asks me to come up to help her with the show that's been rescheduled. Ben's barn is still under quarantine, though, so I don't know when he and I will meet up.

Mom's riders are all doing pretty tame, lower-level stuff in my humble estimation and to prevent myself from getting bored, it occurs to me that I could take Fortune's Fool. Fortune was an absolute machine as a jumper. Even though I decided not to focus on show-jumping, no one could touch him when I trotted him around at some of the nice little rated shows Daniel used to take us to in Vermont, to keep his horses and riders sharp for stadium.

But when I mention that to Max, he looks sad. "I had the weekend off. I was going to go riding."

"Freddie will give you something to ride when Fortune's away." Max doesn't lesson with Freddie although every now and then he'll take a jumping or dressage lesson with one of the young trainers at the barn. He doesn't want me to teach him. Then I get an idea. "Scratch me riding. You haven't shown in a while. Why don't you come with us and do a couple classes?"

"The last thing your mother needs is a fourth ring in her three-ring circus. Besides, I've told you, I'm not a competitive person."

"Fortune needs to show every now and then. I don't want him to get dull. And you competed sometimes at Daniel's."

"Yes, but you see, I kind of like the slightly less brilliant Fortune. All of my body parts are moving as they should be right now, and I'd like to keep them that way."

I grin. "I'm not going to kill you Max, I have a personal and vested interest in keeping you in working condition. I think you can handle .90m without dying."

We arrive late the night before the show, get Fortune settled in at Mom's barn. We leave Mom there, still teaching. I'm glad to learn that she no longer has kids sleeping at the house overnight (she used to do that at our old barn, I think because she didn't trust the parents to get the kids up at 4 or 5 a.m.). I take Max up to my old room.

It's still the same. Same old books, same old drawings. Like I could walk back to that world and wake up in it again. Wake up to getting bashed in high school. Wake up to still being convinced that deep down I was God's gift to the horse world and someday I'd show them all.

"I always feel strange sleeping in your childhood room," says Max.

"Well, you don't have much choice unless you want to sleep in Sean's bed."

"I assume he doesn't have the complete collection of the *Black Stallion* books." Max looks at some of the drawings I did of horses and of anatomically correct naked men, disembodied hands and feet, and also the endless geometric shapes I drew over and over again when I was bored. I could do that for hours, draw for no reason at all.

I stare at the pieces of sketch paper tacked to the wall long after Max loses interest in them. They're actually better than I remember them. Another lifetime. I haven't drawn in so long, I know I won't be as skilled if I go back to it. Use it or lose it they say. But suddenly I want to, it was another way out of myself, another world to escape into like science fiction novels and stuff like that.

The next morning, Mom, Max, and I get to the barn as the braiders are working. I have to braid Fortune because I like to do that myself and he can get antsy in the crossties if he doesn't know you're the kind of person who won't put up with his crap of stomping and nipping. I know it's jumpers and it doesn't matter but I want him to look neat. As part of standard practice, his door's got a sign telling people to stay away from him and not to touch him. So people keep back, which is just as well, not because he's sick though. (We brought our own buckets and feed tubs). After I'm done, Mom and I inspect the work of the professionals. They've done a good job, and we start moving our things into the big rig. The riders will follow in their cars, Max with Fortune in our trailer.

"Small crew," I observe as I get out to give Fortune a final once-over, making sure he hasn't found a way to get manure on his neck or face or any other place not covered with a turnout rug or wraps.

"Most of the top juniors are going next week with Bob to an away show. The crowd is thinner than I thought it would be—" I know Bob is the head trainer, he's kind of a big name in the hunter and equitation world, mostly for juniors. "These are the girls who like to go to more local rated shows, except for Danielle who is looking for a less competitive venue to pick up some easy Marshall & Sterling points. Still, we want to do well." I hear in her voice, I need them to do well, Simon, so I can prove myself to Bob. Mom almost sounds scared, which I haven't heard her sound in forever, not since she left my dad. She was so confident at her old barn but then again she was head and hands better than anything and everything about that ratty old place. She was better than it deserved.

"They'll do great mom, you're here," I say.

When we arrive, Max is quiet. He's wearing his breeches, his Boggs, and a light jacket against the early morning chill. It's been a long time since I've seen him in show clothes. I'd like to flirt with him to get him to loosen up, but I feel weird doing that in front of Mom. I shouldn't but I do.

Unloading, one of the horses, a fine-boned bay with a flashy blaze and four white socks named Mr. Darcy, bursts out of the trailer like someone lit a match under his ass. The girl who owns him looks nervous but she cracks jokes to cover it up. "There's a nip to the air," she says, dryly, "And he seems to be feeling particularly good." I gather one of the reasons we're here this early is because of this horse. Without asking her, I take the gelding. All the grooms and working students are all off with Bob or back taking care of the few horses remaining at the barn.

There is also a pony kid named Brooke, who's riding a tiny, perfectly coal-black pony named Teddy Bear's Picnic. He looks like a mini-Milton. While he's not completely evil by pony standards, the girl and her mom are so nervous that he starts acting up, giving tiny rears, feeding off of their anxiety.

Brooke's riding in the short stirrup eq and hunter classes, which come after the beginner beginner mini-stirrup stuff. Mom tells me I can get Brooke through the warmup ring or I can lunge Mr. Darcy in the grass right now. I pick schooling the pony.

"If my pony acted like that you'd tell me to sort it out myself and send me to work him in the field, get his bucks out and go in," I say. I'm a little surprised how hand-holdy Mom is with these people. She was always really adamant about people at least trying to do it themselves first with the school horses they'd ride.

"If that pony bucks once, Brooke's mother will have a heart attack on the spot. She's a lawyer, by the way," she says. I noticed that Brooke's mom had open-toed sandals on and was carrying a fancy purse, not a show mom grooming bag, so I'd already pegged her right away as a civilian, big time.

"I liked it better at the old barn when all the parents just showed up at the ring and knew they didn't know what they were doing and the kids did know what they were doing," I say.

"Don't whine, Simon," says Mom.

"I'm not whining," I whine.

"This mother has made a major investment in this pony."

On the lunge line, Darcy starts giving some colossal-sized bucks worthy of a bronco, not the Baby Green hunter that he is.

"I did Prep him," says his owner to me. "I swear, he's the only horse that gets pumped up on that stuff, rather than calmer."

"Make a nice event horse," I say, grinning. "Maybe that's his real talent." Well, some things never change, I think. Some of the fashions have changed since I last was in the hunter-jumper world (I don't count going with Daniel, since we definitely went to those shows for experience, not for championships). But most things remain the same.

"By the way, Simon O'Shaughnessy, I'm Corrinne," says Mr. Darcy's owner. "We were all excited to hear that you'd be coming today. Your mom's told us all about you. I was actually considering not showing after Darcy was so bad at his last lesson, but I thought it would be worth it to meet a famous eventer. Mind you, I'm too much of a weenie to event myself, but I love watching it. I hold a plastic glass of wine at Rolex with the best of them."

Despite it all, I kind of like Corrinne by now, not just because she complimented me but because she can laugh at herself. I guess she can't help how deep she's in what I consider the bad stuff of her world. I was snottier about it when I was a teen, but now that I've been kicked around my own little pocket of the horse world, I'm starting to feel as if being in horses is just a series of ethical compromises and the question isn't if you stay pure but how many layers will be stripped away when you're done.

"What did my mom tell you about me?" I say, warily, ready to play innocent.

"All good things," Corrinne says, so I know she's lying about something.

I'm about to follow the pony Teddy Bear to the schooling ring when another pony comes charging through, this one without a rider or a trainer attached to it, just a flapping lead rope. Again, I'm reminded of Milton, although this one's about 12h high so I'm not exactly going to get on him. The idiot trainer is following, yelling. Well, there goes Teddy Bear's competition, I think.

Of course, this completely blows Darcy's mind and he really lets Mom have it on the lunge line, bucking and pulling. Mom's face and hands are taunt and she has a thin smile on her face. As long as the pony doesn't run her over, she's fine. She ignores him.

The loose pony stops to graze. The idiot trainer keeps running after the pony and of course the little guy runs away again.

Max walks over to the crazy people, tells them to stop and slowly follows the pony from a distance. The pony looks at him, thinks about running and for whatever reason, the pony decides that's enough fun for the day and Max leads it back to the owner. Or it's just Max's way. He seems to make all animals calm, which is great as a vet although not so much when you're jumping in a speed class. I'll be schooling him later, I think. Max. Not Fortune, who will be fine.

"Way to go, Max. Now our kid has more competition in the ring," I say, grinning. The mom of the kid I'm supposed to school looks pale as if it was her pony running, not some other barn's.

Young as she is, Brooke doesn't have a bad position but she's nervous and stiff in her arms and honestly, I have to put the fear of God in her to keep her from holding her little push-button darling back. But we manage to walk off with Champion in the short stirrup hunters and do respectably in the eq classes.

I'd be more interested in schooling Mom's young preteen Danielle in her Marshall & Sterling class and truthfully, I feel the short stirrup pony ring is way beneath me, but again, it's Mom, so what can I say? Brooke and her mom don't know who I am, don't even know who mom was when she was a junior. They hand the pony over to be put in the trailer, take the ribbons and they're gone. I don't know why people like that don't just do traveling soccer or whatever but maybe it's not expensive enough to impress people.

"Short stirrup was dull today," I say to Max. "None of the kids fell off."

Apparently, Darcy calmed down enough under Mom's supervision to win some blues, reds, and a yellow in the hack, enough to get him Champion in the Baby Greens. Corrinne looks ecstatic and has Mom take a million pictures, "To prove to my friends my horse is not always trying to kill me," she says.

"I like that horse," I say to Mom.

She rolls her eyes. "You would. It feels like it's been a long day, somehow, and it's only 10 a.m. And we still have several more hunter classes to go."

"And Max. Don't forget Max still has to go in the jumpers."

"I wash my hands of that."

"I don't understand why you still don't like Fortune. He took me up to Intermediate and now he pilots Max around. He's a great horse." Mom just doesn't like him because I proved her wrong with him when she told me not to buy him, I know.

The other horses left aren't nearly as entertaining as Darcy and apparently require not much hands-on (and no chemical) preparation at all. Mom goes off to school the older kid Danielle and since I'm there, I ride another, more complaint bay in the warmup ring, just so he can look at the jumps because the rider is moving up and Mom's worried she'll get nervous and affect the horse's way of going. Before Mom leaves with Danielle, she tells me, "Don't you dare get that horse amped up, Simon."

"Ma, I'm not a kid anymore, I'm a professional and that only happened at a schooling show." She's referring to the time I had to school a hunter for her and just for fun I raced the horse around the jumps because I was bored in the warm-up ring. I mean, I was sixteen and that feels like forever ago. I don't think the rider knew what hit her when she went into that Hopeful Hunter class afterward. The horse took the first five-stride line in three, and it got even more entertaining after that.

Max is a different story. I go over the course with him and explain how and where he can save time, that he needs to get to the first jump with enough momentum, and above all that he has to keep Fortune balanced. "He's a big horse, and that's his one disadvantage against these little guys," I say, looking around at the competition. He's definitely the biggest horse here but also, I know, the most athletic and the best-conditioned.

The first class Max goes clear but I'm about to throttle him because he makes these wide, loopy turns. "Jesus, I practically fell asleep before you got to the last jump. I told you to gallop," I say. There's only five others at the .90m level here and Max gets second.

"Why risk it," he says, "When there was only one horse to go after me?" I sigh.

The next class, a knock-down-and-out speed class, however, is going to be hell to watch, I know. In a speed class there's no jump-off. It's just one round and the horse with the fastest time and the fewest faults wins. Max goes clear again but third place is pretty bad when there are only five in the class and one of the other four went off-course. I glare at him when he just shrugs.

"It's like you don't even care," I say.

The third and final class Max and Fortune actually hit their stride and ride it like I told them to in the first place.

"I'm pretty pleased with a second, a third, and a first, Simon, given that I hardly ever show," says Max. "It was you who wanted me to do this." I'm amused that he's annoyed by my annoyance.

"I hate to see you dragging on his face like that and taking a scenic route in a speed class," I say.

Max sobers. "You mean you think I'm hurting his value or reputation or whatever? I know he's not the same horse now with mainly me riding him as he was when you got him up to Intermediate."

"Honestly, that was partially luck that I got him so far," I admit. "And it's not his value, I'm worried about. If I had wanted to make a profit, I would have sold him as soon as he did respectably well at Intermediate, like, immediately."

"Simon, I'm just having fun. Please. Relax."

I see Mom walking back with Danielle on her large blue roan pony Zooey. Kid got first and looks ecstatic. "Nice, Mom," I say.

The mood is light in the van as we drive back. Bob will be pleased and things are looking up for Mom. She still hasn't found a horse that's right for her, but I know she feels that she's rebuilt at least part of the life she lost when she married my dad, had kids, and then had to claw together a living for all of us to continue riding after the divorce. Of course, none of her riders know this, that every day Mom shows up for work she's trying to make up for lost time.

"Do you know Ben Hillard?" Danielle asks me, as she unwraps the blue roan back at the barn.

"Ben Hillard?" I say and practically spook just as bad as a nervous horse. Then I realize it's not so unusual that a horse-crazy thirteen-year-old, even one from the hunter-jumper world would know about one of the hottest young eventers out there (riding-wise and otherwise). "Um, yeah, I know him. Why?"

"Did you know his horse just died?" I'm standing there, kind of dumbfounded. She shows me her phone, which is apparently how I find out about everything nowadays. It's Ben's Instagram account, the one I creeped all that time ago when I was trying to figure out his sexuality. But this time, it's just a photo of him and Jasper jumping over a coop. *The best horse ever* ...begins the caption.

"EHV is no joke," says Mom, overhearing us.

Danielle goes to withdraw her phone from my gaze. I reach over and pull back her hand, I'm so desperate for information I don't even want to fiddle through my pockets for my own phone. But Ben's caption just ends with the words: ...*the best horse ever, gone but never forgotten.*

I can feel Max looking at me but I don't care for a second. Jasper, Jasper the sweet, willing, perfect horse, the one good thing in the whole competitive mess you could never say anything bad about, who never put a foot wrong. I feel sick, and I feel like I need to get out of this barn now, back home to where I belong.

I'm in my own head as I wander down the barn aisle, but I stop for a moment to see Corrinne, finishing unwrapping and unbraiding Mr. Darcy. She puts some more shavings in his clean stall, carefully banking them in just the right way, goes to fill a third big water bucket, which the worker who cleaned the stall evidently forgot to do, takes a minute to debate if Darcy needs one or two blankets and in what combination.

"He's a big drinker," she says, thinking I'm staring at the third bucket. "And the automatic waterer in his stall is broken."

I'm a little bit surprised. Corrinne might be slightly scared of this beautiful, highly-reactive horse when she's on his back but she's not only a decent enough ammie as a rider, she's clearly a former barn rat. What she's doing is simple, but she moves with no hesitation and works quickly and efficiently. I look at Corrinne, Danielle, and think about the pony mom and kid that bolted as soon as they got the ribbons in their fists.

"You've got the whole gamut here, Mom," I say.

"What? You mean ages?"

"No, riders. Horsemanship."

"That's how it always is Simon."

"No, not always." I could never work at a place like this again but I decide that mom isn't on quite the lowest rung of hunter hell as I thought.

Mom, Max, and I go to get dinner afterward and although losing Jasper makes me feel like I've been punched in the gut, I've barely eaten since yesterday so I know I'm going to eat now. The hunger's so strong it's taken over all the feelings inside of me. Plus, this is real Jersey pizza, my favorite food in the world.

Max is still quiet, I'm not sure why. Maybe he thinks I'm still thinking about Ben, not Jasper, because he saw how I reacted? I don't know. Mom and I decide to get a half-plain pizza (I want something with meat on it but Mom draws the line at pepperoni, says that her middle-aged metabolism can't handle it).

Max tries to order a chef's salad.

"A salad? What are you, a supermodel?"

"It's a chef's salad, not kale."

"We'll have too much left over if you don't eat some, Max, or I'll eat too much," says Mom.

"I'm sure Simon is capable of handling any leftovers."

"Max watches his macros," I explain to mom. "Pizza has too many carbs, right Max?" Mom goes to use the restroom.

"Simon," says Max, and I brace myself for something bad, "I have to say something."

Pause.

"I think you were overly harsh on me today. I really didn't appreciate being yelled at like that."

That's what he's upset about? "You weren't riding well, Max, and that's the truth. It's not unexpected, I mean, I know you haven't been riding as much because the practice has been busy."

"Well, after today, I don't think I'll be showing that much again. I don't appreciate being yelled at like a twelve-year-old in public by you. Maybe little Danielle doesn't mind being reprimanded like that by her trainer but I do."

"I don't understand Max, you did get a first." He got a blue ribbon for fuck's sake. I just don't get it at all. Doesn't he want to know he can do better?

I watch Max methodically eat his salad, carefully getting the right proportions of ham, turkey, and chopped egg on every forkful as I slurp down the molten hot cheese of my slice. Even with all the stress and hurt I've been through over the past twenty-four hours, I can't help it, it tastes pretty amazing to me.

I don't really slow down until I'm halfway through my second piece and then I think to offer Max a bite. I hand what's left over the table. He takes it and finishes it. "You're a bad influence on me," he says, and I reach for a third. I feel at least relieved that as perceptive as he is, he can't see the movie running through my mind about Ben and Jasper.

We have to leave for Maryland right afterward. I kiss Mom goodbye on the cheek, squeeze her, and lift her up a bit. To my surprise she half-embraces Max. She holds him very briefly but says, "Take care of Simon for me, if you can."

"I try," he says.

## Quick Bright Things Come to Confusion

We're on fumes so we stop at a Wawa and gas station combination store on our way out of the state. Like an asshole, I get out to pump and then remember I'm in Jersey. Max always finds it funny that there's no self-serve here. "What, you people are too delicate to pump your own gas?" he says. Then we go inside to get some snacks, since we're not stopping again until home.

Some guy in front of us where we go to pay looks familiar and I hope he won't recognize me but it's a long line and he does.

"Hey, Simon." He sizes me up and down. I'm in jeans and Boggs and even though I'm not in breeches I still reek of horse. "Still with the ponies?"

"Keith," I say. I grit my teeth but since Max is here I try be human. "Guess I should have known I'd run into someone from high school if I stopped at a Wawa. I was in Jersey visiting my mom."

"I'm still at Rutgers," he says. I didn't remember that or care where he went, although I vaguely remember him being in my English and History classes. I do distinctly remember him calling me a faggot on numerous occasions. He was a jocky type, on the football team but I could outsprint and outshoot him in gym class in basketball and soccer. It's been awhile since I lifted but I wonder if I got back into it I could beat him at that. Maybe not. He's a big, thick lumbering guy and he's got acne on his neck and cheeks.

"I didn't go to college," I say.

"Did you make it to the Olympics yet? Or to the Triple Crown?" he kind of sneers when he says that even though to an outside observer in the line it might look like an innocent question.

He's paying now and I hope he'll leave but he doesn't. He lingers in front of the register. I pay for both Max's and my food at the same time—Mountain Dew, Fritos, Snickers, a protein bar, almonds, and water—and I can feel him notice that somehow as he stands there and the fact the two of us are standing so close together.

"So you make a living doing that? Riding?" he says.

That's a really interesting question. I'm not really sure how to answer it. I shrug. "I guess you're going to tell me I shouldn't because the horse does all the work?" The girl beside him, one of those Jersey blonde types with beach-bleached hair and plastic nails, giggles.

"Well, that's what it always looked like to me. But what do I know other than I always lose money at Monmouth Park?" he says, grinning.

"We have a long drive in our trailer," I say, gesturing with my head to where we're parked. "And a horse waiting inside for us."

"Can't keep the horse waiting," Keith says. The girl finds this statement absolutely hilarious and begins to giggle.

I touch Max on the shoulder and motion for him to follow me. As soon as they think we're out of earshot—or maybe, deliberately before we are, who the hell knows—I hear the girl say, "Are they?"

And of course, Keith responds, "Of course."

I drive in silence for a few minutes and Max says, "Don't let people like that bother you."

I can't deny that Keith did get under my skin. Not just the general stupidity, the reminder that even if I did get to the top level of my sport, with all the sweat, blood, money, and sacrifices it will require, in the civilian world it means nothing. If Keith had seen me beat my brother in that stupid 5K or deadlift four hundred pounds then he might have some tiny, tiny bit of respect for me. But it doesn't matter to him, it has no currency, all of my accomplishments with horses are worthless outside of my professional country, like the few euros in my breeches I brought home from Germany and forgot to exchange. Like pictures on a piece of paper. Monopoly money.

"You shouldn't care," says Max. But how can I have any sense of dignity and not care? "It's in the past." Although I can put a bad schooling session behind, stuff like that still lives inside me. I can't help it.

"If I stop caring about that, you'll know I'm dead," I say, and shrug. I can't even drive fast and reckless to burn off the rage because I'm pulling a trailer.

I unscrew the Mountain Dew and take a swig. It's sweet and acid and bitter all at once and the first gulp always hurts but maybe that's why I like it so much, it takes my mind off everything else. Fortune starts to stomp and I focus on the road and navigating through the cars piloted by civilians that have no idea how to drive with a trailer on the road. *Behold the fields where I grow my fucks ...* no, that doesn't work anymore. Even if I wanted it to, it doesn't.

CHAPTER 45

# MORE GHOSTS IN THE (IPHONE) MACHINE

The quarantine is lifted for all the barns up and down the Mid-Atlantic states and things get back to normal. Sort of. Because I'm still thinking about Ben. I know I have to talk to him. I can't leave some stupid social media post about how I'm sorry about Jasper or whatever. I need to see him. So I call. I know there isn't a good time to do it but I call in the morning, hoping at least he's more likely to be alone then.

"Ben, it's Simon." Duh. Of course he recognized the number. Deep breath, trying not to seem like an idiot (although there is something about Ben that always seems to bring out the idiot in me). "I just had to say that I heard and saw about Jasper. That's a really hard break."

"We still don't know how he got it. We'll probably never know. I thought he was going to pull through. I mean, he probably wouldn't have been the same horse but at least I thought he'd be okay. The vet said that the neurological damage was just too much."

"Yeah, I learned that's always the big question." I could add that my SO is a vet but I don't.

"I'm sorry I was such a dick to you," says Ben. "I really regret it, I just want you to know that. I'd like to see you again."

"You know I'm in a relationship."

"Of course I know, I know everything," says Ben. "But I'd still like to see you."

"I'm not free this weekend."

"But I am. Free enough, anyway. You've traveled far enough for me, often enough. Would you like to meet for lunch ... or something?"

"Where are you right now? Who's that I hear in the background?"

"It's not a *who* but a *what*. Those damn turkey vultures squawking. Remember them?"

Yes, I remember that day. "Are you on a horse now?"

"Yes, I'm on Patty."

I hear a voice call Ben's name above the birds. "Who are you with? Girlfriend or boyfriend?"

"I guess I deserved that and I'm with Sasha right now. She's riding Tess. She really likes her. I'll be riding Tess at Training and Patty at Intermediate now that the quarantine's been lifted and I'm just putting some miles on both of them to get them fit again. It's been tough not being able to leave the grounds of the barn because everyone's so worried about EHV, and obviously since Jasper we've had to be especially careful."

"How is Tess doing?" I ask. "I think about her from time to time." Like the ghost of my old horse flitting through my brain, here but not here, her but not her.

"I'm glad. I'm glad to hear you think about her." I hear the vultures again, they must have found something. Ben says that Sasha's not that confident riding out and he needs to hang up. He doesn't trust Tess with Sasha's fear at the reins. Well, that's fine because I don't trust myself with Ben.

Even when I'm not away, weekends are always busiest because that's when most people have time to lesson and train. Plus, although

Freddie's home for now, he's doing a clinic this weekend and then heading right back to the UK. His father's apparently much worse than they thought he was, and they're getting it sorted so his dad will have full-time live-in care in a smaller house where he can't hurt himself. But the old guy can still be reasonably independent, which is good.

I meet Ben at a hole-in-the-wall sub place that's mostly populated by college kids (civilians) at the tables.

Ben texts me he's almost there so I order us both food (I'm not sure what he likes so I order us the same thing, ham and cheese) and I sit in the corner, sip my Mountain Dew and wait. When I see him, well, it's just the same as when I saw him that first time. Yes, he's paler and thinner and more haggard, but he's Ben so he's always put together in his preppy polo, jeans, and loafers. But still, even if I don't have a prayer with him, even though I don't want to leave my current life, the wanting to be like him and the wanting to be with him hits me with the force of caffeine in my bloodstream.

I didn't have the time to make myself look even halfway desirable. I'm just in my stained schooling breeches, shirt with hair and horse slobber on it, and tall boot socks. Didn't bother with a belt, so I'm definitely in George Morris heart attack territory here.

Ben sits down. His mismatched eyes bore right into me. "You look the same," he says. His eyes. The one thing he can't coordinate perfectly.

"How is everyone else at the barn doing?" I ask.

"Jasper was the only one we lost. Monica, the assistant trainer—her horse also got it bad. He'll be okay for lower-level stuff but not a full recovery like we hoped."

I think of the running, the CrossFit, all the stuff I did not so long ago and I say, "It's so much easier in a sport when you just have to worry about a person's body."

"True. Jasper was the best. I've never had a horse that loved his job like Jasper. He was a once-in-a-lifetime horse."

"I've never quite had one of those. All of the ones I've ridden had some kind of quirk. Well, maybe not Pearl. She has real potential."

"You've done well with her."

"Yes, things are pretty good right now—if I can avoid messing them up."

"You mean, if I don't mess it up?"

"I don't begrudge you any success you might have on Patty or Tess," I say.

"Or with anyone else?"

Is there anyone else? I've been telling myself I'm not that tempted but the idea of Ben with another guy still eats at me. Not enough for me not to eat, of course, which I do in great honking bites while Ben more politely finishes his food. But that idea bugs me just like it bugged me a little bit to know that Sasha was riding Tess.

I remember how in Germany I wanted Ben so bad. I know now that he's not perfect and life can hurt him just like it can hurt me but I still want him all the same, want him more in a way. I can't explain why, I just do.

There's a park near the sub shop. It's secluded enough in one very deep place, where they haven't cut back the trees or bushes in a while, where people never go because it's mostly non-horse people and they're not going to sit on a muddy, rusty bench and get their work clothes dirty and where there might be ticks and things. I've only been to the park once before and yet I know why I picked the sub place, despite the dumb jocks and the sorority-type girls making a racket giggling and snorting in the background. It's just like that first time with him, when I had hope.

I still carry that stupid knife he gave me long ago in my pocket. Just this morning I used it to help one of the guys slit open a stubborn bag of shavings. Its sharpness has come in too handy for me to throw away.

I start kissing Ben and I grab for his belt (which of course he's wearing because even in jeans he's never without one, plus they'd probably fall down if it weren't in place since he's obviously lost even more weight he can't afford to lose). I tell myself it's just a quick hook-up, so quick I'll forget it in the rush of things I'll have to do when I'm back at the barn and we're barely finished before some suburban mom-types come strolling by with their kids.

When I hear them Ben and I get up off the dirty bench with a jerk (I don't even bother to brush myself off given there's no point with these old, threadbare breeches). I sit down again and he sits down beside me. The moms look at us as they pass and at first I'm convinced it's because they know somehow, not just that we hooked up but that I cheated on Max. Then I realize it's my breeches, blue-and-white plaid tall boot socks with my Converse sneakers and my ratty old Killers t-shirt. With Freddie gone, I let myself get away with some fashion choices I might not otherwise. When the cat is away …

"I'll see you at Crossview Creek," I say, referring to the next event coming up in our schedule. I might be riding both Pearl and Jazz, since Freddie's likely to still be away. I suddenly realize that means I'll be competing at Advanced and Intermediate, while Ben will be at Intermediate and Training. I mean, I'm not exactly Boyd Martin or Phillip Dutton riding six million horses at one event and they won't be there. (They'll be competing at an even bigger international venue that weekend). But in a way I have moved ahead, only briefly, of course, until Ben is back to his usual form. Until he finds Jasper's replacement. Which I'm sure he'll do speedily, because look how quickly he replaced me and he didn't even have to.

When I get back to the barn, I have five more horses to ride plus lessons. I get home dead tired and fall asleep on the sofa. Max is out doing the grocery shopping and doesn't wake me and when I regain consciousness the next day I'm so hungry and messed up with my time and eating schedule he can't smell the guilt on me.

*Quick Bright Things Come to Confusion*

I'm a terrible liar, even to myself but the stuff in the park feels so dream-like I tell myself it took place in some kind of stopped time, that it doesn't matter at all.

    I'm just the same as I always am with Max and I don't even feel bad anymore as he makes me my eggs and bacon on toast to go as I hurry out the door for my packed Sunday schedule. I stuff the hot sandwich in my face and plan my rides. Pearl has her head out, waiting for me when I arrive. She knows I know how to ride her well. That's all she cares about. That's all that matters.

## CHAPTER 46
# CROSSVIEW CREEK

Freddie comes back then leaves again for the UK when his father takes a turn for the worse, they think it's 'it.'

So I'm on Jazz at Crossview Creek. Jazz is a big rangy horse that can be hard to put together but you'd never know that when Freddie's riding him at dressage. I still remember watching the two of them for the first time and envying how easily Jazz would come into a frame, melting into one with Freddie. I like the horse a lot. He's a really fun ride. I'm not really expecting to get as good of scores as Freddie does in the sandbox but I'll do my best ...

The Iceman and Nebraska Sky are back in true form at Crossview. Lisa's not riding anything. I was wondering if she'd be taking Lexi out *again*, to put the mare through her paces *again* to see if they could unload her on someone else *again*. Any questions about whatever happened to Matt aren't of much concern now—people are too focused on the questions of the course and how they're going to be riding.

Matt and Nebraska score in the low 40s, though, which is better than they have been doing. Jazz and I score 40 exactly, with freakishly unusual agreement between the judges, still not cracking the 30s but good. I don't see Matt's test but I can't help wondering if he's riding as if he has something to prove. He may be the Iceman, but he's got to have been shaken just a little bit in recent months. There's no deathbed conversion for Matt, no evident change of his attitude, demeanor, or ways, other than the fact that he seems to be riding with more focus. Maybe even he's savoring the moment of being alive just a little bit, with cheating whatever they threatened him with before they let him go.

Freddie's wife Cheryl and the kids come the next day to see the cross-country. The children love Jazz, and Winnie even puts her arms around the gelding's neck and hugs him. Jazz is one of those horses that's fairly calm when he's not in the ring or on course, one of his many virtues. I'm eager and chomping at the bit myself and kids bug me at times like this, but since they belong to my boss and Jazz isn't upset, I wait until Winnie's done.

    Jazz is BTDT so keeping him warm and listening to my aids rather than getting him to settle is the objective. I go over the course in my mind. I'm beyond words. Off the horse, the words my mind tend to stray to are "Matt" and "Milton" and "Ben."

    Despite being out in the open, the first jump has images of blue ribbons flanking it and Jazz looks at them slightly, I think mainly because of the odd way the sun's hitting it, so we jump somewhat crooked, but I'm able to settle him down and establish a controlled enough gallop so we're ready for the next question. "Good boy," I mutter, as he remembers his job and pricks his ears forward.

I go clear on Jazz, no time faults. I have to hurry, even though my rides are staggered, to get ready for my trip with Pearl. Riding over to the warmup with her, I pass Patty and Ben. Ben grins and nods his head.

    "Have a good ride," he says.

    "You too," I say and despite all the stewing competitive juices in my gut ... when I see him in that moment, I mean it ... and I don't.

Jazz was pretty much flawless cross-country. He almost makes it feel easy but I know from my course walk that the Intermediate cross-country course isn't that much less challenging than Advanced and Pearl's greener so in some ways this will be harder. I just try to keep her focused and not to think of how my competition is doing—for now.

We're out of the starting box at a good pace and Pearl is soft and easy in my hands, nicely shortening in the first question, two tables that are right on top of one another. She's bold to the water and doesn't look at any of the brightly-colored coops or potentially frightening flowers. But there's a skinny that's so skinny, with such high sides (similar to what I encountered on the Advanced course) well, it hardly looks like a jump. I can feel her almost trying to bear away from it. I remember thinking when I walked it, the jump looks more like a piece of scenery than something anyone in their right mind would go over, and Pearl being in her right mind, is having none of it. I correct her as she goes to the left—but I over-correct and then she goes too much to the right, around it.

Shit.

I circle back, go over it, but it's over. I don't push her hard for the rest of it, just get her through it as a school. I'm so upset I hardly speak to the groom that's waiting, and I'm not like that. I pat Pearl, loosen her girth and roll up my stirrups, and take a walk to let go of my anger. It's one thing to have a refusal or jump badly, it's another humiliation entirely to do a drive-by.

"Shame," Cheryl says when she sees me and I tell her what happened. "But you're top of the leaderboard at Advanced." I try to feel happy and ignore the sinking sense of failure of letting down my other horse.

I check the results for Intermediate thus far. Ben and Patty have a great time, no faults. No surprise.

"A lot of people lost their way at that jump," says Cheryl.

"We were three-fourths of the way through. I don't blame Pearl. It was my fault, I shouldn't have pulled so hard to the other side to get her over. I was too eager." I know what I did wrong, I tell myself to let it go and learn from my mistakes. Stupid course designer, though, with those nonsensical skinnies with the high sides.

Matt and Nebraska's results are in for the Advanced—no refusals or anything but he has a time fault.

I'm pretty proud of Jazz and me because we've done better than Freddie has recently. I remember the first time I saw Freddie riding Jazz in person, how in awe I was of him, how calculated and controlled he could be while still keeping the horse looking forward and eager. I can't watch myself while I'm riding, of course, and I'm not going to review any available video until after this is all over, but I must have channeled at least some of that energy to be where I am now.

But Ben and Patty's perfection eats at my soul, just like my crappy ride on Pearl. I'm so wound up, I can't sleep in the hotel room so I actually go down to the bar downstairs. Two riders I recognize, Todd Anderson and Phillip O'Reilly, are there before me, and I order a beer and join them.

"How's Freddie?" they ask me. "Still in England? How's his dad?"

I tell them what I know, that Freddie's okay although he and his dad were always close and he's taking it hard. "His dad is still hanging on. Jazzy is a nice horse," I add, letting them know how grateful I am that Freddie is allowing me to ride him.

"Yes, he's taken Freddie to a number of wins over the years—of course it's been hell for anyone to beat Hillard lately, but of all the upper level horses competing right now, Jazzy is certainly one of the ones I wouldn't mind sitting on," says Todd. "Hillard. I have underwear older than him." I laugh and I kind of like the fact Todd talks to me as if I'm as old as him. People often do, I don't know why. It's something about my attitude, I guess.

"Shame about Hillard's Jasper," says Phillip. "Really nice horse. Goes to show you never know."

"No, you don't," I say, sipping my beer and looking at the callouses on my hands.

I remember to check to see how Tess is doing at her baby stuff, and she's okay, solid dressage score, only one rail at stadium, kind of the middle of the pack now (the lower levels here are doing cross-country last). It's not like she's gunning to win at Training, she's just here for the experience of course, to see if she has potential or if the barn will sell her soon. My old horse Damsel could jump a stadium Training course in her sleep, the thought flickers in my mind. But the way that OTTB was she'd be spooking at the starting box, never mind the jumps outside.

The stadium course is straightforward and although Jazz and I have one rub, the jump stays in its cups (my fault, I was trying to make up for slowing down at the first one and didn't collect him enough to jump round at the last). I hand Jazz off and now I have to get Pearl ready. I try to ride her as if cross-country doesn't matter to me at all, try to forget yesterday, but we still pull the last rail.

I've won the Advanced. Pearl and I are twentieth at Intermediate. Ben wins it all at Intermediate.

"I'm so happy for him," I hear someone say. "His heart horse just died, you know."

Jazz and I have a victory celebration to go to, a plate, a blue ribbon. I scratch him behind the ears. He's Freddie's boy, of course, through and through, but at least I was able to ride him well enough, which I certainly couldn't have when I first laid eyes on him. And Pearl was good, too. I'll learn, I'll get better; it will still take time.

I think of Ben on Patty, her orange soup chestnut color a stark contrast against Ben's white breeches and the green of the world around us. Who is better? I think, looking down at Jazz as he waits, quiet as a school horse. Half of my heart is happy but the other still is thinking, *Shouldn't have pulled so hard at that skinny yesterday. It's your fault, Simon.* Max would say, "See, competition is pointless because you're always unhappy. It's never enough, even when you win at Advanced." When I won on Pearl at Intermediate all I could think was Ben was better because he was winning at Advanced and even now I'm haunted by the question of will he catch me and Pearl when he and Patty move up, which they surely will soon.

Patty, Paparazzi, is well named because Ben's going to be mobbed by his fans thanks to his miracle comeback from his loss. No matter what I do.

Let him go, I tell myself. Let him go. Jazz snorts as the ribbon goes 'round his dark, muscular neck, so carefully conditioned by Freddie for so many years.

He's content, he did his best, but I'm not. No matter what, it's never enough if it's not always blue. Always have to get back to the field of competition. Except for that one dark time, the fields of my fucks are always crying out for more but I can't go back to the way I was because I know no matter how much it hurts to care, it hurts more not to care so much worse.

CHAPTER 47

# REIN IN HELL?

"Nice, Reece," says Lisa. She's standing in the middle of the ring, my old ring, talking two lesson kids through what's just a little bit above a Novice stadium course. "More pace to the first jump. Don't be so timid."

I notice, extremely grudgingly, that Lisa is a good teacher. She's firm yet specific, critical yet doesn't throw a shit fit and take it personally if the kid doesn't get it right the first time. She sees me at the arena door and walks over to me.

"What do you want Lisa? Your message said it was about Milton," I say. I don't even try to be polite. My voice sounds as thin and strained as my patience. She said that Matt wouldn't be here; he's off teaching at a clinic for the weekend, and while I don't trust his wife, I did verify this online so I came. I tell myself I have nothing to lose. Well, maybe a bit of dignity but that's about it.

"You'll have to wait until the end of the lesson," she says, apologetically. I'm pissed and ready to burst but like it's an unwritten code of horse people, I understand and politely watch the kids finish until they're cooling out the horses, leave the arena, and then when they're out of earshot, I go up to Lisa.

"Is Milton back?"

"No, he's still at the rehabilitation place," says Lisa, picking up the lunge line she must have used earlier in the lesson and a pair of spurs and a bit that she must have taken away from one of the riders and switched for something less severe (I'm guessing because both of them were just in little Prince of Wales nubs and snaffles). "Simon, Milton's not getting better. He's not going to be the same horse. He's not going to be able to jump again."

"What do you mean? He's gotten this far. Horses come back from stifle injuries all the time."

"And some are permanently crippled by them. He can still move around. He'll be okay for walk, trot, canter. In fact, they've been exercising him on the lunge, or trying to, but they're frankly kind of scared of him there. It's not a good situation for a horse with a strong temperament."

"What the hell are you saying, Lisa?"

We're walking through the aisles now, the aisles I trod so many times with Milton and the other horses. I recognize some of the horses I've ridden although there are some new faces as well. We pass Lexi. I put out my hand and she presses her crazy chestnut face into mine and I give her candy. I don't know what they're going to do with her now that two sales have gone bad. As if reading my thoughts Lisa says, "She's leased out to a guy riding her at Novice, right now. He's an okay rider, but they're struggling."

Of course they are. I feel an irrational desire to grab the mare and throw her in my trailer. "She could have been a good horse if Matt hadn't messed her up, like he's messed up all of the horses here."

"Simon, that's really unfair. Look at Geronimo, who won for all these years and who's just been retired—he's going to have one of the kids riding him at the lower levels next season. Look at Nebraska Sky. Both healthy, sound, and successful."

"Survivors. Just because a few horses can survive a crappy program doesn't make it right. Winning doesn't necessarily mean good horsemanship. How many horses were sacrificed to this program?" I sound like Max, I think. Well, they say if you live with someone long enough, you start to pick up their little tics. So be it. Sounding more like myself, I add, "Freddie's—and Daniel's—programs are proof that you can treat the horse well and still win."

"There's more than one way of doing something. I do respect Freddie, Simon, and Matt does too."

"He sure as hell better. But Matt just isn't different, he's wrong, Lisa. He didn't do right by Lexi, by Milton, and frankly he didn't do right by me."

"I know, Simon."

Pause.

"We were friends once," says Lisa, finally. "I miss you."

"I don't—miss being here or who I was when I was here. What's going to happen to Milton? Or did you already have him put down?"

"No, but I wanted to tell you to your face so you didn't have to read about it third-hand."

"Sell him to me."

"What?"

"Sell him to me for a dollar. I'll take him."

"Simon, you don't understand; he's not going to come back."

"Is he in pain? Or is he just useless as an event horse and difficult to handle on the ground?"

"Our thinking is that he can't jump and he's not able to do any dressage above, say, Training level, most likely, and the type of rider that would want a horse that limited wouldn't want a horse with the temperament of Milton."

"That's what I thought. I can handle him. And there are plenty of farms that take retired racehorses in my area. And as long as he isn't worse than he was with me, I think I can keep him moving a few times a week."

"Simon, I can't sell him to you."

"Just write up a bill of sale, sign Matt's name, and I'll take him. What, is he going to sue me for the horse so he can put it down versus leaving Milton at peace? Your husband's an asshole, but he's not going to survive that kind of publicity. They're still whispering about what he did to have someone threaten to break open his face and leave him wandering down a highway."

"Matt would never forgive me."

"So you'd rather him put a horse down for no reason?"

"It's not for no reason!"

"It is if there's a better way."

I follow Lisa into Matt's office. Or their office. She sits down, buries her face in her hands, and begins to cry.

"You don't understand Matt, Simon. He's had a hard life." And she goes on and on about how he grew up at the track and his dad was rough with him and his mom left when he was young, but I don't care, I just don't care because we all have sad stories and no matter how and what you ride there are people who treat horses right and people who treat them like shit, and as much as you blab on about other stuff that's all it comes down to as far as I'm concerned. Who cares if you're depressed or miserable or poor or whatever? The horse doesn't know. The horse just knows if you're treating him right and there are no excuses with horses, none at all as far as I'm concerned.

I think back to the first time I saw Milton, how healthy he looked and how I ignored all the signs, all the things everyone said about Matt. Matt thought I was like him, that I just wanted to get ahead and because Fortune improved so much, so quickly, I could do the same with Milton, fix him, and then he could ride him himself and I was too dumb and blind to see that. And I was young, with no reputation and not much of a record that reflected my ability so he thought he could control me.

I see that all now like a map of the past before my eyes, as Lisa talks. The Iceman's strategy. And I used to make fun of Max for not being able to see more than two moves ahead on a chessboard when I played with him.

Lisa's still heavy, but she's wearing some new breeches—buff and spotless, as clean as the ones Mom used to wear when she was teaching lesson after lesson at that old crummy barn she was at after divorcing my dad. No matter how many horses she helped with all day and how messy and dirty our house and cars were, Mom always looked like she stepped right out of a SmartPak advertisement. And Lisa's eyes suddenly remind me of Mom, but an earlier version of Mom, before the divorce, back when she was married to my father, the man who hated horses and somehow the man who got me into this whole thing, leaving me his money. The sagging skin around Lisa's eyes is dull and yellow, tired and worn out from lack of sleep, lack of something.

I don't contradict Lisa, just watch her mouth move until she writes up the bill of sale and I leave with it. I don't hear half of what she says. I'm bored and sick to death of it all. Assholes, all of them. I'm not sure if I mean men, heterosexual men, or people who treat horses like hell regardless of sexual orientation or gender. Or all of humanity. But assholes, fuckers, all of them.

I pull out of the driveway slowly, like I always do driving out of a horse farm and then step on the gas when I'm on the road with civilians who can take care of themselves and should know to stay the fuck out of my way. Hell, I think. I'm not going back there again. I'm still mad at Lisa, although for a flickering second I wonder—if I were Lisa, what would I do, if I had no options other than to marry Matt and have what she has now?

I get the feeling her husband doesn't 'allow' her to compete right now, given that her record wasn't that great with Lexi. But she's still teaching and riding for a living and around horses every day. She doesn't have to go back to the box, the cubicle, the twelve-hour a day, sitting-on-her-ass grind and just riding when she can slip it in like she did before. I can't sort out the answer to that, I can only thank God I don't have to make that choice. That I have a boyfriend who is a vet, and I have some money and we both have jobs and so we have options. Plenty of options. Not everyone does but I can't worry about everyone.

## CHAPTER 48

# MILTON AT REST

I park the trailer in the dirt lot. There's one other trailer so at least one other group of horse people will be out there. Might be a good thing (people are more inclined to be watchful if there's a lot of us out there), might be bad (a bunch of inexperienced little kids or dumb people with Western saddles that don't know how to ride going trail riding).

It's been a long six months of many MRIs, stall rest, having one of the working students at the barn come and visit Milton and hand walk him, which required giving Milton a mild sedative at first so he didn't eat her alive (although now he tolerates her without it, much to my surprise).

I unload Fortune, give him to Max, and then take Milton. Milton rolls his eyes, looks around, and I can tell he's thinking of bolting, but my gloved hand is steady on his halter. This might have been a bad idea, but I'm getting a bit stir crazy just walk, trot, and cantering in the ring with him (the working student uses the lunge line or a lead rope with a chain across his nose, I'm still the only person who will ride him). And I think the confines of the arena are getting to him as well.

"Maybe you should have just gone alone," says Max, tacking up Fortune who's snorting, pawing, soaking up Milton's dark energy.

"It's better for him to have a steadying influence of another horse," I argue.

"So two crazy horses are better than one, that's your logic?"

"Surprisingly, I have actually found that to be the case," I say. "Trust me."

I know that Max is feeling particularly brave today because he just learned this morning that an article he worked on is getting published in some prestigious veterinary journal. It was on something like the use of cryotherapy on laminitis, and the title was about a million sentences long to say basically that when a pony founders, cold can be helpful, but I'm proud of him just the same.

Once we get on the trails, Milton's his usual looky self, snorting, rolling his eyes, and essentially giving shade to every rock and tree. But then he settles and just follows the white tail in front of him.

Max has been riding more. Now that he's been at the practice longer, his schedule is more regular. He's even been to two schooling shows in the past few weeks, which is huge for him. I took some of the lower-level riders to a local hunter-jumper show to put some stadium miles on them.

It hasn't been decided if I'll move up with Pearl to Advanced or wait. Ben and Patty already have, but Freddie thinks it might be good to have one or two more trials at Intermediate before she does.

Between my own competing and the whole Milton situation and Max, I haven't seen Ben outside of a competition since that one last time, after Jasper died. I've never mentioned what we did together to anyone or even talked about it with Ben at all.

The ride is uneventful other than Milton trying to spin and run at the sight of a family in reflective gear in broad daylight. The kids are riding those training wheel-type bikes. I have to turn Milton's nose to my bootleg practically, but I get him to stay in place and then move forward as they gawk in terror at us. Oh well, my fault having him lead the way, even for a little bit and I have Max get in front of me again.

"Other than almost killing a small child that went rather well," says Max.

"It wasn't that bad. Don't exaggerate."

Max looks Milton over, flexing the horse's bad leg as I hold Milton's bridle. We did a little bit more cantering today than usual and Max says he seems none the worse for wear. Milton's due for another trip to the vet clinic in a few weeks to check on his progress.

I know Milton will never be the Milton I thought he'd be, no matter how much better he gets. I guess you could say he's my trail horse, and somehow that seems appropriate, that if I do have a trail horse it's one like Milton.

I drive carefully, navigating around cars and SUVs and minivans on the road, rushing to the cubicle or supermarket or wherever people go on Monday afternoons, one of the few afternoons I have free to do things like this. At a red light I instinctively reach over and run my finger over Max's palm. He squeezes my hand but then I have to take it back to drive again.

I like to think, when I think about it, which isn't often, that I've been good for Max, that I've helped him get out of his shell. If it weren't for me, he'd still be living in rural Vermont working at a practice where they always dumped the worst assignments on him because he was young but more importantly because he'd take it. Now we actually have something of a social life here, when we can fit it into our schedules, which we try to, as best we can. I notice as I look over for the first time that he has a few grey hairs, just a few, but I can see them because his hair is so dark. I know he hasn't seen them, and when he does, he'll probably bitch about it. And Fortune's grey hairs are all over his pants, too, of course, but that he can see.

Fortune's going back to Freddie's. Max drops me and Milton off at the rehabilitation-slash-retirement place where Milton will probably be for a while longer. It's cheap enough and they know how to handle horses with a few screws loose, since most of the other horses are OTTBs. Milton gets his own paddock.

It's a bit too cool for a bath today, but I curry him and groom him until he gleams, which isn't hard with his smooth, impenetrable black coat. It shows the dust but it doesn't get gross, muddy, and matted like Fortune's or Pearl's.

I turn Milton out in his paddock. He trots away from me when I take off his halter, goes to the fence, paces back and forth, always watching. Waiting for something I can't see. I stay there until he begins to graze although just when I'm about to leave his head jerks up and he snorts, looks around, then finally goes back to eating. There are invisible ghosts and demons, somewhere. A plastic bag, a shadow on a tree. All of these things could have killed his ancestors, so you never know, it's better to run than to stick it out. He's sweaty again from nerves.

I guess you'd call Milton a very expensive, high-maintenance pasture ornament. For a brief second, I wonder how many others are like him out there, that I've driven by or walked by without knowing. My great Advanced mount that was going to take me up the levels so quickly. I wonder if in some dim way he misses it all, even messing with my mind like he did sometimes? But then again, I never felt he had the competitive drive of the man that bought him or his rider, me. Milton Keynes, a mundane town in England. I guess he was named right. I just didn't know it.

I turn away. I have a full schedule tomorrow. Milton might be okay with things now but I know I never will be. That no matter how many moments I have like this of pure peace staring at a horse, I will always be driven to get back into the grind of things, lash myself to the wheel, get back into the game, whatever you want to call it. If I'm not moving forward to a finish line, I'm not me, and I can't settle in a box, not ever. The only good box is a starting box as far as I'm concerned and I'm always waiting for the sound of the gun, straining to move forward, to win. But I also know looking at Milton that at least I can do this, at least I can make sure that he's where he should be right now. This grazing area is his resting place but it's not mine, I'll never rest content until I'm in the ground pushing up the grass myself.

THE END

# ACKNOWLEDGEMENTS

The eventer Doug Payne's eventing helmet cam videos have been an invaluable resource for me as a writer. Not only do they give the viewer the visual experience of riding a complex cross-country course from the safety of an armchair—Doug's voice-overs are incredibly useful for suggesting the thought processes of the rider (and the horse) while on course.

As always, many thanks to Denny Emerson's continued wit, wisdom, and sanity on his Tamarack Hill Facebook page, as well as his incomparable *How Good Riders Get Good: Daily Choices That Lead to Success in Any Equestrian Sport*. His book is a must-read for all equestrians, not just eventers or professionals, and many of his tips are useful for success in any difficult career (like writing). *Modern Eventing with Phillip Dutton: The Complete Resource: Training, Conditioning, and Competing in All Three Phases* is also a remarkably clear and lucid introduction to the sport of eventing and contains tips that are useful for all equestrians, regardless of the level at which they are riding.

Thanks to Horseback Reads, the wonderful collaborative of equestrian authors for their support and also for publicizing and sustaining interest in equestrian fiction. If you liked this book and have already read the first book in the series, *Fortune's Fool*, check out some more horsey authors on their webpage!

And thanks as always to my friends and family for putting up with my incessant chatter about my writing and marketing of my book.

Cover image Credit:
©iStock.com/Click_and_Photo

# ABOUT THE AUTHOR

Mary Pagones is a New-Jersey based writer and editor. Her previous works include *The Horse is Never Wrong* and *Fortune's Fool*.

    Mary has a slight (*cough*) Internet addiction and loves to interact with her fans (or any people who love horses and reading). Please feel free to "friend" and "follow" her on Facebook, Twitter, and Instagram. And if you liked this book or any of her other novels, please let fellow readers know and leave a review on Amazon, Goodreads, or both!

Made in the USA
Middletown, DE
15 June 2018